THOSE BLOODY WOMEN

THOSE BLOODY WOMEN

*Three Heroines of the
Boer War*

Brian Roberts

JOHN MURRAY

© Brian Roberts 1991

First published in 1991
by John Murray (Publishers) Ltd
50 Albemarle Street, London W1X 4BD

British Library Cataloguing in Publication Data

Roberts, Brian, *1930–*
Those bloody women.
1. Boer War. Role of in; Hobhouse, Emily.
Warmelo, Hansie van. Wilson, Lady, Sarah
I. Title
968.048

ISBN 0-7195-4858-6

Photoset by Rowland Phototypesetting Ltd
Bury St Edmunds, Suffolk
Printed in Great Britain at
The University Press, Cambridge

For Jean and Peter Pitchford

Contents

Illustrations

Credits
Nos 7, 10, 11, 12, 13, 15, 17, 19, Transvaal Archives. The remainder,
Author's collection.

Acknowledgements

The research for this book has been conducted over many years and includes material collected when working on related subjects. The lapse in time between researching and writing makes it impossible for me to acknowledge all those in Britain and South Africa who have given me help. But there are some debts I cannot ignore. First, and most important, I am deeply grateful for the continuing support, advice and encouragement of Mr Theo Aronson, who not only suggested many much-needed changes to my first draft but whose help with translations has been invaluable. My sincere thanks must go also to the following for kindly answering my enquiries and helping in a variety of ways: Mr Charles Adams, Mrs Alison Adburgham, Miss Fiona Ashby-Lloyd, the late Mr Toby Barker, Mr George Bishop, Mrs C. Cassidy, Mrs T. W. Du Plessis, Miss Jane Ellerton, Mr John Fuller, Mr Harold Foster, Mrs Maureen Hargraves, Mrs E. M. Johnstone (*née* Keeley), Mr Jonathan Kerslake, Mr F. Kelly-Davies, Mrs J. W. Louw, Revd R. J. Lucas (Rector of St Ive, Cornwall), Mr J. E. Malan, Mrs S. Minchin, Mr Colin Noble, Miss Mavis Orpen, Mr T. G. Wormald and Mr Alan Williams.

I have had help from several public institutions and would like, in particular, to thank: Mr David Doughan and staff of the Fawcett Library, London, Mr G. J. Renecke and staff of the Transvaal Archives, Mrs S. Bane and staff of the Frome Library, Somerset; also the staffs of the South African Library, Cape Town, the State Library, Pretoria, the Cory Library, Rhodes University, Grahamstown, the Cape Archives, Cape Town, the British Library, the Public Record Office, the National Army Museum, London, the Bath Reference Library and the Bristol Reference Library. Although I have listed all the works consulted in the Bibliography, I am particularly indebted to

Acknowledgements

the autobiographical writing of the three main protagonists in this book as well as to *Methods of Barbarism* by S. B. Spies and *Emily Hobhouse: Boer War Letters* edited by Rykie van Reenen.

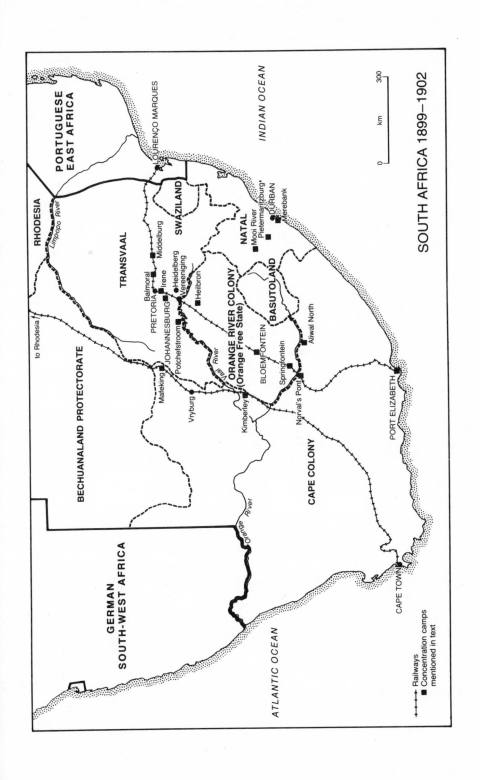

SOUTH AFRICA 1899–1902

+–+–+–+ Railways
■ Concentration camps
mentioned in text

GERMAN
SOUTH-WEST AFRICA

ATLANTIC OCEAN

BECHUANALAND PROTECTORATE

to Rhodesia

RHODESIA

PORTUGUESE
EAST AFRICA

Limpopo River

Lourenço Marques

TRANSVAAL

SWAZILAND

Balmoral
Middelburg
PRETORIA
Irene
JOHANNESBURG
Heidelberg
Vereeniging
Potchefstroom
Heilbron

Vaal River

Mafeking

Vryburg

Kimberley

ORANGE RIVER COLONY
(Orange Free State)

BLOEMFONTEIN
Springfontein

Norval's Pont

Orange River

BASUTOLAND

Aliwal North

NATAL

Mooi River
Pietermaritzburg
DURBAN
Merebank

INDIAN OCEAN

PORT ELIZABETH

CAPE COLONY

CAPE TOWN

0   km   300

1

Society Butterflies

'PLEASE UNDERSTAND', runs Queen Victoria's celebrated remark to the minister who had come to reassure her after a series of British defeats during the opening weeks of the Anglo-Boer war, 'that there is no one depressed in this house; we are not interested in the possibilities of defeat; they do not exist.'[1]

The old Queen's intransigence was not assumed. Although she was no warmonger, Queen Victoria was unshakeable in her determination that her armies should emerge victorious from the war in South Africa. Her interest in the hostilities which had broken out in October 1899 between Britain and the Boer republics of the Transvaal and the Orange Free State was intense. To all things military she responded with an aggressiveness that belied her failing health and eclipsed her many personal problems.

The opening months of the war saw her at her most purposeful: reviewing troops about to sail for the Cape, visiting the wounded in hospital, sending condolences to the bereaved, organizing comforts for her 'dear brave soldiers', doing her utmost to bolster morale.

Nothing was too complex or too trivial to escape the Queen's attention: she offered advice on the choice of army officers and became incensed when changes were made to the military command without proper consultation; she cross-questioned her ministers on reports from the War Office and showed concern for the well-being of horses transported to South Africa. As cataracts were steadily clouding her eyes, she had large-scale maps of South Africa prepared so that she could follow every battle and locate every remote farmstead skirmish.

Daily and weekly newspapers enabled her to compare popular reports with the news she received through official channels. If any journalist dared to criticize the conduct of the war she made no secret of her displeasure.

'Against the Press she is very irate', noted one of her ladies-in-waiting in February 1900. 'The "Morning Post" is banished from the Palace and we are forbidden to touch it . . . I do not think Lord Glenesk [the proprietor] will bask any longer in Royal favour.'[2]

But not all newspaper comment was so imperiously dismissed. Some news items, particularly those coming direct from South Africa, the Queen took very seriously indeed. This was certainly true of the accounts published early in 1900 concerning a social disturbance in Cape Town. A situation was developing, it was reported, which was not only having a detrimental effect on public morale but was threatening military discipline. This the Queen found extremely disquieting. Sending for the Colonial Secretary, Joseph Chamberlain, she demanded that something be done to restore order. It was a command that was easier to give than to carry out. Trouble had been brewing in Cape Town since before the war.

As early as August 1899, when hopes of a peaceful settlement with the Boer republics were fading, British citizens in the Transvaal had begun to take fright. Alarmed at the thought of being stranded in a hostile country, perhaps interned or being made to fight for the enemy, many of them decided to join their kinsmen in the Cape or Natal – both of which were British colonies. The order of their going was largely decided by the size of their bank balances. First to leave were the rich business and professional men who, with their families and servants, travelled to the southern colonies where some had houses and others could afford to move into hotels. They were followed, as tension mounted, by ever increasing crowds of miners, engineers, artisans, clerks and shopkeepers; anyone, in fact, who could scrape together the train fare and rely on friends or relatives to give them shelter. By the beginning of October, with time rapidly running out, the orderly exodus had turned into a stampede. Committees were formed and arrangements made for the evacuation of any British resident in the Transvaal, however poor, who wished to leave.

Altogether some 20,000 *uitlanders* (foreigners), as they were known to the Boers, took refuge in Cape Town, putting a severe strain on the city's limited resources. Things were not helped by the constant flow of troops who passed through the sea-port on their way to the front, nor by the stream of sick and wounded sent down from battle zones who had to be accommodated. Overcrowded, disorganized, lacking amenities, and with the control of the city divided between the civil and military authorities, Cape Town was more like an urban transit depot than a place of refuge.

But it was not this that worried Queen Victoria. Upheavals of one sort or another were to be expected in wartime and, while she sympathized with the refugees, there was little she could do to help them. What decided her to intervene was an invasion of a very different sort: an invasion which threatened to turn the chaos into a circus.

For it was not only refugees who flocked to Cape Town. Hardly had war been declared than the London shipping offices were besieged by a strange assortment of civilians frantic to book a passage to South Africa. 'Foreign countries sent spies,' it is said, 'stock exchange operators sent observers, so as to know when they could hope to handle Rand gold shares again, and besides these extraneous and unwanted persons, there were a whole host of others. Every boat came out crammed with men and women who wanted to be "in" all the excitement. Especially women.'[3] And it was these women, mostly the rich, bored and frivolous wives of army officers, whose embarrassing behaviour was regularly reported in the popular press, who attracted the Queen's wrath.

They were an oddly-assorted crowd. Although the majority of them were related to men serving in South Africa, there were a great many others who had come out purely on a whim. Professing to answer the call of patriotism, few of these flighty visitors had anything to offer in the way of skills. Some, admittedly, arrived with stylishly-designed nurses' uniforms and volunteered to work in the hospitals but, with little experience and no training, they were usually more trouble than they were worth. 'I have heard many Society women,' wrote a journalist, 'thinking that they would like to do a little work, say "O! I love nursing" and then go pottering about the wards in flounces and furbelows, hindering the nurses and irritating the patients. All this is wrong, and should not have been allowed. If ever there is another big war, a good deal of attention, I should think, will be paid to the keeping back of Society women.'[4]

An even greater nuisance were those intrepid ladies who arrived, gamely equipped with tents and camp beds, fully expecting to rough it at the front. Keen to reach the battle areas, they pestered the authorities for railway passes and gave no thought to the risks involved or the problems created. 'They will insist on going to Bloemfontein at a time when the enemy is rife in the country . . .' sighed Sir Alfred

Milner, the harassed governor of the Cape, 'without stopping to think that every time they take a journey [in hostile country] it means pilot engines and all sorts of extra precautions.'[5] It was certainly not the sort of behaviour expected of sedate Victorian women. '*They are so daring*', exclaimed Sir Alfred.

But these mavericks were the exception. For the most part, the women who stepped ashore at Cape Town showed very little interest in the war. They had come to South Africa for fun and were determined to enjoy themselves. Crowding into the already jam-packed hotels they demanded the best rooms, expected every comfort, bullied the overworked staff and complained loudly about the lack of fashionable entertainments. Starved of amusement, they organized their own: dinner parties, afternoon teas, *soirées*, daily canters on the lower slopes of Table Mountain, charity bazaars, picnics and dances. Their prime aim was to attract the equally bored staff officers stationed in Cape Town. One senior officer warned his wife against coming to the Cape because, he said, 'every hole and corner is crammed with ladies who alternate squabbling among themselves with the washing of officers' faces.'[6]

Harmless as most of the socializing was, it seemed singularly inappropriate to the time and place. So stark was the contrast between the merry-making in Cape Town's hotels and the plight of the refugees, the suffering of the wounded soldiers and the news from the battle front, that it was bound to cause offence.

One of the more vehement critics was Mortimer Menpes, the artist, who had been sent out to South Africa as a representative of the weekly illustrated magazine *Black and White*. Arriving in Cape Town in March 1900, he found it 'loathsome', filled with 'heartless Society butterflies' who, he claimed, 'were receiving more attention than they could hope to do in a whirl of London seasons. The dinner parties given to silly young staff officers – the giggling, the tittering – all seem terribly incongruous . . . Fathers and brothers would have been much better without having about them womenfolk, who are always out of place, and apparently hopelessly incapable of appreciating the terrible solemnity of the scenes they witness.'[7]

The fashionable, newly-opened Mount Nelson Hotel was the main centre of revelry. Here were quartered not only the wives of high-ranking officers and some of the senior army personnel but a fair sprinkling of wealthy Johannesburg refugees. It was a rich but far from edifying mixture. 'I dined at the Mount Nelson Hotel,' wrote a volunteer nurse, returning from war-torn Natal, 'where I must own I was most astonished – the dresses, the babble of both men and women was bewildering.'[8] She found it difficult to reconcile such frivolity with the 'realities' of war. Mortimer Menpes considered the atmosphere of the hotel positively corrupting. 'Not only did these women do no good,' he fumed, 'they did a great deal of harm also, for with their gay dinner parties they enticed young officers to neglect their work; and whenever I saw a staff officer at a dinner party, or lounging about at the Mount Nelson Hotel, I resented it and felt that he should be swept out of the place and given healthy work to do.'

It was the reports of journalists like Mortimer Menpes which so incensed Queen Victoria. Having always despised what she called 'the frivolity, the love of pleasure, self-indulgence and idleness' of fashionable society, she had no intention of allowing these useless creatures to undermine the conduct of the war. Her views were summed up in a telegram which Joseph Chamberlain sent to the governor of the Cape in April 1900.

'The Queen', he wired, 'regrets to observe the large number of ladies now visiting and remaining in South Africa, often without imperative reasons, and strongly disapproves of the hysterical spirit which seems to influence some of them to go where they are not wanted. I conclude their presence interferes with work of civil and military officers.'[9] He suggested that Milner send him a telegram pointing out that the ladies were impeding the war effort and asking for a notice to this effect to be issued. 'This', Chamberlain concluded, 'I would submit to the Queen and Her Majesty would instruct me to publish.'

What Queen Victoria called 'the hysterical spirit' was indeed largely responsible for the rush of civilians to South Africa. Never before had such large numbers of British women travelled so far to be near the fields of battle, never again would they do so to such little purpose. There was no rational explanation for their presence in Cape Town: most of them were responding, purely and simply, to the explosion of jingoism which accompanied the declaration of war.

'One is almost smothered', complained Jessica Sykes in November 1899, 'by unceasing Press issues, and deafened with exaggerated tales of slaughter, shouted in triumphant tones by their vendors. The theatre and the music-hall are equally devoted to clap-trap sentimentality, and exhibitions of so-called patriotism taking the form of perpetual brag and boast, as to our superiority over other nations, these claims being based on the fact that we are "English Men". Such exhibitions of national vanity . . . are social conditions we should first condemn, ridicule, and even regard as dishonourable were they carried on in any other country but our own.'[10]

But even Lady Sykes was not impervious to the call to arms. That same month she joined the exodus to South Africa. Her excuse was every bit as vague as those of her more hysterical compatriots. 'I had some unoccupied time at my disposal . . .' she coolly observed, '[so] I thought I would go out to the Cape and spend six or seven weeks there, and see if I could not be of some little use or service.'

Her attitude was typical of a good many other women with time on their hands and cash to spare. Few of them bothered to enquire deeply into the rights and wrongs of the war. 'Whatever the individual opinion may be as to the necessity, justice and advisability of this particular war,' declared the nonchalant Lady Sykes, 'we are face to face with the fact that a *war is here*, and that every day, and all day, healthy, courageous, fine young Englishmen are in deadly peril.' That was all she needed to know. That, in fact, was all that most of the passengers sailing to the Cape – including a majority of those 'fine young Englishmen' – wanted to know. There was a great deal of flag-waving, bands played 'Soldiers of the Queen' and 'Goodbye Dolly Gray', crowds cheered as the troopships left, and there was plenty of talk about Empire, Duty, Patriotism and National Honour but, for the most part, Kruger was merely a name with which to frighten children, and Africa – its peoples, its problems and its tortuous history – remained a mystery.

One person who was in a position to be slightly better informed was Lady Edward Cecil. She was the daughter-in-law of the British prime minister, Lord Salisbury, and she had arrived in South Africa with her husband, Lord Edward Cecil, three months before war was declared. When hostilities began Lord Edward was in Mafeking, where he was appointed chief staff officer to Colonel Baden-Powell, and his wife was living at Groote Schuur, the beautiful Cape Dutch house belonging to Cecil Rhodes, in a suburb of Cape Town.

A bright, attractive young woman, Lady Edward was no empty-headed social butterfly. She had been born into a politically aware family and, during the opening weeks of the war, served on a committee set up to assist the homeless refugees from the Transvaal. Later Groote Schuur was turned into a convalescent home for sick soldiers and Lady Edward and her friend Lady Charles Bentinck supervised the running of the house and helped to administer a Red Cross fund.

Lady Edward Cecil never forgot her wartime experiences in South

Africa. She was to recall them, fifty years later, in her book *My Picture Gallery*. In this she devotes a chapter entitled 'What It Was All About' to examining the background to the war. Her account is merely a summary of the complicated series of events which led to the outbreak of hostilities but, as far as it goes, it reflects the broad views of many intelligent British men and women of her generation. That it is biased is hardly surprising. Emotional propaganda, both before and during the war, made a lasting impression. Not until many years later did historians produce more objective verdicts. But if Lady Edward's interpretation is one-sided, so too were many popular accounts which supported the Boers; both sides could justify their points of view. What needs to be remarked, however, is that once war was declared the Boers, facing a threat to their homeland, had no option but to defend themselves while the British, not directly threatened, travelled thousands of miles and – in the case of the soldiers – were prepared to die for a cause which few of them fully understood. Just how little the British public knew about the South African situation is illustrated by the significant gaps in Lady Edward's short chapter of events.

She starts by explaining how the British first came to be in South Africa. Quite correctly she points out that British troops were sent to the Cape during the Napoleonic wars, when they 'twice wrested it' from the Dutch. Then, with the coming of peace in Europe in 1815, Britain took legal possession of the Cape Colony. It was able to do this by agreeing to accept financial responsibility, amounting to £6 million, for the commitments of the Dutch government towards other European powers. In this way, Britain obtained the right of purchase, as well as that of conquest and occupation.

Lady Edward says little about the resentment which this transfer created among the Cape Boers, who now had to acknowledge new overlords. She merely observes that they 'disliked their new government with its impartial justice between white and black men, its orderly administration and its progressive spirit.' That is far from being the whole story but there is some truth in what she says. The Boers undoubtedly objected to the new laws which, championed by missionaries, granted limited – but by no means impartial – rights to the black population, culminating in the abolition of slavery in 1833. But even more fiercely they resented the claims made upon them by the British administration and the erosion of the relative independence they had enjoyed under their former rulers.

The extent to which the freeing of slaves influenced future events is a matter of dispute among historians. But there is no denying that an accumulation of grievances led, a few years later, to a mass exodus of Boers from the Cape. This desperate attempt to escape the clutches of British authority – known as the Great Trek – was an epoch-making event in the annals of Afrikanerdom. After suffering many hardships and clashes with the African tribes that they encountered, the migrant Boers eventually established two republics in the north: one in the Transvaal and the other in what was to become the Orange Free State. In this way the white settlements in southern Africa divided: the Boer republics in the north and the two British colonies – the Cape and Natal – in the south.

Lady Edward skips lightly over the next sixty years. Of the Boer republics she says, not without reason, 'the old autocratic rule of the landowners was re-established and the natives were reduced to near slavery.' But she ignores, or perhaps was ill-informed about, the uneasy relationship which continued to plague the British and their northern neighbours. This is important in any catalogue of events and deserves a mention even in the briefest of tellings.

At first the British refused to recognize the independence of the Boer republics. The Cape authorities insisted that the migrants were simply renegade subjects of the Queen and were still within British jurisdiction. But eventually the cost of controlling the vast, turbulent interior came to be regarded as a waste of resources, and the freedom of the Boers was formally acknowledged. By the Sand River Convention of 1852, the independence of the Transvaalers was recognized, and two years later the Bloemfontein Convention withdrew British sovereignty from beyond the Orange River. 'Pharaoh', as Professor Eric Walker put it, 'had promised to trouble the people no more.'

Unfortunately, the Transvaal proved a sorry Promised Land. Known officially as the South African Republic, it was a huge territory. Parts of it were wild, unproductive and malaria-ridden. Bickering among factions of the trekkers, as well as constant threats of insurrection from the indigenous black population, made it a country that was almost impossible to administer efficiently. So dramatically did the economy of the Transvaal decline, so lax was its government, that by the 1870s the republic appeared to be on the verge of collapse. This gave Pharaoh the opportunity to break his promise and reassert his authority.

The excuse for intervention was both timely and welcome. The British Colonial Secretary, Lord Carnarvon, was intent on federating the states of southern Africa and saw the independence of the Boer republics as an obstacle to his plans. Failing to win over the Boers by diplomatic means, Carnarvon embarked on a course of deliberate coercion. He started with the Transvaal. Using the near bankrupt, ill-organized state of the country as an excuse, and spurred on by a recent bungled campaign against the Bapedi tribe, he sent a British Agent and a small police force into the Transvaal to bring it under British protection. It was an audacious move, but it succeeded. Military garrisons were established in the Transvaal and, in 1877, the former republic was proclaimed a British crown colony.

This high-handed takeover was denounced by some of the government's opponents in England, but the public was assured that the Boers had welcomed British intervention. Events were to prove otherwise. Over the next three years the Transvaal Boers protested, petitioned and sent delegations to London demanding the restoration of their independence. They got no satisfaction, and their patience finally ran out. In December 1880, they rose in rebellion and sparked off the first Anglo-Boer war. The British garrisons were besieged and a relieving force, sent from Natal, was attacked and disastrously defeated at Majuba Hill, near the Transvaal–Natal border. This crippling defeat brought the fighting to what many in Britain regarded as an inglorious end. 'Avenge Majuba!' was to become a patriotic rallying cry in the years ahead.

A peace settlement was reached in Pretoria, the Transvaal capital, in August 1881. Under the terms of the Pretoria Convention, the Transvaal was handed back to the Boers; Britain however retained what was vaguely called 'suzerainty' over 'native policy' and foreign relations. These terms were amended three years later by a second convention signed in London. The validity of the so-called suzerainty was to be hotly disputed when Britain made claims on the Transvaal later.

The next event to convulse the Boer republic was of a very different nature. In 1886 gold was discovered in the Transvaal. Rich strikes were made in an area known as the Witwatersrand, some thirty-five miles south of Pretoria, and the hitherto poverty-stricken republic was transformed, almost overnight, into a nineteenth-century Eldorado. News of the discoveries, coming as they did in rapid and startling succession, reverberated around the world: prospectors of every nationality flocked to the Transvaal in their thousands.

At this time Paul Kruger was ruling in Pretoria. Then in his early sixties, the thick-set, heavily-jowled Kruger had been elected president of the Transvaal three years earlier. He, more than anyone, was aware of the danger that this invasion of *uitlanders* posed to the Boers' independence. A child of the Great Trek, steeped in the Calvinism of his people, Kruger had very little time for foreigners. His philosophy was that of the Old Testament; for him the Boers, like the Israelites, were an exclusive, chosen people who had a God-ordained mission to fulfil. While he welcomed the discovery of gold as a godsend to his country's economy, he had no intention of allowing it to interfere with the destiny of the Boer nation. He was determined that the forces of Mammon should be kept at bay.

To this end, President Kruger set about hemming the newcomers in with restrictions. He allowed them mining rights but withheld concessions for transport and vital mining equipment; he burdened them with heavy taxes but gave them no say in the running of the country. Having insufficient burgers to handle the concessions, he granted monopolies to favoured outsiders and left the control of the main mining town, Johannesburg, to inefficient appointees. In this way he hoped to regulate the life blood of the new community, but his grip became a stranglehold.

The voteless *uitlanders* found themselves frustrated at every turn. They began to agitate for control of their own affairs, they wanted a say in the government which was supported by their money and labour. Demonstrations were staged, petitions were circulated and protest meetings were held to demand that the vote be given to everyone who qualified by length of residence in the Transvaal – whatever their origins. Kruger quickly found that his financial boom had developed into a hydra-headed monster. Only too aware that the *uitlanders* far outnumbered his burgers, he knew that giving them the vote would mean the end of Boer rule. That was something he had no intention of allowing to happen. 'Wealth cannot break laws . . .' he protested. 'Is it a good man who wants to be master of the country, when others have been struggling for twenty years to conduct its affairs?'[11] He had a case but he lacked the tact, diplomacy and persuasiveness to pacify his opponents. The *uitlanders* soon realized that if they were to obtain justice they would have to call on outside help.

They found a champion in Cecil Rhodes, the powerful mining magnate who had recently seized control of the Cape's diamond industry. Rhodes also had a sizeable stake in the Transvaal gold fields; more importantly, he had reasons of his own for wanting to bring about Kruger's downfall.

Cecil Rhodes, like Paul Kruger, was a man with a mission. Where Kruger saw the Boers as a chosen people, Rhodes believed that the British were 'the best, the most human, most honourable race the world possesses'. He had stated this plainly in a testament he had written at the age of twenty-four. 'I contend', he declared, 'that we are the finest race in the world and that the more of the world we inhabit the better it is for the human race.'[12] This had become his aim in life: starting with Africa, he intended to bring the entire world under the sway of Britain. There could be no question of allowing President Paul Kruger to stand in his way.

But it took time for Rhodes to stand up to Kruger. First he had other goals to achieve. In 1891 he became prime minister of the Cape, and that same year he despatched a pioneer force to occupy the vast territories – later to become Rhodesia (now Zimbabwe) – north of the Transvaal. He was hoping that in these northern regions gold would be discovered. He needed gold to finance his grandiose schemes. But he was disappointed; very little gold was unearthed and he had to look elsewhere. Then it was that he turned his attention to the Transvaal. What Rhodesia could not provide, the Boer republic would be forced to yield.

Rhodes's plan for seizing the Transvaal's gold was as simple as it was foolish. Like Lord Carnarvon, he intended to send an agent to annex the Boer republic, only his agent would not be accompanied by a band of policemen but by a well-armed force. The man he chose as his agent was his friend Dr Leander Starr Jameson. It was Dr Jameson who was to muster a military detachment on the border of the Transvaal and then, at an agreed time, lead his men into the Boer republic where he would claim to be answering a call to free the *uitlanders* from 'Krugerism'. Before this could happen, however, arms were to be smuggled into Johannesburg so that, when word was received that Jameson was on his way, the *uitlanders* could rise in rebellion. It was to be the sort of madcap adventure in which schoolboys and mercenaries delight.

But there was no delight in the outcome. Things did not work out as planned. The Boers got wind of the plot and were waiting in ambush for the raiders; last-minute attempts to stop Jameson embarking on the raid failed and the *uitlanders*, confused and at odds with each other, called off the rebellion. The expedition ended in disaster. Jameson was captured, sent to England to stand trial and imprisoned. Rhodes was summoned to appear before a committee of inquiry and, although let off with a reprimand, never fully recovered from the disgrace. Later it emerged that Joseph Chamberlain had known about Rhodes's plans and had given the raiders his tacit approval. The *uitlanders* had genuine grievances but their cause was exploited and undermined by political and financial opportunists.

So unprincipled, so predatory and dishonest were the instigators of the raid that Jameson's unprovoked attack won international sympathy for the Boers. President Kruger was loudly applauded in Holland, France and Germany (the Kaiser sent him a congratulatory telegram) and in Britain a small group of Liberal politicians – who might otherwise have questioned the Transvaal's self-righteousness, comparing it unfavourably to the treatment meted out to the republic's black inhabitants – now joined the ranks of those who championed Kruger.

Had the Boers had any doubts about the forces ranged against them, those doubts were dispelled by the Jameson raid. Now fully on their guard, they began to arm themselves. In March 1897 President Kruger visited Bloemfontein, the capital of the Orange Free State, to negotiate a new treaty of political alliance with the newly elected president, Marthinus Steyn. Under the terms of this treaty the two Boer republics agreed to assist each other should their independence be threatened. The following month, Britain made a conciliatory gesture by sending a new governor to the Cape. Ostensibly the task of this governor was to heal old wounds and bring about a peaceful settlement with the Boer republics. The man appointed to this mission was Sir Alfred Milner.

This is where Lady Edward Cecil picks up the story again. That she felt qualified to do so is understandable: in 1921 Alfred Milner became her second husband, and it is upon his published papers that her account is based. She says nothing about the controversy surrounding the Jameson raid but concentrates on the injustices suffered by the *uitlanders*. The situation of the 'Transvaal British', she says, was intolerable. She also claims that it was the intention of the Boers to eliminate British influence and establish 'a Boer republic over the whole of South Africa'. This was popular hearsay at the time. But, although later events show that it was not entirely unfounded, there is no reliable evidence to prove that, as Lady Edward implies, the Boers were then actively plotting to take over the Cape. There was more to the growing hostility than that.

If the British government genuinely wanted reconciliation with the Boers it had chosen the wrong man to act as negotiator. Alfred Milner was a man whose prejudices far outweighed his undoubted talents. A self-confessed 'British Race Patriot', the new governor was every bit as determined as Cecil Rhodes to secure English-speaking dominance throughout southern Africa. But on arriving at the Cape, he made all the right noises: he denounced the Jameson raid and expressed the hope that the dispute between Kruger and the *uitlanders* would be settled internally. His peace-making efforts were short lived. Within nine months of taking office Milner's attitude began to change; it became increasingly obvious that he was simply playing for time. 'There is no way out of the political troubles in S. Africa', he wrote to Joseph Chamberlain in February 1898, 'except reform in the Trans-vaal or war.'[13] And a few weeks later he was talking openly of working up a crisis 'by steadily and inflexibly pressing for the redress of substantial wrongs and injustices.' His wish, he confessed, was to bring about 'the great day of reckoning'.

That day came when Milner and Kruger met at Bloemfontein in May the following year. Milner arrived for the talks determined to put Kruger on the defensive. Convinced that the Boers were arguing from weakness, he intended to call their bluff. When he demanded a prompt and wholesale reform of the Transvaal franchise, Kruger cried: 'It is our country you want!' He was right. All the president's attempts to bargain were imperiously rejected and the conference ended in stalemate. It was no longer a question of whether or not there would be a war, but of when the fighting would start.

The next few months were tense. As the Boers continued to amass arms in the Transvaal, British troopships were diverted from India to the Cape. One of the first British officers to arrive was Colonel Baden-Powell, who was sent north to raise an irregular force in Bechuanaland (now Botswana) and Rhodesia. In Natal troops were moved closer to the Transvaal border and preparations were made to defend Kimberley, the centre of the diamond industry, in the Cape. Members of the Transvaal Volksraad (parliament) made bellicose speeches and were supported by their counterparts in the Orange Free State. Although Kruger continued to negotiate, the drift towards war was unmistakable.

At the end of September 1899 the Transvaal forces mobilized and a few days later those of the Orange Free State followed. Then, on 9 October, President Kruger issued an ultimatum. Its terms were uncompromising. It demanded that all points of difference between the two countries be referred to arbitration, that British troops be removed from the Transvaal borders, that all reinforcements that had arrived in South Africa since the first of June be withdrawn, and that troops then on the high seas be forbidden to land at South African ports. The British were given forty-eight hours in which to reply.

There was no chance of these terms being met. The Transvaal's demands were seen for what they were: a declaration of war. 'They have done it!' exclaimed Joseph Chamberlain when the ultimatum reached London. That evening the British government cabled a formal rejection and the following day, 11 October, Britain was officially at war with the Boer republics.

By issuing the ultimatum Kruger had cast himself in the role of aggressor and so played into his opponents' hands. Britain's case, observed an official at the Colonial Office, could not have been strengthened more had Chamberlain dictated the ultimatum himself. Lord Lansdowne, the Secretary for War, agreed. 'Accept my felicitations,' he wrote to Chamberlain. 'I don't think Kruger could have played your cards better than he has . . . My soldiers are in ecstasies.'[14] Even some of Kruger's sympathizers considered his demands deliberately provocative.

The jingo press was jubilant. When the Transvaal's demands were published, they were greeted with scorn. The republic was derided as a 'trumpery little State' and the Boers' challenge was dismissed as farcical. 'One is in doubt', declared the *Daily Telegraph*, 'whether to laugh or to weep.' *Punch* published a cartoon of a robust John Bull declaring, 'As you will *fight*, you shall have it. *This* time it's a fight to a finish.'[15] Majuba, it seemed, was to be avenged at last.

Those opposed to the war despaired. 'I can remember no case within the last forty years', wrote James Bryce, a former Liberal government minister, 'in which the real facts regarding a grave crisis have been so far from adequately conveyed to the British public by the press.'[16] But men like Bryce were very much in a minority. Their protests were lost in the avalanche of lurid headlines and bellicose editorials. Who wanted to listen to the cooing of doves when the bugles were sounding, when the Boers were reported to have crossed the Natal border and laid siege to Mafeking and Kimberley in the northern Cape? 'Give it to the Boers!' yelled the crowds who watched the troopships pull away from the Southampton docks. 'Bring back a piece of Kruger's whiskers!'

Even so, the jingo journalists and dockside crowds were not representative of the whole British public. For the most part news of Kruger's ultimatum was received calmly. War fever, like most fevers, undergoes an incubation period before temperatures rise and pulses pound. In London, fashionable circles remained unruffled, treating the news as something of a joke; only an excitable few succumbed to what Queen Victoria called the 'hysterical spirit'. But lack of numbers did not prevent ready-made patriots from reacting with vigour. This was certainly true of the women who formed a nucleus of 'society butterflies'. Hurriedly packing their summer dresses, their parasols and feather boas, these optimistic ladies set off for South Africa in high spirits, hoping to arrive in time for the victory celebrations. Few thought the war could last more than a couple of months. How could it? What hope had the ill-disciplined, haphazardly assembled Boer commandos of withstanding the regimented might of the British empire?

What was not appreciated was the lack of urgency with which the British War Office had responded to Milner's request for reinforcements. At the outbreak of war, when the Boers invaded Natal with an estimated 21,000 men, there were only some 13,000 British troops in the field. Moreover the newly-appointed British Commander-in-Chief, Sir Redvers Buller, had not then left England. He did not sail for the Cape until four days after war was declared. The early British defeats, which culminated during 'Black Week' in December when the imperial troops were repulsed in the Cape (halting the advance to relieve Kimberley and Mafeking) and Buller suffered a disastrous reverse at the battle of Colenso in Natal, were as unexpected as they were dispiriting. Talk of a quick and easy victory gave way to a mystified gloom.

Attempts to brighten things up may have contributed to the jollifications in Cape Town. Disappointment had to be met with a show of confidence; the gay chatter at the Mount Nelson Hotel reflected the need for diversion as well as the need to stave off boredom. On both counts the 'society butterflies' were only too willing to play their part. They seemed blissfully unaware that they were making pests of themselves, that their behaviour was regarded as scandalous and that they were thought to be hindering the war effort. The last thing they were expecting was a blast from Queen Victoria. With so many of the culprits being influential society women, some of them married to high-ranking officers, it required more than a little political courage to send them packing. Not until he received Joseph Chamberlain's telegram, carrying with it the Queen's authority, did Milner feel he had the backing he needed. His answering telegram was, as promised, immediately published.

According to Lady Edward Cecil, there was 'a great deal of cackle about this message.' Even so, Sir Alfred's strictures appear to have had little effect. Cackle the ladies might but few of them were prepared to leave, and ships arriving from England were as crowded as ever. Indeed, Lady Edward was soon reporting the arrival of another batch of titled women, including one of Queen Victoria's relations – the young Duchess of Teck. (Her 'semi-royal position', says Lady Edward, 'made her very acceptable for opening bazaars, sales of work and the like.') Some of these new arrivals came, as before, in the guise of volunteer nurses but they were no more qualified than their predecessors and spent as much time in the hunting field – on horses provided by Sir Alfred Milner – as they did tending the sick.

But at least the parties at the Mount Nelson Hotel became less rowdy, with fewer staff officers in attendance. This however was brought about by the bullying tactics of the newly-arrived army chief of staff, Lord Kitchener, rather than by the finger-wagging of Alfred Milner. Once Kitchener became aware that military discipline was being undermined, he briskly set about putting things to rights. 'You hear amazing stories', wrote a visiting journalist, 'of how Lord Kitchener will suddenly enter a club, or the Mount Nelson Hotel, in mufti, and with a few words of command will sweep the place of young staff officers who are more or less idling away their time, giving a choice of starting for the front or for England within twenty-four hours . . . One hears from officers and men that everyone is afraid of him.'[17]

Fear triumphed where royal wrath had failed. It was the threat of military transfers rather than talk of official displeasure that finally brought the merry-making in Cape Town to an end.

The first rush of women to the Cape had been a spontaneous event, more of an emotional response to a crisis than a loyal closing of ranks. Those who arrived later were far more purposeful. Sir Alfred Milner's cautionary announcement had been published in England as well as in South Africa but it did little to stop the steady flow of women to the Cape. It was these women, women who were prepared to defy officialdom, who reflected the new spirit of independence which, in all classes, was beginning to make itself felt in late Victorian England. To think of such women as crusaders for the feminist cause would be misleading. For the most part they were from the upper and middle class and would have disowned any suggestion of radicalism. They insisted that their motives were purely patriotic, often inspired by loyalty to their husbands who were serving in South Africa. All the same, by ignoring Sir Alfred Milner's warnings and going where they were not wanted, they were displaying – whether they acknowledged it or not – a disregard for authority that would have been unthinkable to an earlier generation. If they were not rebels in the accepted sense, they were decidedly more assertive than their mid-Victorian mothers.

The nineteenth century can hardly be described as the age of female emancipation, yet it is to the second half of that century that the beginnings of the struggle for equality of the sexes can be traced. From the 1850s onwards there was, as one historian has so elequently put it, 'a stir, it assailed all ranks of femininity, the stir of adventure and new ideas, comparable with the agitation which may be noted in a flock of migrants impelled by the lure of new worlds.'[18] The awakening was slow, progress erratic, but the trend was irreversible. By the late 1880s important gains had been made with the emergence of the first woman doctor, Elizabeth Garrett, the founding of women's colleges at Oxford and Cambridge and the crusades for social and political reform led by women like Josephine Butler, Annie Besant, Barbara Bodichon, Helen Taylor, Emily Davies, Sophia Jex-Blake and Lydia Bekker.

Although only a few of the women who went to South Africa during the Anglo-Boer war were active in the campaigns for equality, many of them had benefited from the battles waged on their behalf. This was particularly true of the passing, in 1870, of the Married Women's Property Act. By this act a wife, if she had money of her own, was able to escape economic bondage to her husband. Among the more fortunate beneficiaries were women from the families of landed gentry or wealthy merchants who, having inherited a fortune, had previously been forced to surrender all rights in their property to the man they married. Financial freedom had given these women a new sense of purpose, a self-assurance and a confidence in their own judgement which made them unwilling to submit to male dominance. They were the sort of women who could afford to follow the flag to Cape Town in spite of the protestations of the Cape authorities. Vague as many of them were about the purpose of their visit, they had little doubt about their ability, and their right, to play a part in the conflict. News items from South Africa, during the early months of the war, had assured them of this.

Not every journalist, when looking for diversions, had confined himself to the doings of the 'society butterflies'. One of the most widely-read newspapers of the day, the recently launched *Daily Mail*, had some very different stories to tell. The *Daily Mail* was the brain-child of the enterprising Alfred Harmsworth (the future Lord Northcliffe) and was designed to appeal to a mass market. On-the-spot reporting during the first months of hostilities had boosted the *Mail*'s sales and ensured its popularity. Not the least of its many wartime scoops had been its success in acquiring a correspondent in beleaguered

Mafeking whose escapades during the siege had not only excited readers of the *Mail* but had been widely reported by rival journalists. Even more remarkable was the fact that the correspondent was a woman, and an aristocratic one at that.

She was the thirty-five-year-old Lady Sarah Wilson. Married, with two sons, she had been born Lady Sarah Isabella Augusta Spencer-Churchill, the youngest daughter of the 7th Duke of Marlborough. Her presence in South Africa at the outbreak of war was purely fortuitous. A few months earlier she had been touring Rhodesia with her husband, Captain Gordon Wilson, an officer of the Royal Horse Guards, and they had broken their tour in July to visit Cecil Rhodes in Cape Town. At Rhodes's house they had met Colonel Baden-Powell, just arrived from England with instructions to raise an irregular force. This chance encounter had led to Gordon Wilson being appointed, as aide-de-camp, to Baden-Powell's staff. Sarah, alive to the possibility of war, had insisted on accompanying her husband when he travelled north to take up his duties. In doing so she set in motion a series of events which were to earn her a reputation for daring, drive her into enemy hands and launch her on a career as one of the first women war-correspondents.

Lady Sarah Wilson was, on the face of it, an unlikely trail-blazer. A daughter of the Victorian establishment, a woman whose upbringing was rigorously conventional and who, like the rest of her family, was an outspoken opponent of women's rights, she appeared to display all the prejudices of her class and age. But there was more to Lady Sarah than met the eye. Beneath her restrained exterior she was a lively, assertive, impetuous and extremely strong-willed woman. She had more than her share of that independent spirit which had brought so many of her contemporaries to South Africa. Indeed, if the ladies who arrived in Cape Town needed proof that the bugles had sounded for heroines as well as heroes, they had only to look to the exploits of Lady Sarah Wilson.

2

An Enterprising Churchill

OF ALL HIS female relatives, young Winston Churchill disliked his Aunt Sarah most. Sarah was the youngest sister of his father, Lord Randolph Churchill, but this close relationship did nothing to warm Winston to her. Nor, for that matter, did Sarah look fondly on her nephew. Ten years older than Winston, Sarah appears to have expected a deference from him which he was incapable of showing; this lack of respect led to a mutual antipathy which lasted throughout their lives.

In many ways Sarah and Winston were very alike, displaying all the recognizable Churchillian traits. That was part of the trouble. Not only were they both headstrong, opinionated and outspoken, but each resented the other's tendency to hog the limelight. So competitive were they, so jealously did they guard their respective claims to fame, that even when they were sharing the headlines in a common cause – the war in South Africa – they studiously avoided mentioning each other's exploits. But the common cause had nothing to do with their hostility towards each other: that had its origins in earlier events.

If Sarah objected to her nephew's impertinence, Winston was no less incensed by her maddening interference in his personal affairs. This was something he found intolerable. His youthful letters are peppered with jibes aimed at his meddlesome aunt. Things came to a head in 1893, shortly after the nineteen-year-old Winston had completed his first year at Sandhurst. Then it was that, in an attempt to raise some extra cash, he decided to sell an old pair of field glasses and advertised them in the magazine *Exchange and Mart*. Somehow or other, Sarah got to hear of this and jumped to conclusions. Thinking that the glasses were his father's, who was abroad at the time, she assumed that Winston was secretly trying to dispose of his father's property and, without making enquiries, she reported the sale to her mother, the Dowager Duchess of Marlborough, as well as to other members of the family. Winston was justifiably furious. In an angry letter to his mother he proved the glasses were his – his father had recently replaced the glasses with a new pair – and roundly denounced Sarah: 'such a cat', he fumed. 'Such a liar that woman is. I will never forget her kindness as long as I live.'[1] Nor did he forget. This trivial incident continued to rankle and ended all chances of a reconciliation between aunt and nephew.

Winston was not the only member of the Churchill clan to be outraged by Sarah's mischief-making. The animosity she aroused in the wife of another of her nephews was every bit as fierce.

In 1892 Sarah's eldest brother, George, the 8th Duke of Marlborough, had died and the title passed to his twenty-one-year-old son, Charles. To ensure both the succession and the family fortunes, the 9th Duke married, in 1895, the rich and beautiful American heiress Consuelo Vanderbilt. After their widely publicized wedding in New York, the couple honeymooned in Europe before arriving in England where they travelled, via London, to Blenheim Palace, the Marlborough seat in Oxfordshire. They were met at the railway station by a formidable array of Churchills, with Sarah well to the fore. At dinner that evening it was Sarah's sharp tongue that Consuelo found most frightening. When the conversation turned to the wedding, the bridegroom's mother complained that she had not been able to attend because her son had refused to pay her fare to America. 'Then', says Consuelo, 'Sarah tittered and also regretted that she had not been present. "But", she added, "the Press did not spare us one detail", and I felt the word "vulgar" had been omitted but not its implications.'[2] Consuelo never forgot that ill-considered remark. Years later when she came to write her memoirs she painted an acid picture of Sarah. 'Lady Sarah Wilson – a Churchill – was quite different', she says. 'She told me to call her Sarah since she thought herself too young to be an aunt, and I felt an enmity I could not account for. She seemed to me as hard as her polished appearance, and her prominent eyes, harsh and sarcastic laugh made me shudder . . . To me she was kind in an arrogant manner that made me grit my teeth.'

'Arrogant' was a word often applied to Sarah. It suited her. She had a blustering, bullying way that made people nervous. She could never, it is said, 'resist a pungent comment or a withering gibe'. But Consuelo was wrong in thinking that Sarah regarded her as a vulgar, title-hunting parvenue. Nothing in fact could have been further from the truth. Sarah's haughty manner resulted from her upbringing and in no way reflected her true feelings. She had been trained to put people down, whatever their origins or background. After the death of her father in 1883 she had become her mother's permanent companion, and the Dowager Duchess of Marlborough was an extremely fearsome woman. 'She ruled Blenheim', says one of her daughters-in-law, 'and nearly all those in it with a firm hand. At the rustle of her silk dress the household trembled.'[3] Years of dancing attendance on the Duchess had given Sarah an exaggerated idea of her own importance, had made her imperious, demanding and patronizing. By imitating her mother, she had acquired the mannerisms of an autocrat. But this façade was easily demolished. Anyone who replied to her in kind (always excepting her cheeky nephew) soon found her willing to laugh at herself. Certainly she could have had no objection to her nephew marrying a rich American: such unions were, by the 1890s, part of a well-established Churchill tradition.

Not only had Lord Randolph Churchill married, in 1874, the dazzling Jennie Jerome, daughter of an American financier, but fourteen years later Sarah's eldest brother, the divorced 8th Duke of Marlborough, had taken for his second wife an even richer American woman, Mrs Lily Hammersley (she shortened her first name from Lilian because it rhymed with million). Sarah was very friendly with both these sisters-in-law and remained loyal to Jennie Churchill long after Lord Randolph's death. Far from scorning American women, Sarah appears to have shared the family penchant for them. In later life one of her dearest friends was the highly attractive Nancy Leeds, the granddaughter of an American doctor, who in her twenties had married, as her second husband, a self-made multi-millionaire from whom she inherited a vast fortune, which enabled her to settle in Europe where she met and married Prince Christopher of Greece. Nancy Leeds was only one of Sarah's unorthodox friends; another was the captivating Alice Keppel, King Edward VII's last mistress. Riches and beauty would always mean more to Sarah than an aristocratic pedigree.

Had proof been needed of her readiness to embrace new money, it could be found in her own marriage to Gordon Chesney Wilson. It was said of Sarah that 'her brothers possessed genius, her sisters stately homes'.[4] By accepting Gordon Wilson, Sarah altered the family pattern. Gordon Wilson's parents had no stately home; in fact when they were in England they had to lease Disraeli's old home, Hughenden, as a country residence. Sir Samuel Wilson, Gordon's father, had started life as a farmer's son in Ireland, but at the age of twenty he had emigrated to Australia where, after working as a miner, he had made his fortune cattle-ranching. In 1861 he had married a daughter of the Honourable William Campbell and from that time on the family of four sons and three daughters had divided their time between England and Australia. Not until after he had been knighted for his services in the Legislative Assembly of Western Australia did Sir Samuel settle, more or less permanently, in England. In 1886 he became the Conservative M P for Portsmouth but neither this, nor his wife's titled connections, prevented the Wilsons from being regarded by their snobbish neighbours as *nouveaux riches*.

While his family were in Australia Gordon was at Eton, where he was to be remembered for the records he set as a runner, and for his singular feat in saving the life of Queen Victoria by striking the gun from a would-be assassin on Windsor railway station. From Eton he went on to Christ Church, Oxford and then, in 1887, he joined the army. He was a lieutenant in the Blues (Royal Horse Guards) when he and Sarah first met and their romance is said to have been encouraged by Lady Randolph Churchill. That encouragement was needed is not surprising. Sarah, then in her mid twenties, was not the most sought-after young woman of the day. Most men found her brusque, schoolmistressy manner distinctly off-putting and Gordon, although a lively enough young man, was a far from dynamic suitor; he was too easy-going and unassuming to battle for a woman's hand. And neither of them had much to recommend them in the way of looks. Sarah was attractive and knew how to present herself. In carefully-posed photographs she appears an elegant, handsome woman, with her wide-set eyes, firm down-slanting mouth and snub nose. But this is because she insisted on facing the camera with her head held high, and was always immaculately dressed. Caught unawares in a snapshot, she is seen to be short, squat, with a receding chin and large bulbous eyes – making it easy to understand some of the less flattering remarks made about her. Gordon, for his part, was an undistinguished, homely-looking man with a large, untidy walrus moustache which, despite his laughing eyes, gave him a somewhat gloomy look. For a military man he was surprisingly round-shouldered.

For all that, it is not difficult to appreciate the mutual attraction. They had many interests in common; both prided themselves on their horsemanship, and Sarah came to share Gordon's passion for hunting.

Temperamentally, each supplied the other's defects, her assertiveness complementing his imperturbable good-nature. Between them they built a comfortable, if prosaic, relationship.

Their wedding at St George's, Hanover Square on 21 November 1891, attended by the Prince of Wales and other members of the royal family, was considered one of the great social events of the year. Only the bride's nephew, young Winston, failed to enjoy it. Having been given special permission to attend the ceremony from Harrow, he complained bitterly about being bundled back to school just as the fun was starting.

Married life suited Sarah. No longer a mere junior member of the Churchill family, an echo of her formidable mother, she now took her own place in society. Within no time she was being reported in the social columns as one of 'the smartest of the young married women'; stylishly dressed, she was seen at every fashionable gathering. Fully sharing her husband's love of the turf, she was thrilled when his horse Father O'Flynn won the Derby in the first year of their marriage. A few months later her first son, Randolph Gordon, was born and the following year saw the birth of another son, Alan Spencer. This completed the Wilson's family. They did not, however, allow the ties of parenthood to interfere with their social life. Gordon was still a junior army officer but he and Sarah lived like plutocrats. Although they were by no means the richest couple in London, they were well able to keep up appearances and match the grander members of Sarah's family.

To what extent Sarah had been influenced by the Wilson fortune in her decision to marry Gordon, it is impossible to say. She had some money of her own but it is unlikely that she was indifferent to the fact that her husband came from a rich family. Judging by later events in her life, it is obvious that money fascinated Sarah: she mixed only with the very rich, and tended to choose her friends by the size of their incomes or the extent of their influence. Her preoccupation with money amused the ever-critical Winston Churchill. When old Sir Samuel Wilson died in 1895, Winston was delighted with a rumour that Sarah had been passed over in her father-in-law's will. 'The common report is', he gleefully informed his mother, 'that the old boy has left it all to the younger children and they get nothing more. I hope this is so most sincerely. Seven or eight thousand a year is quite enough & more money would only increase her conceit & arrogance.'[5]

Seven or eight thousand was indeed a sizeable income in the 1890s. But Winston was wrong in assuming it was enough for Sarah. She had much higher ambitions, and was always looking for ways to increase her fortune. It was a financial involvement which first interested her in South African affairs.

In 1891 Lord Randolph Churchill had paid a controversial visit to southern Africa. The reason given for this visit was that he intended to investigate the suitability of central Africa for British emigrants. Cecil Rhodes had recently sent his pioneer force to occupy Mashonaland (later, part of Rhodesia) and Lord Randolph claimed to be interested in plans to settle British people in the territory. Privately he was every bit as interested in Mashonaland's potential for speculators: the region was then thought to be rich in gold deposits. He was to be disappointed on both scores. The mining expert who accompanied him found few traces of the rumoured gold and Lord Randolph, in a series of provocative newspaper articles, damned the territory's prospects as a colony. But this did not destroy his hopes of a profitable investment. On his return journey he stopped over at Johannesburg and, after consulting leading financiers, invested £5000 in gold claims. It was later revealed that he was acting on behalf of a syndicate which included various members of his family. When, after his return to England, the syndicate was converted into a limited company, one of the listed shareholders was his sister, Lady Sarah Wilson.

Lord Randolph had been terminally ill on his Mashonaland trip. Four years later, in January 1895, he died. After his death Sarah became actively involved in the transactions of the gold-mining company. One of her first moves was to visit South Africa. She and Gordon travelled to the Cape in December 1895 with Alfred Beit, the influential gold-magnate and ally of Cecil Rhodes. Beit it was who took the Wilsons to Groote Schuur and introduced them to Rhodes. Although never at his best in the company of women, Rhodes seemed to take an instant liking to Sarah and invited the Wilsons to lunch on Christmas Eve. The lunch was a great success. Most of the talk was political but Sarah, who was enchanted by Rhodes, found her host somewhat preoccupied. On hearing that Sarah and Gordon were about to leave for Kimberley, Rhodes pressed them to stay with him on their return and then appeared to have second thoughts. 'My plans', he explained as they were leaving, 'are a little unsettled.' Just how unsettled those plans were, not only the Wilsons but the entire world was soon to learn.

Sarah is vague about her reasons for visiting Kimberley – the so-called Diamond City – but there may well have been a financial incentive. As it happened, financial considerations were forced to take second place to a more explosive event. The Wilsons had hardly arrived in the town before they became aware that trouble was brewing. On the voyage from England Sarah had heard Alfred Beit and others talking of a plot to force President Kruger into granting concessions to the *uitlanders* but, or so she claims, she failed to recognize the significance of what was being said. Now, it seemed, all was to be revealed. Her suspicion that she had arrived in South Africa in 'stirring times' was to be confirmed.

First there were rumours of tension in Johannesburg. Sarah was told that some women who had been preparing to leave for the Transvaal had received telegrams advising them to delay their departure. Then the newspapers published details of a manifesto issued by the *uitlanders*, setting out their grievances and calling for a mass meeting. Two days of anxiety followed. Nearly everyone in Kimberley had a friend or relative in Johannesburg, and the possibility of a rebellion there was a cause for alarm. That possibility increased when they received the most stunning news of all. On 30 December it was learned that Dr Jameson – himself an old Kimberley resident – had invaded the Transvaal with an armed force. The people of Kimberley found this impossible to believe. The idea of Jameson, a local hero, leading an invasion force was incomprehensible. When it was later reported that most of the army officers accompanying him held imperial commissions, the feeling of incredulity gave way to one of bewilderment. 'One heard perfect strangers', says Sarah, 'asking each other how these officers could justify their action of entering a friendly territory, armed to the teeth.'

Not until Jameson and his men were captured, on 4 January, did the truth strike home. Then the citizens of Kimberley forgot their former doubts and rallied behind the defeated doctor, turning their anger on those who had deserted him – the perfidious mining magnates of Johannesburg who, they claimed, had sacrificed Jameson to save their own skins.

Sarah and Gordon did not stay to see the demonstrations which, over the next few weeks, were staged in support of Jameson. They decided it would be unwise to travel on to Johannesburg and returned instead to Cape Town. Here they found 'everything in a turmoil', although most people they met appeared thankful that war had been averted. They were still in Cape Town when a few days later Rhodes, who had resigned as prime minister, left for England to, as he put it, 'face the music'. The Wilsons went to see him off on the mail ship and

Sarah seized the opportunity to consolidate her friendship with the instigator of the Jameson Raid. She had no doubt that Rhodes would survive the crisis, and told him of a bet she had with a friend that he would return as the dominant figure in South African politics within a year. Rhodes was not so sure. 'It will take ten years', he told her; 'better cancel your bet.' They were both wrong. Rhodes was to die six years later without ever regaining his political influence.

With Rhodes gone, Sarah's thoughts again turned to the Transvaal. Her purpose in coming to South Africa had been to familiarize herself with the mining industry and this made a visit to Johannesburg essential. But how to get there? Rail travel between the Cape and the Transvaal had been seriously disrupted; the only alternative route was by way of Natal. This meant travelling by sea to Durban and taking a train from there to Johannesburg. Unfortunately, most of the coastal steamers were already fully booked. Sarah, never backward in flaunting her family connections, turned for help to the governor of the Cape, Sir Hercules Robinson, who obligingly arranged for the Wilsons to travel as 'indulgence passengers' in a troopship which was being sent to Durban to pick up Dr Jameson and his men. Having been handed over by the Boers, the raiders were now being taken to England to stand trial. Sarah was delighted. She was not certain whether the curtain had just come down on a farce or a drama, but having said goodbye to the luckless producer she was anxious to catch a glimpse of the leading actors.

A glimpse was all she did catch. Not until Sarah and Gordon were about to disembark at Durban did the bedraggled, forlorn-looking prisoners scramble aboard the troopship. Recognizing some friends among the army officers, the Wilsons exchanged a few hasty words with them. Sarah even managed to greet Dr Jameson before she was hurried ashore. This was her first meeting with the man she came to admire for his charm of manner and 'absolutely fearless disposition'.

Before leaving South Africa, Sarah was to catch sight of another local celebrity. In Johannesburg most of her time was taken up in consultations with Lord Randolph Churchill's mining expert, but she did manage to squeeze in a day's visit to Pretoria. It was here that she and Gordon spotted the redoubtable Paul Kruger. They were being shown over Pretoria's handsome main square when the solemn old patriarch, flanked by four burgers, came shuffling down the steps of a government office and entered his carriage. 'We took a good look at this remarkable personage', says Sarah. 'Stout in figure, in a somewhat worn frock-coat and rusty old black silk hat, President Kruger did not look the stern dictator of his little kingdom which in truth he was.' She had to remind herself that Kruger, for all his homely looks, was 'in his ignorant fashion, a man of iron like Bismarck'.

The Wilsons' first visit to South Africa was remarkable for its timing and for its effect on Sarah. In the space of a few hectic weeks she had visited most of the important centres in the country, befriended its influential English-speaking leaders and become acquainted with its politics and the problems of the white communities. Although she acknowledged the genuine grievances of the Boers, her sympathies remained firmly with the *uitlanders* who, in her opinion, were battling to ensure the economic prosperity of the Transvaal. Ignoring her own financial interest in the outcome of the struggle, she lauded the mining magnates as crusaders in the cause of progress. Only the obstinacy of their opponents and the foolhardiness of their hot-headed partisans prevented them from achieving their goals. On her return to England, Lady Sarah Wilson emerged as a fervent champion of the powerful Randlords.

She was not alone. Sarah's views were echoed by most of her fashionable friends. These were the years when London society embraced the *nouveaux riches* of Johannesburg and rejoiced in their gold. 'The Nineties', says a historian of the period, 'were the high and palmy days of the great Randlords . . . Johannesburg seemed nearer to London than any English town.'[6] With gold fever running high, Sarah was much in demand. Not the least of her attractions was her ability to produce at short notice one of her new South African friends, whose presence was guaranteed to brighten any dinner party. The most sought-after guest was the dashing Dr Leander Starr Jameson, the man who in Sarah's circle had come to be regarded as a hero of Empire.

Jameson's farcical invasion of the Transvaal had in no way diminished his reputation. His failure to seize Johannesburg was dismissed as an unfortunate mishap. At his trial in London, he had been sentenced to fifteen months' imprisonment, but ill-health had gained him an early release. It was during his convalescence after he left prison that Jameson came to know the Wilsons well. When he was fully recovered he was happy to be introduced to Sarah's friends. It was in the company of Dr Jameson that, three years later – in May 1899 – Sarah and Gordon returned to South Africa for their second visit. On their arrival at the Cape, they left immediately for Rhodesia where, in Bulawayo, Jameson handed them over to his friend Major Heany.

For the next five weeks, Heany – a red-bearded American who had been involved in the Jameson Raid – played host to the Wilsons. Sarah, who had brought her German maid, Metelka, with her – having left her small sons with Gordon's mother – was delighted to be back in Africa. 'A curious thing about that continent', she remarked, 'is: you may dislike it or fall under its charm, but in any case it nearly always calls you back. It certainly did in my case.' One of the reasons for this visit was that Sarah wanted to inspect some mines of which Major Heany was a managing director. They also found time to indulge Gordon's passion for hunting. Game was scarce, the lions kept well hidden and they were caught in some violent thunderstorms, but the country was 'pretty and well wooded' and Sarah loved the rough-and-tumble of camp life. It all seemed a million miles from civilization. But news from the outside world did occasionally reach them. They were made aware of the tension then building up in the south: the political wrangling, the failure of the negotiations between Kruger and Milner, the threats and demands on both sides. There was no escaping the fact that they had again arrived in Africa at a time of crisis. This time, however, it was not a military escapade but a full-scale war that seemed 'exceedingly likely'.

It was a cable from Cecil Rhodes, inviting them to stay at Groote Schuur, that finally decided them to return to the Cape. They reached Cape Town shortly after Rhodes arrived from England – he had cabled them from the ship – and they were able to witness the hysterical demonstrations that were staged to welcome him. Whatever the rest of the world now thought of Cecil Rhodes, he was left in no doubt about the loyalty of the citizens of Cape Town. The Wilsons attended a monster meeting held for Rhodes in the Drill Hall. As he mounted the platform, says Sarah, 'the cheering went on for ten minutes, and was again and again renewed, till the enthusiasm brought a lump to many throats.'

Even so, the threat of war overshadowed all other considerations in Cape Town. At Groote Schuur, every conversation tended to centre on which side would make the first move. Oddly enough, Rhodes was one of the few who thought the crisis would pass and that a settlement would be reached. He was convinced the Boers would eventually be forced to climb down. 'Kruger', he was fond of saying, 'will bluff up to the cannon's mouth.' Gordon Wilson did not agree. As a professional soldier he had little faith in the predictions of politicians, and recognized the need to prepare for the worst. That need became more apparent when, on 25 July, Colonel Baden-Powell arrived in Cape Town.

Baden-Powell had come with instructions to raise an irregular force which would guard the Rhodesian border and, if necessary, distract the Boers from advancing southwards through the northern Cape. Apart from those instructions and a small body of officers, the dapper, forty-two-year-old Colonel had little else. During the short time he was at the Cape he attempted to recruit men and raise money, but on both counts he was frustrated by the Cape authorities, who were afraid he would alarm 'the Dutch'. Undeterred, Baden-Powell instructed his chief-of-staff, Major Lord Edward Cecil, to remain at the Cape and use his influence – as son of the British Prime Minister – to obtain guns and ammunition, and then left for Bulawayo where he intended to raise his troops. He had been strictly forbidden to station men at Mafeking, the principal town in British-controlled Bechuanaland. However, he could congratulate himself on one stroke of luck. Although he had been unable to enlist men at the Cape he had obtained the services of an additional officer, in the person of Captain Gordon Wilson. Whether he was also pleased to have the company of Lady Sarah Wilson is another matter: like so many Victorian army officers, Baden-Powell had little time for women. But, wanted or not, Sarah was determined to accompany Gordon to Bulawayo and the two of them left for the north in August 1899.

Waiting for a war in Bulawayo was a tedious experience for Sarah. The primitive little town, not much larger than an English village, had been established some five years earlier and, although now connected to the Cape by rail, was still relatively isolated. News was unreliable, often contradictory, and the local newspapers were often reduced to reporting pointless gossip. 'It can easily be imagined', says Sarah, 'that there was little else discussed then but warlike subjects, and these were two dreary and anxious months.'

On the rare occasions when Gordon was in town, the monotony was slightly less oppressive. During the day Sarah was able to watch the officers drilling their new recruits and in the evening members of Baden-Powell's staff would join the Wilsons for a hand of bridge. There were even times when they were allowed to continue their excursions in the veld, visiting the homes of nearby mining managers and exploring local beauty spots. But such activities were rare. More often than not Gordon was away on duty, unable to return to Bulawayo, and out of touch with Sarah for days at a time.

Baden-Powell, obeying the letter if not the spirit of the Cape prohibitions, had established a second recruiting base at Ramatlhabama, a few miles north of Mafeking. He claimed to have no wish to enter Mafeking, but this did not prevent his officers – dressed in civilian clothes, their luggage marked with a plain 'Esq.' – from becoming frequent visitors to the Mafeking railway station, where they were not only recognized but welcomed. Like the rest of Baden-Powell's staff, Gordon spent a great deal of his time dashing backwards and forwards between Bechuanaland and Bulawayo. During his absences, Sarah amused herself 'learning how to bandage on the lanky arms and legs of a little black boy'.

By the end of September, hopes of peace were running out. Kruger ordered his men to mobilize. In the western Transvaal commandos were formed and massed on the border of the northern Cape. At last Baden-Powell was given permission to move his troops into Mafeking. These were the men he had mustered at Ramatlhabama; the other half of his force – the men recruited and trained at Bulawayo – were under the command of Colonel Herbert Plumer who was now detailed to provide a mobile patrol. It was Plumer's task to defend the Rhodesian border and reduce pressure on Mafeking. Several months were to pass before Baden-Powell's divided force came together again.

With war imminent, Gordon Wilson was ordered to join Baden-Powell in Mafeking. Sarah decided that the time had come for her to return home and it was arranged for her to travel to the Cape, from where she would sail for England. Her friends in Bulawayo warned her of the risk she was taking. Now that there was a real threat of war, they said, any train travelling through South Africa 'might be stuck up, fired upon and the like'.[7] Sarah refused to listen. She had no intention of sitting out the war in Bulawayo and, in any case, she was secretly harbouring thoughts of playing a more exciting role when war was declared.

'Lady Sarah Wilson arrives, I believe, one day this week', wrote Lady Edward Cecil from Groote Schuur on 2 October.[8] But Lady Sarah did not arrive. She got no further south than Mafeking. In fact, she had never seriously contemplated making for the Cape, and had changed her mind about returning to England.

On 3 November 1899, the *Daily Mail* published a letter which it had just received from Lady Sarah Wilson. Published under the heading 'Our Life in Mafeking', this letter was announced as the first of a series 'recording the events on the Frontier from a woman's point of view'. Why or how Sarah came to send this despatch is not clear. The most likely explanation is that she, along with the rest of her family, had contacts in the newspaper world and had seized the opportunity to exploit them. By choosing to write to the *Daily Mail* she displayed characteristic shrewdness. At that time few newspapers were more popular than the attention-grabbing *Mail* and the promise of 'war letters' from a titled woman correspondent guaranteed acceptance and a generous reward. Sarah would not have overlooked such considerations. And she was right. Having recently failed to persuade Winston Churchill to act as a correspondent, the *Mail* was only too pleased to accept Sarah's services. She was promptly enrolled as a Special War Correspondent and hailed as 'the only woman acting as such for any paper in South Africa'. Her first report was said to have created a 'great sensation'.

When she wrote this report, on 7 October, Sarah had been in Mafeking for a week and was staying at Dixon's Hotel. Conditions in the town were chaotic. War had not yet been declared but Baden-Powell had not allowed this to interfere with his plans. On entering Mafeking he had immediately set about preparing for a siege. All able-bodied men were enlisted in a town guard, a chain of outposts was established, trenches were dug and defence works started. Stock was taken of the town's supplies and arrangements made for women who so wished to leave for the Cape. Most of Mafeking's inhabitants, noted Sarah, were in a state 'of serious alarm'.

With an attack expected at any moment, rumours of the Boers' approach buzzed as incessantly as the locusts that plagued the town. Sarah was assured that 5000 Boers were in laager on the border and were preparing to advance on Mafeking in a couple of days' time. This proved to be untrue, but one scare was quickly replaced by another. There was talk of spies and traitors, of mysterious horsemen sighted in the distance and of reinforcements arriving for the Boers from Pretoria. So persistent and convincing were the rumours that there was a constant ringing of alarm bells calling out the town militia, and at night the firing of rockets into the air would send the bemused population scurrying to their posts. These night alarms became so frequent that most people took to sleeping in their clothes.

For all that, for all the sleepless nights and rumour-mongering, Sarah was enjoying the crisis enormously. 'In spite of wars and rumours of wars', she wrote, 'we eat and drink and have our joke, even play a game of bridge after dinner, though this is apt to be abruptly broken in upon by one of the party being mysteriously "wanted" outside, or having to ride out and see the outposts are bright and awake."⁹ There were several of her London friends attached to Baden-Powell's staff – including Lord Edward Cecil and her cousin by marriage, Captain Charles Fitzclarence – and in no time she began to feel very much at home. She even bought a white pony called Dop from a Johannesburg polo-player and spent her mornings and evenings riding round the outskirts of Mafeking inspecting the fortifications. It all added to the feeling of suspense and urgency.

After a while Gordon and Sarah rented a small cottage in the town, but they continued to eat at Dixon's Hotel. It was an arrangement that suited Sarah for, although she found the hotel food 'weird', she enjoyed the lively company of the army officers who gathered there. The only thing that spoiled her fun was the thought that she might suddenly be ordered out of Mafeking. Baden-Powell, as she well knew, was doing his utmost to clear the town of unnecessary liabilities. When Dr Jameson arrived unexpectedly, hoping to play a part in the siege, he was sent packing 'with more haste than courtesy'. The little doctor was so hated by the Boers that Baden-Powell told him bluntly that if he meant to stay it would take a battery of artillery to defend the town. Jameson left, protesting that he had intended to travel on to Natal in any case.

Sarah was aware that she was equally unwelcome. 'Colonel Baden-Powell', she wrote in her memoirs, 'did not look on my presence with great favour, neither did he order me to leave, and I had a sort of presentiment that I might be useful . . . Therefore, though I talked of going South every day by one of the overcrowded trains to Cape Town, in which the Government was offering free tickets to any one who wished to avail themselves of the opportunity, I secretly hoped to be allowed to remain.' This was written years later. At the time she made no secret of her determination to stay. Not only did she promise the *Daily Mail* a series of letters but, by renting a cottage in the town, she made it clear that she was not a bird of passage. Nor was she alone in her defiance. Another officer's wife, Mrs Godley – a sportswoman after Sarah's own heart – had followed her into the town and the two of them joined forces. It was their intention, they declared publicly, to stick it out. 'There is no rush to take advantage of the railway facilities', wrote a war-correspondent; 'many of the bolder spirits, led by Lady Sarah Wilson, flatly refuse to leave and have banded them-selves as Red Cross nurses.'¹⁰

But they were reckoning without Baden-Powell. On 8 October – the day after Sarah first wrote to the *Daily Mail* – Mafeking received details of the ultimatum which Kruger was about to serve on Britain, demanding the withdrawal of troops from the Transvaal borders. This gave Baden-Powell his deadline. He sprang into action and redoubled his efforts to strengthen the weak spots in Mafeking's defences. 'In the little time that is left to us', reported Angus Hamilton of *The Times*, 'we hope to ensconce ourselves behind something of an impregnable defence.'[11]

For her part, Sarah moved to the house of Mr Benjamin Weil, a well-known Mafeking merchant. Weil lived in the centre of the town, close to the railway station, and his house was considered 'comparatively safe'. Sarah hoped to turn part of it into a hospital. There was no longer any question of her returning to the Cape. Traffic to the south had come to a halt and there was talk of the Boers tearing up the railway line.

But Sarah was not to remain in Mafeking. With the ultimatum running out, Baden-Powell decided to expel all unwanted visitors, particularly the women visitors. Late one night he sent a staff officer to inform Sarah of his decision. A Boer force, she was told, was expected to arrive at Mafeking the following day. It was thought they would rush the town: she must leave for a place of safety immediately. This was an order she could not ignore. As an officer's wife and a descendant of the great Duke of Marlborough, she was far too conscious of her duty to challenge a military command. Reluctantly she bowed to the inevitable.

Sarah had been about to go to bed when the staff officer arrived; now she changed into travelling clothes. At first it was suggested that she make for a mission station in the Kalahari desert, but this plan was quickly abandoned. The mission station was extremely isolated and it was thought that supplies might run short. Instead she was told to head for Setlagole, some forty-six miles from Mafeking, where she could be accommodated at a trading store. There she would be on the direct route of any relieving force arriving from the Cape.

Her preparations did not take long. She and her maid, Metelka, hurriedly packed two handbags which they strapped to a Cape cart. The cart, drawn by six mules, was to be driven by a Cape 'coloured' man, and a Zulu servant, Wilhelm (whom Sarah mistakenly called Vellum) was to ride behind on Sarah's pony. Wilhelm, who had once been employed by Dr Jameson, was to remain at Sarah's side throughout the hectic days ahead. 'Beneath his dusky skin beat a heart of gold', said Sarah, 'and I could safely have confided countless treasures to him.'

The preparations complete, they sat waiting for the dawn. As the night wore on the wind howled mournfully round the house, making all thought of sleep impossible. Shortly before daybreak they got ready to leave. Struggling to keep calm, Sarah said her goodbyes and, after a last hug from Gordon, climbed on to the cart beside Metelka. The driver flicked his whip and the little party trundled forward. They drove through the dawn-dark streets, bumped across the railway lines, and headed for the open veld.

At about the same time, another party set out in the opposite direction. Mrs Godley had also been given her marching orders, and was making for Bulawayo. 'Both wished to remain handy', said Major Godley, 'for the few weeks during which, if it took place at all, it was expected that the siege would last.'[12]

3

Alarms and Excursions

'So that afternoon [11 October 1899] our burgers crossed the border near Mafeking', wrote Alida Badenhorst from a farm just within the Transvaal; 'they tore up the railway line and destroyed the telegraph wires . . . next morning we heard a deep booming. We could not think what it was, only our hearts beat with anxiety. Soon tidings reached us: war had broken out.'[1]

That morning Sarah also listened to the distant booming of guns. In her little white-washed bedroom at the Setlagole store, she stood transfixed as she counted each dull thud. Altogether, she estimated, twenty shots were fired. The bombardment was followed by an 'impressive silence', made all the more intense by the almost unreal tranquillity of the surrounding countryside. The sky was cloudless; a faint early-morning glow blurred the horizon. Sarah was numbed by a sense of eeriness. She was used to cannon fire – to salutes on ceremonial occasions – but this was different. This was war. Each shot had been aimed at human beings: more than likely at the very men to whom she had recently said goodbye. Realization of this, she says, sent a shiver down her spine 'akin to that produced by icy water'.

Quickly recovering from the shock, she closed the door and started to dress. She was anxious to get away from Setlagole. The store had not proved the haven she had been promised. The whole of the previous day, in fact, had been disastrous. From the time they left Mafeking in the chilly half-light, she and her little party had been at the mercy of the desolate veld. As the sun had risen, so had the wind. Dust and sand had whipped at the cart with a blinding, stinging

35

intensity and the heat had become almost unbearable. 'I have never experienced such a miserable drive', declared Sarah, 'and I began to understand the feelings of people who commit suicide.' The sun was beginning to set when, after jolting across a dried-up river bed, they sighted the Setlagole store. Sarah was never to forget her first glimpse of this dingy grey house, with its wooden trellised stoep, its dilapidated stables and ramshackle outhouses – all tinged in the gold of the fading sun. A troop of donkeys grazed close to the front door, fowls and turkeys strutted nearby and groups of white and black men chatted idly at the entrance to the store. The serenity of this familiar African scene held Sarah spell-bound. 'I, who had left scenes of strife, excitement, and impending horrors of an invested town', she recalled, 'looked with amazement on this calm and peaceful landscape.'[2]

But she was soon forced to face reality. After being welcomed by Mr and Mrs Fraser, the old Scots couple who kept the store, she received a visit from a sergeant of the local mounted police. He told her that a large Boer force was encamped some ten miles away. African runners had reported that they were lying in wait for an armoured train that was expected at Mafeking that night. The sergeant, who was something of an alarmist, thought that it was more than likely that after ambushing the train they would descend on Setlagole and loot the store. He advised Sarah to leave the area as soon as possible. He even suggested that she continue her journey that very night.

This threw Sarah into a quandary. Characteristically, she was not so much concerned for her own safety as she was about the ignominy of a British officer's wife being captured by the enemy. 'I would run no risks', she declared stoutly, 'of capture or impertinence from the burghers, who would certainly commandeer our cart, pony and mules.' On the other hand, both she and her servants were worn out from their journey and the mules were in no condition to start another trek. Her mind was made up for her by the driver of her cart. Boers or no Boers, he flatly refused to move that night.

Once again, Sarah was unable to sleep. Throughout the night she lay, with the curtains open, listening apprehensively to the occasional barking of the farm dogs. At four o'clock the faithful Wilhelm appeared at the window to ask whether he should inspan the mules. Sarah advised him to wait until the sergeant arrived. About an hour later she got up to look at the weather. Then it was that she heard the sound of gunfire.

By the time Sarah had dressed, the farmyard was alive with noisy groups of Africans, all staring in the direction of the firing. Then an

African horseman arrived with news that the Boers had derailed an armoured train. He could tell them little else. When pressed for details all he could say was that the train had 'fallen over'; he did not know whether there had been any casualties, as he had left as soon as the big guns had opened up. This garbled report was sufficient to alarm Sarah. With Boers expected to attack Setlagole, she decided to leave immediately. The mules were harnessed to her cart and, after instructing Wilhelm to remain at the store and collect what news he could before joining her that night, she and Metelka climbed into the passenger seats for their second day in the veld.

They had been advised to make for Mosita, a small African village some twenty-five miles west of Setlagole. Close to the village was a solitary European house owned by a Mr Keeley who, in times of peace, acted as the local magistrate. Here, Sarah was assured, she would be made welcome, and as it was well off the beaten track she would be kept out of harm's way.

Anticipating another gruelling drive, Sarah was surprised to find herself travelling in comfort through fine open country. The vicious wind of the day before had dropped and the parched, stony veld gave way to pleasant grassland. There was not a house in sight and the only sound to be heard, apart from the driver swearing at the mules, was the curious chuckle of the large African pheasants as they started up from the long grass. At the little mud-hut village their arrival created great excitement. Men and youths crowded round the cart and the driver was forced into a long pantomime of the recent fighting ('imitating even the noise of the big gun') before they were allowed to pass on. A mile or so along the road, they skirted a huge dam and drove up to the Keeley farm. Here their reception was by no means as cheerful.

When Sarah marched in and boldly announced that she had come to beg a few nights' lodging, she discovered that Mr Keeley was in Mafeking where he had been detained to help with the defence of the town. His wife, a worried-looking woman in her mid thirties, had not only been left with five children but was expecting a sixth. As the family was known to be staunchly pro-British, Mrs Keeley was afraid of possible reprisals on the part of the local Boers: except for a young brother, she was entirely without male protection. 'At last', says Sarah, 'I had found someone who was more to be pitied than myself.'

At Mosita, Sarah felt completely cut off from the world. With the railway lines torn up, the telegraph wires cut and no newspapers, day after day would pass without a word from a trustworthy source. How the war was progressing or how Mafeking was faring she had no way of knowing; the odd snippets of information brought by African runners all too often proved as unreliable as the depressing local gossip. To be isolated in this way was a frustrating experience for Sarah. 'It often used to make me sigh enviously', she says, 'when I took my evening walk just before sundown, to think of the newsboys in London noisily proclaiming the latest news, here we were in the same continent, and we knew so little . . . [It was] as if we were on another planet, surrounded by vast distances of sandy waste as effectually as if it were by the ocean.'[3]

At long last news of a sort did arrive. One evening, as she and Mrs Keeley took up their vigil on the stoep after supper, a rider cantered up with a batch of letters from Mafeking. They had been smuggled out of the town by Sarah's colleague on the *Daily Mail*, who was on his way south to send off some cables. One of the letters was from Gordon. From it they learned of the unsuccessful attempts which the Boers had made on the town shortly after Sarah's departure. There were also details of Mafeking's first bombardment (which had proved singularly ineffective, the only casualties being one dead hen and a wounded dog). Gordon, who imagined Sarah to be at Setlagole, had ended his letter by assuring her that the Boers had been told she was at the store and asked to leave her unmolested.

This contact with Mafeking, vague as it was, had a heartening effect on Sarah: it convinced her that she had a part to play in the war. If messages could be smuggled out of Mafeking, they could also be smuggled in. Although pitifully short of hard news, she decided to pass on the few scraps of information she had gathered to the invested town. After selecting a loyal African named Boaz as her courier, she wrote a short note, folded it into a used cartridge case and sent her elderly messenger hurrying towards Mafeking. This trial run was to be the first of many undertaken by Boaz. 'His task was of course a risky one', explained Sarah, 'and we used to pay him £3 each way, but he never failed us.'

During the next few weeks Boaz was constantly employed in carrying despatches to and from Mafeking. It proved an important service. Not only was Sarah able to keep the garrison in touch with local rumour but, according to Angus Hamilton of *The Times*, she 'acted as the chief medium by which Baden-Powell managed to get his despatches through to the Government in Cape Town.'[4] Mosita, in fact, became a recognized clearing centre for despatches. 'Sometimes they got through, sometimes not', says Baden-Powell, 'so she took care that her messages had a cheerful tone lest the Boers should think we were weakening.' Nor were her activities confined to Mafeking. Major Dennison, who was operating from Kuruman in the Kalahari desert, says his despatches 'were handed by the natives to Lady Sarah Wilson . . . by whose kind aid the letters were sent on by her trusted boy to their destination.' Sarah, he says, deserved 'great credit for the services she rendered our corps.'5

Once the flurry of excitement created by this new venture had subsided, the household was again thrown back on the boredom of Mosita; the interminable days, the uncertainty of conflicting rumours. Even the despatches they relayed were guarded, often contradictory. Apart from a visit from an English farmer, who told them that the nearest town, Vryburg, had fallen to the enemy without so much as a shot being fired, they could obtain no definite news.

Not until the unexpected arrival of Mr Keeley, early in November, were they given a first-hand account of what was happening in Mafeking. Having served for some weeks in the town guard, Mr Keeley had been given permission to return to his family. He brought disturbing news. The Boers, he said, were now drawing closer and, although the town was not completely surrounded, he had had to ride for his life to escape. There had been several very severe fights but the garrison was still in high spirits and underground shelters had been constructed to provide protection against the daily bombardments. More alarming were the rumours that the Boers intended to step up the shelling with a new siege gun capable of firing a 94 lb. shell.

Depressing as was his news, Mr Keeley's return gave the women new confidence. After days of uncertainty it was a comfort for them to hand over some of their responsibilities and relax a little. Unfortunately this easing of tension did not last long. When the next alarm sounded Mr Keeley was away visiting a neighbouring farmer and the women were left to cope as best they could.

One evening, just as they were about to go to bed, they were startled by the sudden arrival of the police sergeant from Setlagole. He had come to warn them of a new danger. Setlagole, he said, was swarming with armed Boers and he and his men had had to evacuate their barracks. He advised them to drive all the cattle off the farm and prepare for a commando raid. The household sprang into action. Mrs Keeley arranged for the cattle to be dispersed and Sarah buried her jewel case and despatch boxes in the garden. But the Boers did not arrive that night and there was no sign of them the following morning. All day they waited with 'strained nerves and aching eyes'; not until the sun set did they realize that once again they had been misled by the jittery sergeant. The Boers, they learned later, had headed in the opposite direction on leaving Setlagole.

All the same, the possibility of a visit from the enemy could not be ruled out. Most of the surrounding area was now in hostile hands and their Boer neighbours were known to be suspicious of Sarah. There were even rumours that the strange woman at Mosita was really a man in disguise. Mrs Keeley lived in daily fear that her husband would be arrested. When, a few days later, an approaching horseman was sighted, she was convinced that her fear was about to be realized. Telling Sarah to keep out of sight, she sent her young brother to find out what the man wanted. He returned to announce another false alarm. The unkempt rider, wrapped in a long cloak and wearing a slouch hat, was no one more sinister than the energetic Mafeking correspondent of the *Daily Mail*, Mr Hellaway who, having ridden south to send off his cables, was on his way back to the besieged town.

Mr Keeley returned to Mosita shortly after the newspaper correspondent left. One morning he was working in the garden, beating off a swarm of locusts, when Sarah joined him. He asked her to take over while he lit his pipe. Seizing the switch, she made a determined attack on the pests. Many years later this incident was to be remembered as her only attempt to help with the running of things during these weeks. 'The woman', complained Mr Keeley, 'was nothing but a damned nuisance.'[6]

It was not that Sarah was lazy. On the contrary, when the occasion arose she was not only willing but eager to play her part. But it would never have occurred to her to offer domestic assistance. Surrounded all her life by servants, she had never had to consider how her needs were catered for and was oblivious of the work she created for others: such mundane tasks were left to the long-suffering Metelka. Ironically, had Sarah shared some of the household burdens at Mosita she would have found life there less tedious. As it was, she mooned about the farm, bored, restless and dispirited: a burden to herself and an annoyance to others.

At last she could stand it no longer. The time had come, she decided, to take some sort of action. Ever since she had heard that the neighbouring town of Vryburg was occupied by the Boers she had longed to find out what was happening there. What a *coup* it would be if she could unearth military secrets and pass them on to Mafeking. The thought aroused all her espionage instincts. But this was not something that could be left to African runners; only by visiting

Vryburg herself could she obtain the sort of information she was seeking. Once her mind was made up, she began to plan for what she knew would be a risky operation. If she was caught she would most certainly be taken prisoner and she had no intention of exchanging the boredom of Mosita for the isolation of a Boer gaol. First she needed to test the vigilance of the enemy.

Living on a nearby farm was a family of Boers who had taken a lively interest in her association with the Keeleys. The son of the house was captivated by her white pony, Dop. Now, hearing that the boy was about to take some cattle to Vryburg, Sarah offered to lend him the pony. The youngster was delighted. He had no hesitation in agreeing to act as her messenger. She gave him some letters to post for the English mail and a short note to the English-speaking magistrate asking for newspapers and reliable information. She also gave him a cheque to cash at the Vryburg bank. If he managed to get away with such blatant trafficking with the British, she felt she could chance a visit to the town herself.

The boy returned a few days later. Sarah was staggered at how well her plan had worked. Not only had he succeeded in cashing her cheque, but he had brought a reply from the magistrate which, Sarah was amused to see, was an official envelope with the bold 'On H. M. Service' neatly crossed through. The only disappointment was his failure to post Sarah's letters. These had been refused by the post office, not because they were addressed to England but because the stamps were those of the Cape Colony and the postal authorities only recognized Transvaal stamps. Less encouraging were the stories the youngster had to tell. Vryburg, he said, was abuzz with rumours of Boer victories and there were murmurings of reprisals against local people who had sided with the British. The magistrate's letter was equally pessimistic. For all that, Sarah was heartened. Obviously, military discipline was slack and there seemed no reason why she should not visit the town.

She could hardly wait to get away. The very thought of seeing the 'Transvaal flag flying in the town of a British colony' was a challenge she could not resist. Mrs Keeley's brother, young Arthur Coleman, agreed to drive her to Vryburg in a pony trap, and word was spread among the locals that she had toothache and was going to visit the dentist. She was tingling with excitement when, early one morning, they set off along 'the villainous road' for the sixty-mile drive to occupied Vryburg.

Most of the farms they passed were empty and the road was deserted.

In the evening they were given a night's lodging by a friendly Jewish trader, and it was not until they were approaching Vryburg the following morning that they saw signs of enemy activity. A party of horsemen appeared on the brow of a hill and seemed to be riding towards them. Feeling sure that they were about to be questioned, Sarah began to prepare her excuses but, after a casual glance in their direction, the men circled and galloped away.

As they entered the town they got a closer glimpse of the occupying force. Driving down the main street, their attention was caught by the heavily guarded court-house. Armed men were passing in and out of the building, sentries patrolled the streets and more were crowded round a notice pinned on a tree. Through the surrounding trees they could see the boldly striped Transvaal flag fluttering from the court-house roof.

Arriving at the Central Hotel, Sarah marched in and announced herself. The English-speaking manager looked at her aghast. Hurrying her to a side room, he advised her to stay there and on no account mention her name. He told her that earlier that morning a newly-appointed magistrate had arrived and was already making his presence felt. It was rumoured that strict regulations were about to be announced concerning the arrival and departure of visitors. The chances of Sarah being allowed to leave the town, he said, were extremely remote.

Sarah spent the next few days in the hotel. Only once did she venture out. Disguising herself as best she could, she paid a secret visit to the hospital where some wounded British soldiers – captured after the derailment of the train near Mafeking – were recuperating. The men were all well, but it was too risky to repeat the visit. She decided it would be wiser to remain out of sight. Most of her day was spent sitting at the window of her room watching the mounted burgers patrol the town. She was not impressed. 'I could never have imagined', she wrote disparagingly, 'so many men absolutely alike: all had long straggling beards, odd felt hats, shabby clothes . . . Most of those I saw were men of forty to fifty years of age, but there were also a few sickly looking youths, who certainly did not look bold warriors.'

Her main concern was to get back to Mosita. This called for a great deal of thought. Residents were now forbidden to leave Vryburg and anyone travelling on business could only do so on a special pass from the magistrate's office. Armed sentries were posted on all the roads, and vehicles and their passengers were liable to be searched. The hotel manager told Sarah that it would be madness to attempt to leave.

But she refused to be put off. She steeled herself to bluff it out.

Arthur Coleman, who spoke fluent Afrikaans, was sent to the magistrate's office to apply for a pass. He did so by pretending to be a Boer who had come to town with his sister for provisions and now wanted to return home. Crude as it was, the ruse worked. After a nerve-racking wait and some 'pointed questions' the pass was eventually issued. Sarah could hardly believe their luck. She decided to leave before daybreak the following day. The hotel manager lent Sarah a shabby ulster which almost enveloped her; she covered her face with a heavy veil and wound a woollen shawl round her sailor hat which, she says, 'almost completely concealed my identity'. Then they set off.

With Sarah sitting slumped forward beside him, Coleman drove to the outskirts of the town. Here they were stopped by sentries. Numb with apprehension, Sarah climbed down from the cart and stood some distance off while Coleman went to show the pass. To excuse her apparent shyness and muffled appearance, the youngster explained that she was suffering from toothache and had a swollen face. The formalities took some minutes – 'the longest', says Sarah, 'I have ever experienced'. But at last Coleman returned and they scrambled back into the cart and headed for the open road.

They covered the sixty miles to Mosita in one day.

Sarah's first attempt at espionage had proved a disappointment. Cooped up in the hotel she had been in no position to assess the strength of the Boer commandos or to obtain information about their activities. The only news she could pass on to Mafeking had come to her through the hotel manager and concerned the early fighting in Natal. Her despatches, she claimed, were the first to reach the besieged town with intelligence 'from the more important theatre of war'. Unfortunately much of what she had to tell was dated, vague and decidedly over-optimistic. But her letters undoubtedly boosted morale in Mafeking. 'We presume', wrote one of the inhabitants, 'she is in the very best position to give full information.'[7]

This estimate of her worth would have surprised Sarah. Once back in Mosita she felt more isolated, more out of touch and ineffectual than she had ever been. For the first time she became thoroughly depressed. She even began to doubt the rightness of the war and, in arguments with Mr Keeley, questioned the validity of claims made on behalf of the *uitlanders*. 'It seemed to me then', she later explained, 'we were not justified in letting loose such a millstream of wretchedness and destruction, and that the alleged wrongs of a large white population

– who, in spite of everything, seemed to prosper and grow rich apace – scarcely justified the sufferings of thousands of innocent individuals.'

Every bit as unsettling was the precariousness of her position at Mosita. Sarah's visit to Vryburg had intensified the suspicions of the local Boers and she was now told that the rumours about her presence at the farm had grown out of all proportion. Having earlier been suspected of being a man in disguise, she was now thought to be Baden-Powell's wife in hiding or, alternatively, 'a granddaughter of Queen Victoria, sent specially out by Her Majesty to inform her of the proceedings of her rebellious subjects'. Whichever version was accepted, it was becoming increasingly obvious that Sarah's days at Mosita were drawing to an end. Should a Boer patrol arrive in the neighbourhood, she would undoubtedly be sought out.

It was this imagined threat which decided her to return to Setlagole. There was nowhere else for her to go. The road south to Kimberley was blocked; to the west lay the formidable Kalahari desert; to the east the Transvaal. Baden-Powell had told the Boers she was at the store, and it was at least one stage nearer to Mafeking to which, despite everything, she still hoped to retreat. 'I determined therefore', she says, 'to return to Mrs Fraser's . . . With many grateful thanks to the Keeleys, I rode off one morning with Vellum [Wilhelm] in attendance, to Setlagole.' She arranged for Metelka to follow her later with the cart and mules.

Sarah arrived at Setlagole to find the Boers had ended their recent occupation of the store and moved on. Mr and Mrs Fraser welcomed her back. Soon Sarah was to discover that life at Setlagole was much livelier than it had been at Mosita. Hardly a day seemed to pass without bringing some frightening rumour or threat. That the rumours were mostly unreliable and the threats evaporated on investigation did nothing to dispel the menacing atmosphere of the store.

Just how unreliable the news reaching Setlagole was became apparent to Sarah the day after she arrived. That same morning some Africans rushed into the store with what appeared to be well-authenticated news of a British victory just outside Vryburg. They also reported that the railway line was being repaired and that the staff of a nearby station had returned to work. Sarah decided to investigate the railway story for herself. Saddling up Dop she rode to the station, only to find the place locked and barred. Not until she strode over to the station-master's house did she discover the source of the rumours. There, seated on the rickety stoep, she found the stationmaster engrossed in *Nicholas Nickleby*. He told her that he was the only member of the staff who had returned and he was there simply because it was his home: he knew nothing about the line being repaired. Sarah had some sharp things to say about 'vague native rumour'.

But her visit to the station roused her curiosity. It made her wonder just how badly the line had been disrupted by the derailed armoured train. A detailed report on the capsized trucks, she thought, would be invaluable to any plan for relieving Mafeking. Once again she decided this was a mission she would undertake herself. She received no encouragement. Neither the Frasers nor the English-speaking farmers who congregated at the store thought much of her chances of success. The Boers, she was told, kept the railway line under close surveillance.

Not until a Reuters correspondent, a Mr J. E. Pearson, arrived at the store was she able to persuade anyone that the risk was worth taking. The saddle-sore reporter was on his way to Mafeking and had stopped at Setlagole to rest his horse. Pearson, an American, seemed the ideal person to accompany Sarah: for not only could he take a report to Baden-Powell, but he had the added advantage of possessing a camera. The opportunity seemed too good to miss.

Taking an African guide with them, they set off after an early lunch the following Sunday. 'There was not much fear of meeting any Boers', says Sarah, 'as the latter were always engaged that day in psalm-singing and devotions.' She was right. The only sign of life they saw came from wayside African kraals where the startled inhabitants greeted them with shouts and cheers. A woman on horseback was a rare sight and the spectacle of Sarah charging hell-for-leather past their huts caused a sensation. Arriving at the railway line, they left their horses at a Baralong village and walked to the train.

The crumpled wreckage, shimmering in the heat, was a depressing sight. The pilot coach was embedded in the dust, the bullet-ridden engine, with its battered armoured truck, was still on the rails, and the rear carriage was upended in a culvert. Leaving her companion busy with his camera, Sarah scrambled about the trucks trying to assess the damage. There was a chilling silence about the place which made her edgy. She kept a continual watch over her shoulder. 'I should not have been surprised', she says, 'to have seen an unkempt head bob up and ask our business. But all remained silent as the grave.' The only sound came from a swarm of locusts massed under the engine. It was too quiet for comfort. Sarah could not get away from the wreck fast enough. As soon as she had completed her inspection she hurried over to Pearson, badgered him into putting away his camera and hustled him back to their horses. Not until they arrived back at Setlagole did she feel safe.

Pearson left for Mafeking immediately, taking Sarah's report with him. At last Sarah felt she had achieved something worth while. It confirmed her belief that she could be of use as a spy. The only problem was that she no longer had Boaz to act as her runner. Local Africans were not eager to enter Mafeking; too many messengers had been caught to make it a risk worth taking. 'Several of the native runners', says Major Dennison, Sarah's contact in the Kalahari, 'were shot in cold blood by the Boers, many of whom take a delight in putting natives up in the road and coolly shooting them down . . . All are not like this; too many, nevertheless, can be charged.'[8]

Sarah found a solution to her problem a few days later. The intrepid Mr Pearson, having performed the hazardous ride in and out of Mafeking, stopped at Setlagole on his way back. He reported that all was well in the town, although most of the inhabitants were now living underground because of the constant shelling. Aware of Sarah's difficulties, he had brought with him a basket of carrier pigeons. He assured her that by using these birds she would be able to 'communicate swiftly and safely with the garrison'. The idea pleased Sarah, but she was uneasy about managing the pigeons. Pearson quickly reassured her. To demonstrate how simple it was, he suggested that they should send one of the birds on a trial flight. With Sarah's help, he wrote a note to Baden-Powell outlining the situation at Setlagole and ended by saying: 'Lady Sarah Wilson is here doing good work as an intelligence officer.' After selecting a pigeon he clipped the note to the bird's leg and set it loose.

With a flutter of white wings, the pigeon soared into the air, hovered a second, and then – to Sarah's alarm – began to circle wildly. Pearson was unperturbed. The pigeon's behaviour, he told Sarah, was not unusual and this particular bird had been chosen for its prize-winning feats. 'So', says Sarah, 'as it eventually disappeared, I thought no more of it.'

But this was not to be one of the bird's prize-winning flights. Although headed in the right direction, it never reached Mafeking. It came down in the laager of the besieging Boers, settled on the roof of the commanding officer's headquarters and was promptly shot by an observant veld-kornet. A Transvaal newspaper reporting the incident said: 'A carrier pigeon hovering around Mafeking was shot by a burger yesterday . . . One of Lieut. Jooste's men left immediately for Pretoria with the despatch. The contents are still secret here.' They were not to remain secret long.

The Boers arrived at Setlagole two days later. Early that morning a party of armed burgers had left the laager near Mafeking and by midday were seen to be approaching the store. Sarah knew nothing of their arrival until she entered the dining-room for lunch where she was astonished to find two of the male guests hacking away at the floorboards with an axe. They told her that they were trying to widen the trap door of a shallow underground food store. 'We are going to hide, Lady Sarah,' they explained. 'The Boers are on the premises.' Sarah, alarmed but ever practical, pointed out that they would probably suffocate in such a small space and advised them to think again. But they were far too panic-stricken to think. Jumping up they began rushing about the room in search of another hiding place. Sarah watched in amazement. When one of them finally dived beneath a velvet cloth covering the grand piano, she was unable to contain herself. 'The whole scene was so comic', she says, 'that I sat down and laughed.'

The thought of the Boers brought her back to earth. Standing up, she took charge of the situation. First she ordered the skulker to come out from under the piano. Then she gave the pair of them a brisk lecture. Never one to mince her words, she told one he was far too puny to interest the Boers and advised his companion, a more burly man, to lie on the sofa and feign illness. 'And I really believe,' she says, 'anxiety and worry had so preyed on him that he was as ill as he looked.'

Determined not to be flustered, Sarah sat down to eat her cold lunch. A few minutes later Mrs Fraser came panting in to report what was happening. Some thirty or forty Boers 'armed to the teeth' had invaded the store and demanded food. After helping themselves to tins of salmon and sardines, they had been given coffee and were now sitting in the yard devouring their loot. By peeping through the green venetian blind, Sarah caught her first glimpse of a commando in action. Sprawled in the shade the bearded burgers, dressed in an odd assortment of civilian clothes, with cartridge belts slung across their shoulders, seemed to her a motley crew to be challenging the British empire.

All afternoon Sarah paced the darkened room while one of her jittery companions kept watch at the window. The stifling heat, the curtained gloom and the tense atmosphere contrasted sharply with the boisterous behaviour of the men outside. Their meal finished, the

Boers again crowded into the store and Mrs Fraser came flying back to report they were now helping themselves to clothes and cigarettes. She was convinced the store was about to be ransacked. But, to everyone's surprise, the Boers made no attempt to search the house: they contented themselves with some desultory shooting at a row of bottles, set up in the yard.

The reason for their visit became known only after a few of them had helped themselves to some cheap brandy. In a fit of drunkenness the leader of the party turned on Mr Fraser and demanded to know the whereabouts of the newspaper reporter who had written to Baden-Powell. He was also interested in the Englishwoman who had been mentioned in the reporter's note. Mr Fraser pretended not to understand what he was talking about. This produced another outburst. With God's help, the man explained, they had intercepted a carrier pigeon headed for Mafeking and were now waiting for a senior officer to arrive before rounding up the people mentioned in the reporter's note. They had sent for the former owner of the store, Mr Lamb, to help them in their search.

Alarming as was this news, there was nothing to be done about it except wait. Just as the sun was setting that evening, a voice was heard outside joking in English with the Boers. Peering into the gathering dusk, the Frasers recognized the new arrival as Mr Lamb. His coming helped to relieve the tension. Mr Lamb, having lived in the district for some years, knew the Boers well. Within no time he had persuaded them to put down their guns and settle for the night in an outhouse. As soon as the Boers had dispersed, Sarah and her companions came out on to the stoep and sat breathing in the cool night air.

The arrival of Veld-Kornet De Koker the next day quickly put an end to the peaceful atmosphere. Hardly had he arrived when he gave orders for a full-scale search. Sarah immediately sprang into action and hustled the timid lodgers into position. When the search party came crashing into the dining-room she had the satisfaction of seeing her ruse work: both men were completely ignored by the intruders. For the rest of the day the Boer officers remained closeted in the living room. When they finally emerged, the household was assembled and a proclamation was read out. The country, it was announced, was now part of the Transvaal and all the residents must either leave their homes within seven days or enrol as burgers. The occupants of the store were then made to sign a blank piece of paper which, in effect, signalled their acceptance of these terms.

In Sarah's case the conditions did not apply. She was to be taken prisoner. Replying to her flood of protests, De Koker informed her that as she was a foreigner she must remain under arrest until she could produce 'satisfactory credentials' for being in the territory. The veld-kornet then announced that he and his men were leaving for Mosita, which had been mentioned in Pearson's note, and would return the following day. Three sentries were left to watch Sarah. She found this annoying, but seems not to have regretted the fact that she was responsible for getting so many people into serious trouble.

She was, however, distressed to see the Boers bring Mr Keeley with them when they returned the next day. Seething with indignation, she again tackled De Koker about her own position. She was a woman and a non-combatant, she argued, what grounds had he for treating her as a prisoner-of-war? The veld-kornet was polite but firm. Her case, he said, was being reported to Pretoria and, until further orders were received, she was 'on no account to leave the precincts of the farm'. The three sentries would stay to guard her.

As the Boers were about to leave, Sarah scribbled an appeal to the Boer commander and gave it to one of Mr Keeley's escort to deliver. She asked for permission to pass through enemy lines and join her husband in Mafeking. Mr Keeley was not hopeful. He told her that the Boers had been watching her since she left Mafeking and even knew of her trips to Vryburg and the wrecked train. To make matters worse, the Boer laager was now under the command of a General Snyman, a bigoted man who was unpopular even among his own troops. There was little chance of her softening Snyman's heart. The men rode off, leaving Sarah cursing the ineptitude of carrier pigeons.

Early next morning, De Koker returned. He had discovered Sarah's note and had come to offer her a pass to the Boer laager. He volunteered to escort her there personally. The Frasers warned her not to go with him. She thought it wise to take their advice. It took some time to persuade De Koker to accept her refusal but he eventually agreed to leave the pass with her. Shortly after he left, Mr Keeley arrived back at the store. He had been released on condition that he remained neutral. Now, on his way back to Mosita, he had called to deliver the official reply to her note. It came as no surprise. Sarah's request had been turned down. She was to remain where she was under the surveillance of the Transvaal burgers.

Sarah had no intention of doing so. The idea of sitting out the war in an isolated tin-roofed store appalled her. More than ever she was determined to return to Mafeking. She had greatly resented being turned out of the town by Baden-Powell; now that her expulsion had been confirmed by the enemy she was doubly incensed. Seeking an excuse to defy both British and Boer commanders, it was not long before she found one.

The disruption of the railway had affected the entire district. Food supplies had been cut off, provisions were fast running out. On the day Mrs Fraser announced that there was only enough meal to last a week, Sarah decided she had good reason for moving on. She still had the pass issued by Veld-Kornet De Koker and this, she thought, would enable her to shake off her guards. Once she reached the Boer laager, she had no doubt that she could bluff her way into Mafeking. She had a convincing case to present. Not only was there a food shortage at Setlagole, but she had been told that a Mrs Delpoort, a 'Dutchwoman' in Mafeking, was anxious to return to the Transvaal. Surely an exchange could be made? She decided to chance her luck.

The scarcity of food at Setlagole did not prevent Sarah from saddling the Frasers with her maid. 'I did not wish', she explained, 'to expose her to any hardships in the laager.' With Metelka she left her pony, Dop. Then, with Wilhelm driving the mule cart and an African servant riding behind, she set off along the treacherous road to Mafeking. Apparently, although she does not say, De Koker's pass was accepted by the Boer sentries as sufficient authorization for her sudden departure.

The thought of invading the enemy camp was exhilarating. As the hooded cart trundled along, neither the oppressive heat nor the choking dust could stifle Sarah's high spirits. This was far and away her most exciting trip. Whatever happened at the end of it, she would at least have put an end to the interminable days of waiting. That what she was doing might prove dangerous does not appear to have occurred to her.

They rested the mules twice on the forty-six mile trek. The second halt was at the house of Veld-Kornet De Koker. Sarah's pass took her only so far; she needed another to proceed to the Boer laager. It was her first experience of a *platteland* home and she found it bewildering. De Koker solemnly introduced her to members of his large family – few of whom could speak English – and then left her with them, trying to make conversation by nods and winks. They were, she admits, 'all very affable to me, or meant to be so, if I could but have understood them.' She was greatly relieved when, after having been served coffee in the mud-floored living room, she was handed her pass and could make her escape.

At about four that afternoon she crested a slight rise in the flat plain and caught a glimpse of Mafeking, its corrugated-iron roofs shining tantalizingly in the heat-hazed distance. She was seized by an impulse to make a dash for it. By whipping the mules, she estimated that they would be half way to the town before the Boers realized, and Baden-Powell would surely send out an escort to cover the rest of the way. But the two Africans would not hear of it. They assured her that 'many Boer sharpshooters lay hidden in the scrub'.

She was soon to discover how true this was. Having reluctantly turned the cart towards the Boer laager, she drove into a hidden outpost. A Boer officer, every bit as startled as she, ordered her down from the cart and told her she would have to remain there until dark. He pointed out that the road was well within range of the Mafeking guns; she might get shot by her own people. Sarah had no alternative but to obey. Sitting beside her cart, she listened glumly to the sounds of war. Periodic bursts of gun-fire echoed from the town, punctuated now and again by the boom of the Boer cannon. All around her grim-faced burgers sat silently puffing their pipes. Over an hour passed before the officer ordered a party to saddle up and escort her to the laager. An enormous force of armed men came swarming out of the laager as they approached. The cart was quickly surrounded. After her unheroic mishap at the outpost, Sarah now had the satisfaction of riding into the enemy camp in true military style. At last her invasion was being taken seriously.

When news of her arrival at the Boer headquarters reached Mafeking it created a stir. She was already regarded as a heroine by the townsfolk and now her reputation for daring soared. 'General Snyman', it was reported, 'turned out three hundred Boers, armed for battle, who at once proceeded to capture a solitary woman.'[9]

4

In and Out of Captivity

THE EXCITEMENT CREATED by Sarah's detention at the Boer laager was not confined to Mafeking. Within hours of her arrival there, cables were being sent to England telling of her plight and giving colourful accounts of her adventures. Any details left out of the cabled news were obligingly supplied by speculation in the London press. Legends were born which were to reappear whenever Sarah's name was mentioned in the newspapers. There were certain variations but the gist of most reports followed the same line. Sarah, it was said, had originally been sent to Mafeking as 'war-correspondent to a well-known London newspaper' and this had resulted in her falling into the hands of the enemy. 'Lady Sarah', claimed one report, 'has all the courage and intrepidity of her great namesake, Sarah Jennings, the first Duchess of Marlborough and she set off on a two-hundred-mile ride across the veldt in order to get her copy through. However she was taken prisoner by the Boers, and sent to Pretoria to join her nephew, Mr Winston Churchill.'[1]

That Sarah should be linked with her nephew was inevitable. Only a couple of weeks earlier Winston Churchill had provided the British press with one of the few stirring stories to come out of South Africa during the opening stages of the war. His courage, daring and resourcefulness had captured the public's imagination and given a little sparkle to a campaign that was then sadly lacking in heroes.

Winston Churchill had arrived in South Africa twenty days after the outbreak of war. Having turned down the offer to act as a war-correspondent for the *Daily Mail*, he had agreed to represent the

Morning Post in Natal. As a reporter, he had accompanied a military detachment on an armoured train reconnaissance which, on its return journey, was ambushed by a Boer commando. The train crashed into a boulder that had been placed on the line and three trucks were derailed. The engine, which remained on the rails, had been blocked and was powerless to move. With remarkable coolness, and under fire from the Boers, Churchill took charge, despite the fact that he had no military status, and organized the clearing of the line. After working valiantly for over an hour, they freed the engine and sent it on its way. But Churchill remained behind and, together with fifty-seven of the soldiers, was taken prisoner by the Boers. He was sent to Pretoria where he was interned in the Staatsmodelskool (State Model School).

Praises had rung out when news of Churchill's feat reached England. The press was unanimous in hailing him, there were even calls for him to be awarded the Victoria Cross. The *Daily Mail* immediately cashed in by coupling him with its special correspondent. 'Anxieties crowd upon the Spencer Churchill family at the present time,' it announced, 'for in addition to the distress in which they are plunged over Mr Winston Churchill's fate, they are uncertain as to the welfare of Lady Sarah Wilson.'[2] This, at the time, was largely conjecture but it was to be confirmed once it became known that Sarah had also been taken prisoner. For the next few days, Lady Sarah Wilson's fate became a matter of national concern.

Not everyone feared for Sarah's safety. Those who knew her felt confident she would prove more than a match for her captors. This was something Winston Churchill's mother discovered during the weekend she spent at Windsor Castle shortly after news of Sarah's detention was received. 'The Queen', recalled Lady Randolph Churchill, 'was full of enquiries about my sister-in-law, Lady Sarah Wilson, who was then reported to be a prisoner in Boer hands. "They will not hurt her", she said with a charming smile.'[3]

Sarah did not share the Queen's optimism. Her early experiences at the Boer laager shook her confidence. Although she was not worried about her safety, she had little faith in her gaolers' benevolence. Her hopes of a quick return to Mafeking had been dashed.

Things got off to a bad start. When Sarah's cart drew up in front of the whitewashed house which served as General Snyman's headquarters, she was surprised to see that another huge crowd of burgers had gathered round the entrance. News of her arrival had spread and men had rushed from every quarter of the laager to catch a glimpse of the Englishwoman who had boldly invaded their stronghold. 'I was fairly startled', Sarah admits, 'to find what excitement my appearance created.' Much as she would have loved to march into the Boer commandant's office, she was nervous about pushing through the crowd and remained seated firmly in the cart.

But something had to be done. Determined not to appear apprehensive, Sarah demanded in a loud clear voice that General Snyman be told of her arrival. One of the men at the back of the crowd disappeared into the house. Then, after an 'interminable wait', Snyman's secretary came squeezing through the crowd and, much to Sarah's relief, spoke to her in English. The general, he said, would see her immediately. Climbing down from the cart, Sarah prepared to follow the man as he elbowed his way back to the house. Only then did she realize that she had misjudged the burgers. As she stepped forward, the men parted rather sheepishly to allow her a clear passage. They were, she acknowledged, 'very civil, nearly all of them taking off their hats as I passed through.'

Inside the house she was ushered into a low dark room. Seated on a bench in the corner, two old men watched her approach. One of them, a gaunt-faced, steely-eyed burger with a long white beard, was the unpopular General Jacobus Snyman. One glance was sufficient to confirm all Sarah had heard about him: he might not have been the psalm-singing, sanctimonious murderer of women and children that the inhabitants of Mafeking imagined him to be, but he was clearly a man to be taken seriously. His ruddy-faced, bearded companion, Commandant Botha, was more amiable ('a good sportsman', said the British) but on this occasion he looked almost as formidable as his chief.

The interview was polite – Sarah was given a bowl of coffee – but unproductive. Speaking through an interpreter, she outlined her position. She had come to the laager, she explained, at the suggestion of Veld-Kornet De Koker. She had no relations in South Africa, except her husband in Mafeking. She had been forced to leave Setlagole because of the food shortage. She was now prepared to ask Colonel Baden-Powell to exchange her for Mrs Delpoort who, she believed, was anxious to leave Mafeking. She would like General Snyman's permission to apply for the exchange. The two men heard her out in silence. When she had finished, Snyman rapped out his reply. Her request was turned down. The exchange, he said, would not be possible.

Sarah could scarcely believe her ears. It had never entered her head that her proposal would be dismissed so curtly. Snyman's lack of courtesy staggered her. 'Then it occurred to me', she says, 'that this old gentleman meant to keep me prisoner-of-war, and my heart sank to my shoes.' In desperation she pleaded for a respite. Would Snyman at least consider her case before taking further action? To her surprise, the general agreed. But meanwhile she had to remain a prisoner at the laager. The secretary was ordered to take her to the field hospital.

Still dazed, Sarah was led back through the staring crowd to her cart. The hospital was about half a mile from Snyman's headquarters. Arriving there she was shown into a tiny room where she was told she could sleep. There was no bed, only a broken-down sofa, the place reeked of disinfectant and the windows were riddled with bullet holes. The only other furniture was a large centre-table and a dilapidated wash-stand. This, together with the smell, made it obvious to Sarah that she was to be kept in an operating room. It was a depressing thought but, she says, 'I was too tired to care much.'

However, there was no question of her being allowed to sleep. Before he left, the secetary told her that her luggage had be to searched. He took away her bags and called in two nurses to examine her personal effects. The nurses, complaining that searching people was not part of their work, performed their task with surprising alacrity. After turning out Sarah's dressing case, they made her undress so that they could confirm that she had no hidden documents. Meanwhile the men outside were poring over her papers and correspondence. But nothing was found. Wisely, Sarah had destroyed all evidence of her despatch-running before leaving Setlagole.

The search had just been completed when a messenger arrived from General Snyman. Thinking over her request, he had decided to agree to an exchange. He still refused to accept Mrs Delpoort in her place but, if Baden-Powell was willing to hand over a certain Petrus Viljoen, he was prepared to allow Sarah to return to Mafeking. On learning that Petrus Viljoen was a convicted horse thief who had been in the Mafeking gaol since before the war, Sarah was outraged. How dare they think of exchanging a woman for a criminal? The suggestion was disgraceful. She asked for permission to write to her husband. This was agreed to and, making it clear that she would only mention Snyman's proposal as an impossible condition, she scrawled a quick note.

My dear Gordon,
      I am at the laager. General Snyman will not give me a pass unless Colonel Baden-Powell will exchange me for a Mr Petrus

Viljoen. I am sure this is impossible, so I do not ask him formally. I am in a great fix, as they have little meal left at Setlagole or the surrounding places. I am very kindly loooked after here.

There was nothing more she could do. After handing over her note, she settled down for the night on the lumpy sofa. She now had little hope of returning to Mafeking. Her plight was more serious than she imagined: there was a strong possibility that she would remain a prisoner until the war ended. Her earlier activities had been closely watched by the Boers and this made Snyman extremely suspicious. 'What shall I now do with Lady Sarah Wilson?' he wired to Pretoria. 'Please answer speedily. In my opinion she is an important spy.'[4]

On receiving Sarah's note the following morning, Gordon Wilson took it straight to Baden-Powell. Both men agreed with Sarah: the idea of swapping her for a horse-thief was unthinkable. Gordon told her as much in the formal reply he sent to the laager. Knowing it would be read by the Boers, he ended with a show of righteous indignation. 'I fail to see', he declared, 'in what way it can benefit your captors to keep you prisoner. Luckily for them, it is not the custom of the English to make prisoners-of-war of women.' Others would think differently before the war was over.

Baden-Powell was every bit as uncompromising.

Lady Sarah Wilson wrote saying she had arrived at Snyman's laager, [he noted in his diary] but that he would not pass her unless Viljoen were released from prison here. This man has been fined £100 for inciting the natives to rise, and was doing 6 months for theft . . . I replied that women were not usually considered prisoners-of-war; and I could not send a criminal in exchange for Lady Sarah . . . Explained that Mrs Delpoort, for whom he had asked lately, was not sent because she was unwilling to go. On asking her again today she expressed herself willing – so I wrote again suggesting her exchange for Lady Sarah.

But, unknown to Baden-Powell, the capricious Mrs Delpoort was still dithering. After talking the matter over with friends, she let it be known that she was again having doubts about leaving Mafeking. Her shilly-shallying so unnerved Gordon that he offered a reward to anyone who would take her place. Only two women responded. One of them turned the offer down as she considered the reward too miserly; the other backed out at the last minute because 'she had too many children to leave behind'.[5] But this was not the real problem. Until the Boers agreed to negotiate there could be no exchange; it was Snyman's reluctance to reply to Baden-Powell's letter that prolonged the uncertainty.

'White flags of truce are continually going backwards and forwards *re* Lady Sarah Wilson', observed a member of Mafeking's town guard. 'I suppose if it is possible they will get her back into town.'[6] Baden-Powell was doing his utmost to achieve this. After waiting a couple of days for Snyman's answer, he wrote again demanding a reply. But it was to no purpose. The Boer commandant remained inflexible. 'Snyman replying to my letter', noted Baden-Powell, 'says he will not take anyone in exchange for Lady Sarah Wilson except Petrus Viljoen.'

What Baden-Powell did not know was that Snyman was playing a crafty game. From the moment that Sarah arrived at the laager he had determined to use her to secure Viljoen's release. In his telegrams to Pretoria he claimed that the British were proposing to swap 'a certain Jeffrey Delpoort'[7] for Sarah, which he had refused, making no mention of an exchange of women. But unless, for some strange reason, Mrs Delpoort had a man's Christian name, the wily old general was clearly prevaricating. Petrus Viljoen, the man he wanted, was the grandson of a well-known Boer commandant and Snyman obviously thought that in Sarah he had an important enough hostage to effect an exchange.

Sarah was only vaguely aware of these negotiations. Although she bombarded Snyman with imperious protest notes, she rarely saw him or his senior officers. Her contacts with Boer headquarters were confined to encounters with the general's messengers; it was these unfortunate go-betweens who felt the edge of her sharp tongue. For news of what was happening in the laager, she had to rely on the gossip of the patients and their visitors. The nurses, some of whom were German, were far too busy and suspicious of her to be forthcoming. Sarah soon tired of their endless complaints, while they resented the extra work she caused. But it was to a harassed, overworked woman doctor that Sarah took particular exception. Like the rest of her family she was an outspoken opponent of sex-equality, and had been one of an anti-suffrage party known as the 'Churchill lot' who had signed a 'strong protest' against the extension of the franchise to women which was published in the *Nineteenth Century Review*. Now, confronted by a professional woman doing what she considered to be a man's work, all Sarah's reactionary instincts were roused. The 'lady doctor', she sniffed, was 'the first of her species I had ever come across . . . she looked singularly out of place, which I remarked to several people, partly from the irritation I felt on hearing her addressed as "Doctor".

No doubt these remarks were repeated to her, and this accounted for her black looks.'

That the hospital staff were short with her is hardly surprising, but she had no real cause for complaint about her treatment. True, her room was hot and stuffy at night and swarming with flies during the day, but these conditions prevailed throughout the laager. She was awakened with a cup of coffee and her meals were laid out in her room. The food was good and plentiful; on one day only was she left without meat. 'The other days', she says, 'they gave me eggs, very good beef, splendid potatoes, and bread in any quantity. Besides this I was able to buy delicious fruit, both figs and apricots.' And the burgers, almost without exception, treated her with the utmost respect.

Nothing, though, could relieve the boredom. It was worse than anything she had experienced at Mosita or Setlagole. As the days passed without a word from Pretoria, Sarah began to grow desperate. She even toyed with the idea of slipping past the sentries at night and making her way to Mafeking on foot. The only thing that held her back was the thought that, as she had no way of letting Baden-Powell know she was coming, she might be shot as she approached the town. To be under fire from her own side was, in Sarah's opinion, far worse than anything the Boers might have in store for her.

It was while she was pondering this problem that an Englishman arrived at the hospital. He turned out to be a Mr Spencer Drake and he told Sarah he had met Lord Randolph Churchill during his visit to the Transvaal. When Sarah expressed surprise at finding an Englishman in the laager, he was quick to excuse his loyalty to the 'Queen's enemies'. His family (who claimed to descend from Sir Francis Drake) had been settled in South Africa for some years and he was now a Transvaal burger. 'I owe everything I possess to the South African Republic,' he explained, 'and of course I fight for its cause.' This had not always been the case. During the first Anglo-Boer war Drake had fought on the British side, but he had become disillusioned by the capitulation which followed Britain's defeat at Majuba. 'We colonials were very badly treated and thrown over by the English Government in 1881', he argued, 'and since then I have ceased to think of England as my country.'

Having no wish to quarrel, Sarah decided to change the subject. She asked him what his status was in the laager. He told her he was Snyman's adjutant and that he had been away from the camp on business. Hearing that Sarah was at the hospital, he had come to ask whether he could be of service. This was all the prompting Sarah needed. She immediately launched into a string of complaints. Drake was left in no doubt as to what she thought of Snyman and the Pretoria authorities. Rather shamefacedly, he admitted that the general was not easy to handle but promised to do what he could.

Precisely what he told Snyman is not known, but his agency – together with a further blast which Sarah delivered to Snyman's secretary after Drake had left – undoubtedly had its effect. There was more than a hint of panic in the telegram which the Boer general sent to Pretoria that afternoon. 'Please, please send me at once your decision concerning Lady Sarah Wilson', he wired. 'She is most unwilling to stay here any longer.'[8]

The answer to Sarah's pleas came not from Pretoria but from Mafeking. At six o'clock the following morning, Spencer Drake knocked on her door and told her to be ready to leave in half an hour. Baden-Powell, he said, had agreed to exchange her for Petrus Viljoen. As Sarah scrambled into her clothes there can be little doubt that she congratulated both herself and Spencer Drake. In truth, their efforts had been only incidental to her release. Much against his will, Baden-Powell had felt forced to accept Snyman's terms. '. . . Altho. Lady Sarah Wilson is being well treated by the Boers just now,' he noted in his diary, 'there is a very grave risk to her should they suffer – as they most probably will shortly do – a reverse, and have to retreat hurriedly and they might at any time use her as a hostage. It is therefore desirable to get her now at any price.' But he was not prepared to let the Boers think they were getting the best of the bargain. He insisted that he was negotiating Sarah's release 'in recognition of the services she has rendered as an intermediary in carrying despatches between Mafeking and the south.' This was telling the Boers nothing they did not already know and so, with honour satisfied on both sides, a truce was called until eight o'clock in the morning so that the exchange could take place.

Worried that Snyman might change his mind at the last minute, Sarah was relieved when the mules were finally harnessed to her cart. Her farewell meeting with Snyman was formal and polite. He asked some pointless questions and she enquired about his health. 'Then he rose and held out his hand, which I could not ignore,' she says, 'and without further delay we were off.'

At the same time, Petrus Viljoen was leaving Mafeking. A small crowd gathered to watch him being blindfolded and put into an open cart which, driven by Lieutenant Moncrief and flying a white flag, trundled out of town. About half-way between the town and the laager the two parties met. Sarah was delighted to see that her counterpart, Viljoen, looked decidedly miserable. Once the formal exchange had been made, Lieutenant Moncrief swapped vehicles and, heading Sarah's tented cart towards Mafeking, set off across the stony veld.

Sarah was given an extraordinarily enthusiastic welcome. The normally silent trenches came alive as the men flung their hats in the air and cheered. From the first redoubt sprang Baden-Powell and Lord Edward Cecil. Waving their arms they came running to greet her. As she entered the town a mass of people pressed about her cart, shouting her name and reaching up to shake her hand. In the middle of this excited crowd her cart went bobbing through the market square towards her old quarters at Mr Weil's house. She entered with the cries of her well-wishers still ringing in her ears.

But not everyone was overjoyed to see her. There was, for instance, something acid in the comment made by Dr William Hayes, the town's principal medical officer. 'Lady Sarah Wilson has come in', he observed; 'the Colonel exchanged the convict Viljoen for her . . . We have one more lady to look after, that is all.'[9] Others bitterly resented the release of Viljoen. 'We should have liked to have kept that gentleman where he was,' grumbled a war-correspondent, 'as he tried to get the Kaffirs to rise against us before the war.'[10] But the main objection to the exchange was that Viljoen knew Mafeking well and could use his knowledge to assist the Boers. Allowing him to go free was seen as a threat to the town.

As if to demonstrate that such fears were well founded, the Boers immediately stepped up their bombardment. Hardly had Sarah disappeared from view before 'Creaky' – the Boers' great siege gun – sent what she called 'a parting shot'. The cannonade was kept up for the rest of the day. One of those to feel the full blast of the shelling was Gordon Wilson, who narrowly escaped death when a chemist's shop he was visiting was hit and totally destroyed. Others were not so lucky. A passing African was cut to pieces by the same shell: 'parts of him', it was said, 'were found laying about in the road.'[11] That day three men were killed and eight were wounded in Mafeking.

5

Under Siege

MAFEKING WAS A primitive little place, a 'mere tin-roofed village', Conan Doyle called it, plumped down in the stony wilderness some ten miles from the Transvaal border. Established in 1885 to serve as the administrative and trading centre for the surrounding districts, it had grown over the years and by the time war broke out its white population had risen to 1500. But, small and isolated as it was, the town was not devoid of civilized amenities. It boasted a bank, several churches and schools, a library, a race course, a small printing works which published its own newspaper, the *Mafeking Mail*. In peacetime its general stores provided a wide assortment of goods; its three hotels, although not luxurious, offered comfortable accommodation to passing travellers, and the recent addition of the Victoria Hospital, with its forty beds, had given a much-needed boost to the town's scanty medical services. Nor could Mafeking be dismissed as a functionless backwater. Until 1897, when the railway was extended northwards to Bulawayo, it had acted as a rail-head and its workshops, sidings and engine-house still retained an importance in the affairs of the town. Life there might have been dull, but it was not stagnant.

For all that, the town bore the unmistakable stamp of a *platteland* dorp. Originally planned round the dusty market square, its unpaved streets stretched scarcely half a mile in any direction. Architecturally it was featureless. With the exception of the newly built Catholic convent, its mud brick houses, fronted by wooden stoeps and roofed with corrugated iron, were all single-storeyed. It was dust-blown, stark and relieved only by the ragged pepper trees lining its streets. In summer it could be intolerably hot.

About half a mile from the town, but still within the defended area claimed by Baden-Powell, was the African *stadt* or township of Mafikeng (a Tswana word meaning 'place of rocks', from which the European settlement derived its name) where lived an estimated 5000 Barolong. The Barolong were Tswana tribesmen who, after a series of disputes with the Boers, had settled in the area long before the British arrived on the scene. Officially they were supposed to be neutral – the opposing sides both insisting that it was exclusively a 'white man's war' – but the Barolong's long-standing feud with the Boers had ensured their allegiance to the beleaguered garrison. At the beginning of the siege a Barolong delegation had pleaded with Baden-Powell to supply them with the means of defending themselves but their request had been turned down. They were told that their *stadt* had been included within the defences of the town and if they were attacked, 'white troops would do all the fighting' and protect them. But this was said more to counter possible objections from the Boers than to guarantee the tribesmen's neutrality. Not only did Baden-Powell recognize the valuable part the Barolong could play in the 'white man's war' – from the outset they helped to build the defence works and acted as spies and runners – but he must have been aware that, as experienced cattle-raiders, they could assist in replenishing the town's food supply.

The inclusion of the Barolong *stadt* within the defence boundaries meant that the defenders had a larger population to feed, but this was a problem they were prepared to deal with in their own way. As John Comaroff has pointed out, when food supplies began to dwindle 'the fact that the tribesmen were rationed far more severely than the townspeople, and that death from starvation was rife amongst them, did not alter [Baden-Powell's] determination to continue holding out.'[1] He was always to insist that the Barolong would have been worse off in the hands of the Boers. Nor was his refusal to allow the tribesmen the right to defend themselves strictly enforced. Accusations of 'arming the natives' by both sides became a feature of the siege. By the time it ended some 500 Barolong are said to have taken up arms. This is not to be wondered at: the hardships endured by the black population of Mafikeng – mostly from disease and starvation – were enormous. They had every reason to retaliate.

They were not alone in their suffering. In the well-trodden veld outside the town there was another vulnerable enclosure. Known as the 'women's laager', this was a temporary camp set up shortly before the siege began. It was intended to serve as a refuge for women and children who had no reason to stay in the town, and was situated on the northern side of the Barolong *stadt*. Hastily erected, overcrowded and disease-prone, the laager was a squalid and miserable place. Persuading some of the women – many of whom were Afrikaners – to move there had not been easy. One woman, for instance, had to be dragged away and 'during her paroxysm of anger declared she hoped the lintels of the houses in Mafeking would be smeared with the blood of English women and children.'[2] Threats like this were later remembered when lights were seen flashing from the laager at night. 'It is known', wrote the highly suspicious Dr Hayes, 'they signal to the enemy by this means.' Baden-Powell was forced to take action. He issued a decree warning that the flashes were 'most objectionable' and ordered all lights in the laager 'to be extinguished at 9.30 p.m.'[3] But his suspicions were not shared by the Boers. Far from respecting the women's encampment as a sanctuary which housed their own kin, Snyman's gunners seemed to single it out for some of the heaviest shelling. Direct hits were regularly reported and on at least one occasion a woman was wounded by Boer snipers. That many of the more resolute women refused to be separated from their husbands and preferred to take their chance in the town is hardly surprising.

One woman who would never have dreamed of seeking refuge in the laager was Lady Sarah Wilson. Although she had no more reason to be in the town than some of the other women, she could claim the privileges of a senior officer's wife and would have objected strongly to being penned up in a congested, makeshift camp. Not that the possibility of such confinement ever arose. Having returned to Mafeking at her own request she was left, with the help of Gordon, to settle in the town as and how she wished.

The siege had lasted fifty-three days by the time Sarah arrived back in Mafeking. They had been eventful, often exciting days but they had taken their toll. Morale was beginning to sag: the daily shelling, the food rationing, the fading hopes of relief and the recent flooding of the trenches had frayed nerves and encouraged feelings of despondency. To counteract this Baden-Powell seized every opportunity for a display of confidence. His slight, jaunty figure was seen everywhere. Swinging his cane and whistling operatic arias, he seemed assured and tireless. In Sarah he gained a valuable ally. 'She was a most remarkable woman', he was to say, 'and the influence she had on the morale of the defenders was immense.'[4]

Arriving fresh from the enemy camp, Sarah lost no time in spreading her opinion that the Boers were on the point of surrender. The burgers, she assured the war-correspondents who flocked to interview her, were heartily sick of the war and disillusioned with Snyman's leadership. This so impressed Baden-Powell that he immediately addressed a letter to the 'Burghers of the South African Republic at present under arms near Mafeking', advising them to lay down their arms and return to their farms. The only effect this had was to bring a sharp retort from Snyman, who accused the British commander of adopting childish and underhand methods. The trading of insults had become a recognized game in this very communicative siege.

Sarah's first concern was to arrange a bomb-proof shelter for herself. This was essential in a town where most of the population was now existing underground. Not only was it necessary to be protected from the shelling, but anyone straying too far from a bolt-hole risked being picked off by snipers. Sarah was taking no chances. Helped by a group of army officers, she set about constructing a dug-out in front of Mr Weil's house. Some eight feet deep, it was roofed with a double set of steel rails, covered by sheets of corrugated iron and then by a huge tarpaulin on which was piled nine feet of solid earth, and sandbags protected the entrance. The inside chamber was reached by wooden steps. Panelled in white-painted wood, it resembled, according to Sarah, 'the cabin of a yacht', and to add a splash of patriotic colour she hung one wall with a large Union Jack which she surrounded with war trophies. The shelter, she proudly claimed, was 'a triumph in its line'. To inaugurate it, she arranged an underground dinner party for six guests.

Within a few days of its completion, the dug-out was severely tested. A shell exploded at the entrance, killing a linesman who was fixing telegraph wires connecting Sarah with the military headquarters. On another occasion it withstood a direct hit from one of Creaky's shells. 'It is, I think,' boasted Sarah, 'the only shelter in the town on top of which a 94 lb. shell actually exploded – without making the glasses jingle.'[5] The dug-out became one of the wonders of Mafeking. Photographs of the interior were smuggled out of the town and published in London magazines. Sarah was photographed and sketched beside it in various poses and costumes: standing at the entrance in a simple cotton dress, mounting the steps wearing a sun-bonnet and seated on top of the sandbags in a rakishly-tilted boater. It was all very different from life in the insecure women's laager.

Mastering the town's routine was largely a matter of following established practices: instructions given by the military were confined to elementary safety precautions. Shell warning, for example, consisted merely of bells ringing from the look-out posts – Sarah was privileged in being alerted by telephone – and once the alarm was given everyone was expected to take cover. After that civilians were left to amuse themselves.

The number of hours spent underground depended on the Boers' energy and the weather. There was no telling how long a bombardment would last. Stories of near-misses and lucky escapes were legion. Sarah was amazed at the risks taken by men who strolled about the streets whistling and joking, leaving it until the last minute before diving into the nearest dug-out. Equally astonishing was 'the happy unconcern of the black boys, whose lively chatter is wholly undisturbed by these terrible missiles.'[6] But, amusing as some incidents appeared in retrospect, the continual booming of the guns and the daily reports of people being killed or maimed for life were a constant grim reminder of danger. The jauntiness with which Sarah had entered the town did not last long. She was scathing about those who tried to make light of the townspeople's sufferings. 'The siege of Mafeking is certainly no joke,' she reported to the *Daily Mail*, 'as we see in an English paper some individual who left here after the first few days would appear to make out. Death is ever-present with us, a stern reality.'[7]

Like the rest of the town, Sarah looked forward to the interval of peace that came with nightfall. She considered the half-hour between sunset and moonrise to be the most pleasant of the day. Herds of mules would be driven along the dusty streets to be watered; cattle and goats would return from the veld. The townsfolk would sit on the steps or on the sandbags of their shelters, chatting and fanning themselves in the cool evening breeze. Then, when the sun had set, the last hour's bombardment would commence, the thunder of the guns made all the more terrifying by the echoing darkness.

Sunday was a day of peace. By a bizarre mating of piety with war, the Boers had refused to fight on the sabbath. Mafeking, although wary of the truce, was quick to take advantage of the respite. Dressed in their Sunday best, people would saunter about the town, attend church, meet with their friends for afternoon tea and relax, as one of them put it, 'with the knowlege that one might walk anywhere without being killed and carried to the cemetery sewn up in a sheet'.[8] Sunday was the one day on which the women were allowed out of the laager. Their appearance in town, pale and gaunt as many of them were, helped to give a semblance of normality to the usually deserted streets and provided an excuse for afternoon games, concerts and sporting events. Sol Plaatje, a remarkable young Barolong whose work as interpreter for the military had separated him from his wife and son, found the weekly family reunions heartwarming. 'It is really touching', he noted in his diary, 'to see ladies and children from the Women's Laager . . . meet their brothers, husbands, fathers etc. from the trenches. From Monday to Saturday our beleaguered home has the appearance of Judgement Days, while today it looks like a gay Christmas.'[9] The women loathed returning to their camp at the end of the day.

Sarah made the most of the day's freedom. On her first Sunday she was up and on a pony by 6 a.m. and, accompanied by Gordon and some army officers, rode out to inspect the town's defences. Later, after attending church, she visited the Victoria Hospital. She was conducted through the wards by the youthful-looking matron, Miss Hill, who together with her handful of nurses had won the admiration of the entire town. Situated next to the Catholic convent, which as the only two-storeyed building in Mafeking was a natural target for the Boer gunners, the hospital had attracted more than its share of shells. Yet, working in overcrowded conditions, with a minimum of medical supplies, the nurses had created an oasis of cool efficiency amid the horrors of the siege. Their treatment of the badly maimed patients, however, was constantly harassed by the bombardment. Shortly after Sarah's visit, a shell landed in a ward where a serious operation was taking place; by some miracle none of the patients was injured but a woman, who had previously been wounded by a Mauser bullet, died of fright.

In the afternoon Sarah saw a brighter side of siege life. At a gymkhana on the recreation ground, she mingled with a holiday crowd cheering on competitors in some lively sporting events. Baden-Powell, in evening dress and a comic hat, was enjoying himself immensely. Flourishing a ring-master's whip, he jollied along competitors, joked with spectators and served teas to all from a travelling wagon. Dinner at Dixon's Hotel that evening was every bit as merry. Food was surprisingly plentiful: fresh tomatoes, young cabbages, beef and eggs, 'even', says Sarah, 'the stocks of Schweppes soda-water appearing inexhaustible.' Seated at the table, surrounded by her old friends, she felt as if no time had elapsed since she left the town two months earlier.

With Christmas approaching, Sarah decided to make herself useful. Food might have been plentiful at Dixon's, but the poorer sections of the town were beginning to feel the pinch and few expected the festive season to be anything but a sadly nostalgic, decidedly dismal event. Sarah refused to succumb to the general pessimism. Touched by the wan, hungry-looking youngsters in the women's laager, she regarded Christmas as a challenge and set about organizing a mammoth children's treat.

Helped by a committee of energetic women, she explored the town's resources. Old toys were unearthed and renovated, lengths of ribbon, bunting and coloured paper were draped, bunched and twisted to decorate the Masonic Hall. Ben Weil, the owner of Mafeking's largest store, was approached to donate provisions and a Christmas tree; an army of women set to work baking cakes, puddings and mince pies. Army officers were roped in to provide transport to and from the women's laager, and the band of the Bechuanaland Rifles agreed to play for carol singing. The end result surpassed all expectations. 'Great credit is due to Lady Sarah', enthused a member of the town guard.[10]

Christmas Day fell on Monday. As it was by no means certain that the Boers would observe a truce (their own festival was usually held on New Year's Day) Mafeking decided to celebrate a day earlier. A notice in the *Mafeking Mail* invited all children between the ages of three and thirteen to a party on Sunday, 24 December, to be held between 4 p.m. and 6 p.m. Over two hundred and fifty children turned up.

They were brought from the laager, shrieking, cheering and waving Union Jacks, in gaily decorated brakes. The entire town turned out to welcome them. Baden-Powell, the mayor, the nurses, the nuns, all joined in singing carols, serving tea and pulling crackers. A prize given for the fastest run from the laager to town was won, to everyone's delight, by the popular Captain Ronald Vernon. The high spot came when each child marched solemnly up to the sparkling Christmas tree to receive a gift from Sarah.

No Barolong children had been invited. The notice in the *Mafeking Mail* had been intended to celebrate an exclusively white Christmas, even though there were black Christians in the *stadt*. On this occasion, however, the excluded community was not, as so often happened, entirely ignored. Sarah, well trained in the role of Lady Bountiful, arranged for the remains of the children's treat to be distributed in Mafikeng the following day. Sol Plaatje watched the sharing out of these left-overs with mixed feelings. 'Lady Sarah Wilson', he noted sadly, 'sent down a collection of toys and sweets for distribution amongst the children of our village. Contented little black faces musing over their gifts reminded me of a little fellow far away . . . deserving a Christmas box from his father but unable to get it. It squeezed out of my eyes a bitter tear.'[11] His distress is understandable. He had been married for almost two years and had spent most of that time parted from his family. 'To think', he had written the day before, 'that this is the second Christmas of my wedded life and I have to spend it, like the first one, so very very far away from the one I love above all.'[12]

Christmas Day in Mafeking was not the gloomy affair that had been predicted. The Boers observed the truce and most of the townspeople sat down to a hearty Christmas dinner. Sarah and Gordon entertained Baden-Powell, Ben Weil and seven officers to luncheon. There was even a turkey which had been 'overlooked' when all the livestock had been commandeered at the beginning of the siege and, says Sarah, 'in spite of the grilling heat, we completed our Christmas dinner by a real English plum pudding.' But for some this Christmas dinner was to be their last.

The previous evening Sarah had walked home from the children's party with Captain Ronald Vernon. This lively officer, whose high spirits had made him the hero of the day, had been in an expansive mood. Taking Sarah by the arm he had told her, in strict confidence, about a plan to attack a Boer gun emplacement to the north of the town. The sortie was to be made at Game Tree Hill in the early hours of Boxing Day.

Christmas night was clear and cool. As the sun rose, the sleeping town was wakened by the distant rapping of Maxims and the faint crackle of rifle-fire. Sarah was up immediately. She telephoned head-quarters and was told that Baden-Powell and his staff had left at 2.30; the assault on Game Tree Hill had begun. Alarmed, she rushed to Ben Weil's house where she discovered a cockney servant stationed on the roof. From this position he had a clear view of the little hill, surmounted by its solitary tree. Every so often he scrambled down to describe the action to Sarah. His reports were not encouraging. Soon it became obvious that something had gone seriously wrong. The British armoured train had come to a halt and there were no signs of the men who should have been storming the gun emplacement. Sarah, torn by anxiety, paced up and down. Gordon was among the attacking force, as were most of her friends.

For two agonizing hours the firing continued; then it petered out. Weil's servant came down to report that the British were retreating and there were ambulances on the field. As the men straggled back to the town, the dismal story unfolded. A combination of bad scouting, misinformation and security leakages had led them into a hopeless situation. The Boers had been waiting for them and had torn up the railway-line, bringing the armoured train to a halt; the gun emplacement, which had been described as little more than a trench, had been protected by a high wall of sandbags and the force holding it had been strengthened during the night. From their well guarded position the Boers had held off their attackers and, after a few valiant charges, the British had been ordered to retreat. Unexpectedly out-numbered, they had not stood a chance.

Late that night the armoured train returned to the station opposite Sarah's dug-out. It brought back the dead and the wounded. Out of a force of a hundred men, twenty-four had been killed and between twenty and thirty wounded. Among the dead was Captain Ronald Vernon. Watching the slow stream of limping men and covered stretchers leaving the station, Sarah was struck by the contrast to the previous day's merriment. 'I could hardly realize in particular the death of Captain Vernon,' she says, 'who had been but a few hours before so full of health, spirit and confidence.'

But she spent little time brooding. Hearing of the chaos at the hospital, she rushed to offer her services. She was given the task of clearing the wards of convalescents, to make room for the wounded. These patients were to be housed in the Railway Institute and Sarah, with a trained nurse, Miss Crauford, and four other women, set to work preparing the hall for their reception. There were no beds, no cooking utensils, no crockery and no food. Ben Weil was appealed to and, from his inexhaustible store, eventually produced all that was needed. Everything arrived at once – the equipment, the food and the hospital wagons bringing the patients. Confusion was at its height when Creaky thundered forth. A shell passed over an approaching hospital wagon and landed close to the improvised convalescent home. The women and patients took the explosion calmly. By working non-stop, they managed to establish some sort of order. Once the patients were settled in, arrangements were made for Miss Crauford to attend the Institute every day and for other women to take a day's duty in turn. Sarah was to be on hand at all times to supervise the running of the place.

It proved to be a full-time job, made all the more difficult by the arrival at the Boer laager of a new siege gun. New Year's Day, which had been confidently expected as a day of truce, saw the opening of a more determined offensive. Shells rained down on the town and the station area, in which the Railway Institute was situated, became a prime target for the Boer gunners. Patients in the hall were continually being carried to the outside bomb-proof shelter. Sarah, dodging back and forth between her dug-out and the hospital, frequently ran the gauntlet of bursting shrapnel and rifle fire when reporting for duty. 'Lady Sarah', it was reported, 'regarded the explosions with an equanimity hardly outdone by onlookers at Crystal Palace fireworks.'[13]

'She ran some considerable risks . . .' testified Baden-Powell, '[but] just went on with her work for the wounded, giving all a splendid example in her determination to carry on no matter what odds.'[14]

In January Sarah's difficulties multiplied. Miss Crauford, now recognized as one of the town's most competent nurses, was asked to take charge of a hospital in the women's laager and Sarah was left in sole charge of the Railway Institute. Then, shortly afterwards, Gordon joined the invalids in her care: having survived the Game Tree Hill assault, he suddenly collapsed under a sharp attack of peritonitis. There was no room at the hospital and he was left to recuperate in Sarah's dug-out. The strain of nursing him, attending the convalescents and sleeping in the dank shelter was too much for even the sturdy Sarah. Just as Gordon began to mend, she caught a chill which was aggravated by a sore throat and a mild attack of fever.

'I managed, however, to go about as usual,' she later explained, 'but one afternoon, when I was feeling wretchedly ill, our hospital attendant came rushing in to say that a shell had almost demolished the convalescent home, and that, in fact, only the walls were standing. The patients mercifully escaped, owing to them all being in the bomb-proof, but they had to be moved in a great hurry, and were accommodated at the convent.'

Within a few days both she and Gordon were ordered to join the patients. The continuing heavy rains made the stifling shelters extremely unhealthy. Fever and dysentery had spread through the town; an outbreak of typhoid in the women's laager had caused great alarm. The doctors insisted that Sarah and Gordon remove themselves to the convent. Here, at the end of a corridor on the upper floor, they were given two small rooms which, they were assured, were safe from shelling.

Sarah soon had reason to doubt those assurances. Baden-Powell had taken advantage of the convent's deserted upper storey to post look-outs in the empty rooms. From her quarters at the end of the corridor,

Sarah could hear the men shouting to each other as they watched the Boer gunners through a telescope. On her first night, having crawled thankfully into bed, she was suddenly brought to her feet by the sound of heavy boots clattering along the wooden passage. A voice shouted: 'The gun is pointed at the convent!' Then Creaky belched forth. The shell went soaring over the building and buried itself in a cloud of dust about half a mile away.

This was not the only near-miss Sarah was to experience at the convent. She came to dread the setting of the sun and the 'good-night' volleys from the enemy. But it was in the early evening, ten days after leaving her dug-out, that she had her narrowest escape. January 26 was a day of vicious shelling. It started early in the morning when a shell almost demolished one of the town's hotels. Late that afternoon, as Sarah and Gordon were about to sit down to their evening meal, Major Goold-Adams, a former commissioner of Bechuanaland, paid them an unexpected visit. The three of them were chatting when the guns opened up. Within seconds there was a terrifying din above their heads and the wall against which they were sitting caved in. Suddenly, says Sarah, 'all was darkness and suffocating dust. I remember distinctly after my head had been hit twice by something hard and heavy, putting up my hands, clasped to shelter it, and then I recollect my relief to find the bricks had ceased to fall.'[15]

A rescue party quickly appeared and dragged them out. Dazed, covered with brick dust, they were led downstairs. Sarah had been cut on the head and the two men bruised. When the room was examined the next day, it was found that some two tons of bricks and mortar had fallen into a space no more than five feet square. Only the fact that their chairs had been against the wall, not drawn up to the supper table, had saved their lives. Their survival was regarded as little short of a miracle. Not surprisingly, Sarah left the convent that evening. Back in her dug-out she slept more soundly than she had done for many nights.

If nothing else, their short spell at the convent restored both Sarah and Gordon to health. They were on their feet by the time they returned to the shelter and before long Sarah was back in circulation. In addition to her other duties she had been reinstated as the *Daily Mail*'s special correspondent. Her lively despatches were later described as 'one of the sensations of the war'. They were balanced, graphic, high-spirited and surprisingly professional. In one of her early reports she summed up the mixture of realism and defiance which prevailed in the town during the early months of 1900.

Everyone is now more or less resigned to an indefinite prolongation of the siege. We have food and provisions in plenty, and have ceased to believe the many fairy tales of approaching army corps . . . As to our soldiers, they may no doubt think they would like more fighting, though it seems to me there has been enough here to satisfy most people – they may grumble at being cooped up in this little town – but when the history of this war comes to be written, people who should know are of the opinion that Mafeking will be found to have played no small part in the huge task of holding South Africa.[16]

Sarah also appeared to have acquired a rare skill as a journalist. 'During the whole course of the siege,' states a contemporary account of the war, 'Lady Sarah often managed to get her messages through when it was out of the power of other correspondents to do so.'[17] The secret of her success was revealed later by Baden-Powell. Hiring runners to carry her despatches, he claimed, cost her '£15 for each journey'.[18] This, in 1900, was a very large outlay indeed; few of Sarah's rivals could afford to match such extravagance.

The despatch-running was not entirely one way. Sarah received almost as many letters and telegrams as she sent. Indeed some of the information smuggled into Mafeking hardly seemed worth the risk involved. By far the most important message sent to Sarah was the one that reached her at the end of January. It came as a telegram from her sister-in-law, Lady Randolph Churchill, who had just arrived at the Cape on a hospital ship and gave Sarah news of her relations. 'Very grateful: your wire first direct news of family received,' Sarah replied. 'We receive scanty news. Please wire again. Congratulate you on Winston's plucky escape.'

By the time Sarah received Lady Randolph's telegram, Winston Churchill's famous escape from his prison in Pretoria was old news. He had, in fact, freed himself a few days after Sarah's release from the Boer laager. Pleased as she must have been that young Winston was free, she might not have welcomed the fact that his exploit had completely outshone her own adventures.

On the night of 12 December 1899, Winston Churchill had scaled the wall of the Staatsmodelskool, dropped into the garden of the house next door and then nonchalantly strolled through the streets of Pretoria until he reached the outskirts of the town, where he managed to board a goods train on the Delagoa Bay railway line. He remained on the train, buried under a pile of empty coal sacks, until it arrived at Witbank in the eastern Transvaal. Here he made his way to the

Witbank colliery where the friendly English-speaking manager hid him down a mine shaft and arranged for him to be smuggled on to another train which took him to the Portuguese port of Lourenço Marques (present-day Maputo) in Mozambique. The following morning, he boarded a steamer and sailed round the coast to Durban. A huge crowd was waiting to welcome him at the Durban docks. Hailed as a hero, his name featuring for the first time in headlines throughout the world, Churchill had not only gained his freedom but staked his claim to fame.

6

Holding Out

FOLLOWING THE DISASTERS of 'Black Week' in December 1899, Lord Roberts had been appointed to supersede Sir Redvers Buller as Commander-in-Chief in South Africa. His arrival at the Cape, on 22 January 1900, accompanied by his chief-of-staff Lord Kitchener, put new heart into the floundering British campaign and heralded a series of military successes. First, on 15 February, British troops ended the siege of Kimberley. Shortly afterwards a huge Boer force surrendered at Paardeberg and finally, at the end of the month, came the relief of Ladysmith in Natal.

But while Britain rejoiced over these triumphs, the people of Mafeking were sunk in gloom. It took time for the good news to reach them. Lord Roberts's arrival might have boosted British morale at the Cape but it brought small comfort to Mafeking. In a telegram which the new Commander-in-Chief sent to Baden-Powell shortly after his arrival, he congratulated the town on its determined stand but warned that Mafeking was 'too far to attempt relief at present'. Baden-Powell responded by tightening the food ration and strengthening the town's defences: it was possible, he informed Lord Roberts, that he could hold out until the middle of May. His attitude might have been a little different had he known that, before leaving Britain, Roberts had seriously suggested that Mafeking should be left to its fate.

That the siege might last another three months was a daunting prospect. 'Things', sighed Sol Plaatje, 'are looking mighty blue.'[1] He was not the only one to despair. Already worn out by the incessant shelling, the food shortages, sleeplessness, shattered nerves and the endless days of waiting, the townspeople were now beginning to lose heart. 'Days roll into weeks', Sarah reported on 16 February, 'but our life here goes on without much change or variation; and yet there is a sort of change visible from the highest to the lowest. People are graver, there is a tired expression on most countenances, the women look paler, the children more pinched.'[2] Unlike some others, she refused to admit to feelings of despair and put the lassitude down to 'the wear and tear of the mind consequent upon this long bombardment'. This was something on which she was well qualified to speak. Not only had she narrowly escaped death at the convent but, since her return to her shelter, she had experienced another near-miss. One evening as she was walking past the Post Office, a shell crashed into the building and she found herself running through an avalanche of debris to the nearest shelter. 'For a moment I thought I was killed', she admitted.

Only Baden-Powell remained as bright, as active and optimistic as ever. Sarah did her best to imitate him. She saw it as her duty as a member of the ruling élite to set an example. 'Inside Mafeking', wrote Vere Stent, Reuters' correspondent, 'it is no hyperbole or flattery to say Lady Sarah was a star of merry reassurance and cheerfulness under increasing difficulties.'[3] It was Vere Stent who called her 'the good genius of the siege'. Whether the overworked nurses or the harassed women in the laager, not to mention the neglected families in the *stadt*, would have seen Sarah in quite the same light is another matter. But there can be no doubt that she helped to boost morale. She was to be seen everywhere: distributing prizes at the Sunday sports, accompanying Baden-Powell on his rounds, visiting sick civilians as well as sick soldiers. If nothing else, she brought a semblance of normality, a lady-of-the-manor cosiness, to a far from ordinary situation. 'She kept up her vivacity', said Baden-Powell, 'from start to finish.'[4]

More than vivacity was needed to disguise the fact that the enemy was at the door. Every entertainment was overshadowed by the knowledge that, when relaxing, they were particularly vulnerable to attack. This was dramatically illustrated at the festivities staged to counter Lord Roberts's gloomy message. That Sunday, Baden-Powell announced, the regular afternoon concert would be followed by a 'Beleaguered Bachelors' Ball'. The concert, which started at five o'clock, was a huge success. Baden-Powell gave his hilarious impersonation of 'Signor Paderewski, a tousled haired pianist', which, according to Sarah, 'held the hall entranced or convulsed with laughter'. Spirits were still high at eight o'clock that evening when the guests began to arrive at the

Masonic Hall for the Bachelors' Ball. The officers in their dress uniforms and the ladies in their bright, if dated, finery, brought a breath of the *beau monde* to the modest tin-roofed hall. Jet, ostrich plumes and outsized bunches of Parma violets more than made up for the shabbiness of the setting. When the band struck up 'Rule Britannia' it was greeted by enthusiastic cheers; then a mixed assortment of dancers took to the floor. 'Lords, Earls, Lady Sarah, Colonels and Majors,' gushed one excited townswoman, 'down to ourselves all whirling away.'[5]

They did not whirl for long. Hardly had the dancing started when it was stopped by a sudden crash of gunfire. There were a few dazed seconds; then a stampede into the streets. Orderlies galloped past the hall sounding a general alarm and the officers went dashing to their posts. 'It was just like Waterloo,' noted a guest, recalling the Duchess of Richmond's ball on the eve of that famous battle, 'all the officers had to go, and left the civilians to console the ladies.'[6]

The Boers had launched a determined attack on the nearby brick-fields and the sporadic gunfire continued all night. Not until the following day did the activity cease, allowing the bedraggled revellers to emerge from their shelters and return uneasily to their homes.

It was during the month of February that the white population of Mafeking was brought face-to-face with the spectre of any siege – the possibility of starvation. Until then few among the townsfolk had doubted that their provisions would last. So confident were they that, at the beginning of the month, Sarah had been able to write to the *Daily Mail*: 'There is plenty of farinaceous foodstuffs to last three months on our present rations.'[7] Less than two weeks later her reports had become more guarded. 'As regards foodstuffs,' she wrote, 'the town can hold out for some time, if required, but only with the greatest economy.'[8] This change in tone reflected the dismay and uncertainty caused by Lord Roberts's pessimistic telegram. On taking stock, the military authorities had been alarmed to discover that they had scarcely enough supplies to last until the end of April. Rations were reduced and new restrictions imposed.

It was the black population that had to bear the full brunt of the clamp-down. For some time past there had been an acute food shortage in the Barolong township and, as early as December, it had been rumoured that 'natives' were digging up dead horses and eating them. But not until February did Sol Plaatje report that mule flesh was being distributed among some 900 inhabitants of the *stadt*. 'It looked', he wrote, 'like meat with nothing unusual about it, but when they went to the slaughter pole for the third time and found there was no more meat left and brought the heads and feet, I was moved to see their long ears and bold heads, and those were the things the people are to feed on. The recipients, however, were all very pleased to get these heads and ate them nearly raw.'[9] That Plaatje found this disgusting is not surprising: there had long been a strong taboo against horseflesh among the Barolong. Many indeed chose to die of starvation rather than touch the forbidden meat, and the death rate in the *stadt* continued to rise.

The widespread aversion to horseflesh may have contributed to Baden-Powell's decision to disguise the meat ration by setting up soup-kitchens in the *stadt*. A horse-meat factory was started which, besides producing soup for the kitchens, provided sausages and brawn for the town. The soup-kitchens, organized by Gordon Wilson and started towards the end of February, were expected to feed nearly 1000 Barolong daily. Officially the soup was said to be concocted from horseflesh; in fact, any stray animals – including dogs and mangy chickens – went into the cauldrons. Every effort was made to keep the ingredients secret, but the more observant quickly caught on. 'Soup kitchens opened to feed the natives,' noted one of the troopers. 'Dogs not licensed are to be destroyed. Sounds suspicious . . .'[10] For this highly suspect fare the Barolong were charged threepence a bowl, but the destitute received a free ration. Even so it was impossible to overcome the taboo. 'Some', reported Sarah, 'die of starvation owing to their prejudice against horseflesh.'

Sarah's reports on the soup-kitchens earned her criticism. In a despatch dated 25 February, she made the mistake of explaining exactly how the kitchens were supplied and her report was published in the *Daily Mail* under the heading: NOW EATING STRAY DOGS. This led to the accusation that she was sending 'alarming reports as to the condition of Mafeking in February'.[11] But, compared with the reports of other correspondents, Sarah's assessment of the situation was relatively moderate. A week or so earlier Angus Hamilton, the highly respected *Times* journalist, had been far more pessimistic.

'Mafeking at last is siege-weary – and, oh, so hungry!' he complained. 'It seems months since anyone had a meal which satisfied the pangs that gnaw all day. We have been on starvation rations for so many weeks that time has been forgotten, and now there seems the prospect of no immediate help forthcoming! We are sick of it, so tired of malaria, diphtheria, and typhoid . . . we have such sorrows in our midst and such suffering women and such ailing children as would turn a saint to blasphemies.'

But then, suddenly, the tide seemed to be on the turn. First came the news that Ladysmith had been relieved and shortly afterwards it was learned that Lord Roberts had marched into the Orange Free State and occupied Bloemfontein. At the same time rumours swept the town that Colonel Plumer's force (which had been separated from Baden-Powell at the beginning of the siege) was advancing towards Mafeking. Relief was expected within days.

But as hopes rose, so they fell. Plumer had indeed been within six miles of the town but his approach was little more than a tactical move. Hearing that a relief column was on the way, he had made an attempt to draw Snyman's force away from Mafeking; but he had been outnumbered and forced to retire. The following day Snyman wrote to Baden-Powell claiming that the battlefield was strewn with British dead and gave permission for them to be buried. 'Happily,' says Sarah, 'his language was more forceable than accurate.' Out of a force of 350 men, Plumer had suffered forty-nine casualties.

Baden-Powell warned Plumer not to make another attempt until he was sure the relief column was drawing near. At the same time he tried to put Plumer's nearness to good use by asking him to assist in the evacuation of some of Mafeking's black inhabitants. Those he most wanted to get rid of were the hundreds of 'refugee and foreign natives' who had crowded into the garrison at the beginning of the siege.

By this time the plight of the entire black population had become desperate. J. E. Neilly, the *Daily Telegraph*'s correspondent, was horrified by the agonies of the victims of starvation.

I saw them fall down in the veldt [he reported] and lie where they had fallen, too weak to go on their way. The sufferers were mostly little boys – mere infants ranging in age from four or five upwards . . . The Barolongs proper were not so badly off; the least fortunate were the strange Kaffirs who came in from the Transvaal as refugees . . . When the Colonel got to know of the state of affairs he instituted soup kitchens, where horses were boiled in huge cauldrons, and the savoury mess doled out in pints and quarts to all comers . . . One of those kitchens was established in the stadt, and I several times went down there to see the unfortunate fed. Words could not portray the scene of misery; five or six hundred frameworks of both sexes and all ages . . . [wearing] tattered rags, standing in lines, each holding an old blackened tin, awaiting turn to crawl painfully up to the soup kitchen . . . It was one of the most heart-rending sights I have ever witnessed.[13]

There were others among the white inhabitants who were distressed by this widespread suffering. Sarah was not among them. As late as April she was still reporting: 'No native need starve if he will but walk a short distance to the soup kitchen in his particular district.'[14] She appears to have been unaware of the deaths which resulted from the weakened state of the refugees.

These unfortunates had fared worse than the Barolong. They had been the first to be penalized by the clamp-down on rations. Not only had Baden-Powell been forced to close down the town's grain store – the main source of supply for 'foreign natives' – but he had given orders that the refugees were not to be employed in the town. Left to fend for themselves and unable to work, the unwanted outsiders were obliged to beg, steal or scavenge what food they could. Sol Plaatje, who dealt with supplicants at the magistrate's court where he worked, was appalled by the distress this caused. It was miserable, he wrote, 'to be surrounded by about 50 hungry beings, agitating the engagement of your pity and see one of them succumb to his agonies and fall backwards with a dead thud.' Many had given up in despair and braved the dangers of trying to slip through the enemy lines to reach a place of safety. They had been joined by the more desperate among the Barolong. In March, Sol Plaatje – who had helped in taking a census – estimated that the population of the *stadt* must have halved since the siege started. Baden-Powell now intended to reduce it further by organizing a large-scale exodus of refugees.

Parties of Africans, mostly women and children, were sent out of the garrison at regular intervals during the night. 'They are not armed', noted a townswoman, 'and have to walk through the Boer lines. But of the two evils, the risk of being shot at is simpler as it would mean starvation living here.'[15] Faced with these frightening alternatives, over a thousand Africans managed to reach Plumer's advance post. Others were not so lucky. Gruesome stories were told about those who fell into Boer hands. One of the more notorious incidents occurred at the beginning of April when a party of over 600 women was intercepted by the enemy, stripped, flogged and, after having their clothes burnt, driven back naked to the town. On many other occasions both men and women were simply shot at random, even though they left the town carrying a white flag. Precisely how many died on leaving Mafeking it is impossible to say.

Although Baden-Powell officially condemned the atrocities – repeated protests were sent to Snyman – he was undoubtedly pleased with the success of his evacuation plans. At the end of April, he estimated that he could now hold out until 22 June, which was the new date set by Lord Roberts for the relief of Mafeking.

Loyal hearts beat faster when, in April, Baden-Powell received a message of encouragement from Queen Victoria. 'I continue watching with confidence and admiration', she wired, 'the patient and resolute defence which is so gallantly maintained under your resourceful command.' This was the second such message the Queen had sent and it brought home to everyone just how important Mafeking had become. With the other sieges lifted, the dusty little tin-roofed town was the last bastion of British defiance and this gave it symbolic significance. As Lord Roberts's army marched across South Africa, attention was riveted on the town which had become the 'ewe lamb of the Empire'.

'We are resolved to hold out', Sarah declared stoutly, 'for as long as is humanly possible.' How long that might be, no one could say. The bombardment of the town was kept up throughout March and for most of April. There was a great sigh of relief on 11 April when Creaky, after firing its last shot – which, ironically, hit the Dutch church – was sent back to Pretoria. At Easter the churches were full for the Holy Week services and Sarah noticed how, in contrast to earlier days, the rain now fell freely through the roof of the Anglican church. Hot-cross buns were made by stamping the meagre bread ration with a cross.

Hunger, lack of nourishment and the need for more wholesome food now overshadowed all other considerations. There was hardly an entry in a diary or a newspaper report that failed to mention the deterioration of the rations. 'Our bread', Sarah told readers of the *Daily Mail*, 'is now made entirely of oats and is full of husks, which causes a good deal of illness. There are many cases of nervous prostration among the garrison, as well as malarial typhoid.'[16]

A new and bizarre food supplement arrived about this time. Quite unexpectedly a flight of locusts descended on the town. These insects, long considered a delicacy by the San (Bushmen) of the Kalahari, were seized upon by the Africans. The San were in the habit of cramming live locusts into their mouths, but the Barolong preferred them boiled. Once the idea caught on, the townsfolk came to appreciate the insects, describing them as being rather like tasteless prawns. Sarah was among the first to try the new hors-d'oeuvre. She pronounced upon it favourably and wired to her sister in England: 'Breakfast today, horse sausages; lunch minced mule, curried locusts. All well.'

This was not the only message Sarah sent to her sister, Lady Georgina Curzon. For some time past she had been concerned about the people of Mafeking who had lost either their homes or their livelihood, and she had written to Georgina in March asking her to start a fund to help such victims of the siege. Georgina had responded by writing to *The Times* appealing for subscriptions. Her sister, she explained, had implored her 'to bring before the generous British public the destitute condition of the nuns, refugees and civilians generally in Mafeking. She writes with authority, having witnessed their sufferings herself.' The response was immediate, far exceeding Sarah's modest expectations. One of the first subscribers was the Princess of Wales, who wrote to Georgina: 'I hope very soon they will be relieved and I trust your poor sister Sarah will be none the worse for all she has gone through.'

The fate of Mafeking had become everyone's concern. Few doubted that the town would be relieved but even the most optimistic feared for the health and safety of the inhabitants. These fears were heightened when, on 24 April, it was learned that President Kruger's impetuous grandson, Sarel Eloff, had joined the besieging force, bringing with him reinforcements. Self-assured, reckless and ambitious, Eloff soon let it be known that he was determined to capture Mafeking at any cost. He was taken at his word.

The news Mafeking had been waiting for came at the beginning of May. Then it was that Baden-Powell was informed that a relief column, commanded by Colonel Bryan Mahon, was about to approach the town from Kimberley. No official announcement was made but it was not long before Mafeking was abuzz with rumours. Everyone seemed to sense that the long months of confinement were drawing to a close. 'As we near the end of the siege', wrote Sarah on 11 May, 'our conditions in the little town are perhaps becoming more cheerful . . . I have had conversations with the ladies of Mafeking, and they, as much as the men, are determined that the Boers shall not come in here while a particle of food remains.'[17]

She spoke too soon. The ladies might be determined to hold out, but President Kruger's grandson was every bit as determined to come in. Having kept the town on tenterhooks for over two weeks, Sarel Eloff decided to make good his word by launching a surprise attack.

At four o'clock on the morning of 12 May, Sarah was suddenly woken by the sound of rifle fire. Hurrying out of her room, she was met by the noise of bullets swishing past the canvas blind at the end of Mr Weil's stoep. She quickly shut the door, lit a candle, and scrambled into her clothes. Outside everything was pitch dark; from the darkness came sounds of the town springing to life. Footsteps hurried to and fro, now and then a lantern was seen flashing between the houses. In a matter of minutes came the sounds for which Sarah had been waiting: an alarm bugle, followed by the slow tolling of a church bell. It was the signal that a general attack had started.

As Sarah stood at the front of Mr Weil's house wondering what to do, a man came running down the street. He told her that everything was under control; he had just left Baden-Powell and his staff drinking coffee at their headquarters. The rifle fire which could be heard coming from the east, he said, was thought to be a feint; the 'real business' was expected on the other side of the town, near the Barolong *stadt*. Sarah was joined by a group of women and together they stood, straining their eyes, trying to make out what was happening. They were not left wondering for long. From the direction of the *stadt*, tongues of flame pierced the darkness. 'At the same time,' says Sarah, 'a din of confused cries, unmistakably native ejaculations, was borne to us by the breeze along with the smell of burning thatch and wood.'[18] Then, quite close, there was a cheer. They were in no doubt as to what had happened: the Boers had broken through.

As soon as it was light, Sarah decided to go to the hospital. Ben Weil told her she was mad. The worst firing was coming from that direction, he said, and she was bound to be caught in the cross-fire. Sarah refused to be put off. Sending for Gordon's batman to accompany her, she snatched a few things of value and set out. Running along the road, they twice had to flatten themselves against a wall as bullets whizzed over their heads. Once Sarah tripped and fell and the batman had to help her to her feet. Not until they reached the trench leading to the hospital were they able to stand upright and so cover the last 500 yards in comparative safety.

Conditions at the hospital were chaotic. From the beginning of the attack hospital wagons and stretcher parties had been arriving with wounded men. Shortly after Sarah arrived, three wounded Boers were brought in and then came an African with a shattered arm who, it was whispered, had acted as a guide for the attackers. One of the more pathetic cases was a young army orderly who had been shot near the heart while taking a message to one of the outposts. Sarah sat with him for hours, dabbing his head with eau-de-Cologne and brushing away the flies. In the evening he passed into unconsciousness and died shortly afterwards.

The firing continued all day. At the hospital they were aware that a fight was in progress but reports from the town were muddled and they did not learn what had happened until much later. It was more of a skirmish than a battle.

On planning his attack, Sarel Eloff had banked on the support of 700 men. But, after setting fire to the *stadt*, he had counted the raiding party and found that it had dwindled to about 200 burgers and 40 French and German volunteers. With this totally inadequate force, he had pushed on to the old police barracks – now the headquarters of the Protectorate regiment – on the western side of town. He had easily captured the barracks and imprisoned the commanding officer and his staff. Then he had settled down to await the reinforcements he expected General Snyman to send in. He was expecting too much. Snyman, who had been doubtful about the action from the outset, was characteristically half-hearted in his efforts to storm the western defences. Baden-Powell had little difficulty in holding him off. After bravely holding the police barracks throughout the day, Eloff was forced to surrender. The Boers were then rounded up and marched to the Masonic Hall.

News of the surrender was immediately telephoned to the hospital. Later that evening Sarah and two of the nurses slipped away to 'have a peep' at the prisoners. 'A motley crew they were,' declared Sarah, 'representatives of many nationalities . . . who knew they had got out of a tight place and were devoutly thankful still to have whole skins.'

Early the next morning, the town was again woken by the sound of shell fire. One after another, three shells burst and then there was an eerie silence. Sarel Eloff, who had been lodged at Mr Weil's house, explained to Sarah what this meant. The shells, he said, were a pre-arranged signal which, had the raid proved successful, would have been answered by a volley of rifle fire.

As things turned out, these were the last shells fired into Mafeking.

That afternoon the Boer officers were packed off to the gaol where they were to remain until a suitable house was prepared for them. Vere Stent was one of the newspaper correspondents who interviewed them in the prison. He asked them why Sarah had been released from the laager. 'Who could possibly have shot anyone so good-looking?' replied Eloff gallantly.[19] The looks of the African women who were flogged and shot were not, it seems, rated so highly.

Three days after Eloff's attempt to seize Mafeking came the news that Mahon's relief column had already passed Vryburg. That same morning Colonel Plumer's sadly depleted regiment linked up with the column. Together the combined force of almost 2000 men headed towards Mafeking.

News of Mahon's approach roused the townspeople. Clambering on to roof-tops, clinging to chimneys and balancing on ladders, they watched as the dust clouds blurred the horizon. Every drift of dust seemed to tell a different story; now it seemed that the Boer were being reinforced, now that the relief column was drawing nearer. Cynics claimed the whole thing to be another Boer trick, a hoax to throw the garrison off guard. Then, on the second afternoon of watching, artillery fire was heard and there were definite signs of a withdrawal from the Boer lines. Shortly afterwards Gordon Wilson scrambled down from Baden-Powell's look-out and ordered a contingent of horsemen to saddle up. They were joined by Baden-Powell and Major Panzera with some horse artillery. When the party returned later that afternoon, it was learned they had tried to head off an enemy detachment but had been foiled by the gathering dusk. Tired of watching, many people gave up and returned to their homes.

That evening, as Sarah was about to sit down to dinner, she heard a faint cheer. Rushing to the market square, she grabbed the arm of the first man she saw – a dusty, khaki-clad soldier. 'Has anyone come in?' she asked.

'We have come in,' replied the man casually. 'Major Karri-Davis and eight men of the Imperial Light Horse.'

It seemed too astonishing to be true. Here was an advance party of the relieving force, the men they had watched and waited for, yet their arrival was so matter-of-fact that it seemed somehow unreal. There was little visible excitement, no cheering crowds, no bands playing: 'Merely a score or so of people, singing "Rule Britannia", surrounding eight or nine dust-begrimed figures each holding a tired and jaded horse, and a few women on the outskirts of the circle with tears of joy in their eyes.'

Later that night, Sarah was driven to the polo-ground where, in the brilliant moonlight, she joined the crowds watching the relief column limp into camp. But the sense of anti-climax persisted. A Boer force, under their formidable commander, Koos De la Rey, had put up a determined opposition to the column's entry into Mafeking. Weary after the fighting and the long march, the soldiers slumped down beside their assembled wagons and slept.

Sarah spent the rest of the night helping out at the hospital. Not until the following day was the relief force officially welcomed. Then, led by the Royal Horse Artillery and joined by the town guard, the soldiers marched through the town to the market square where, cheered by a huge crowd, they were presented with an address of welcome by the mayor. Sarah watched the proceedings from the convent and was deeply moved. It was a sight she was never to forget. 'Ever since,' she recalled many years later, 'when I see galloping artillery, that momentous morning is brought back to my mind, and I feel a choking sensation in my throat.'

A Reuters' message telling of the relief reached London at about 9.30 p.m. on Friday, 18 May 1900. From the Mansion House, where it was first announced, the news quickly spread throughout the delirious capital. Paper boys raced along the streets giving away special editions that were being churned out from Fleet Street. In music-halls and theatres performances were stopped as the audiences rose to cheer and sing 'God Save the Queen'. Frantic crowds surged along Pall Mall, Piccadilly and Regent Street, singing, shouting, waving flags and bunches of red, white and blue streamers – known as Kruger's Whiskers – blowing whistles and hoisting banners. Lamp-posts were scaled, top hats flung into the air, rockets fired into the night. From West End to East End, from Park Lane to the Bank, one could hardly move for the press of near-hysterical people. A new verb was added to the English language that night: 'to maffick – to exult riotously'.

In Grosvenor Square the mob swarmed about a tall, red-brick corner house on the south side. It was here, said a report, 'that Lady Sarah Wilson's little boys are staying with their grandmother'.[20]

The following morning all other news was swept aside. The papers plastered their pages with pictures of the defenders – Baden-Powell, Lord Edward Cecil, Colonel Plumer and Lady Sarah Wilson – all grouped under the triumphant headline: MAFEKING RELIEVED!

7

'Tommy Atkins, the war has just begun'

THE FRENZIED REJOICING which greeted the relief of Mafeking was misdirected. While there could be no denying the gallant and resolute stand made by the isolated garrison, the lifting of the siege was irrelevant to the progress of the war. Indeed the ending of this, the last of the three long-drawn-out sieges, was an emotional event, of symbolic rather than military significance. Mafeking was too far removed from the path of conflict to be of any strategic value; it would have made little or no difference to the campaign had Lord Roberts obeyed his first promptings and left the beleaguered town 'to its fate'. The real, the more calmly assessed, British gains were being chalked up elsewhere in South Africa.

Lord Roberts's arrival at the Cape, in January 1900, had resulted in a complete transformation of the pattern of war. The sixty-seven-year-old Roberts had been sent to South Africa, at his own request, to replace Sir Redvers Buller as Commander-in-Chief after the disasters of 'Black Week' in mid December 1899. A succession of British defeats in that fatal week – at Stormberg, Magersfontein and Colenso – had so alarmed politicians that the astute Roberts had had little difficulty in furthering his long-held aim of securing for himself the South African command. Roberts's success was overshadowed by personal tragedy. On the day his appointment was confirmed, he was informed that his only son, Lieutenant Frederick Roberts, had been killed while trying to rescue the field-guns abandoned during the

Colenso battle. It was a terrible blow, about which Roberts refused to speak; but its effect was apparent to everyone. When on 23 December he boarded the *Dunottar Castle*, which was to take him to South Africa, it was noticed that many of the officials who had come to see him off, including Lord Lansdowne, wore black in deference to his bereavement.

By the time the *Dunottar Castle* reached Cape Town, Roberts's plan of campaign had begun to take shape. The War Office's proposed strategy of advancing on the Boer republics from the Cape midlands was ditched and replaced by a plan that utilized the Cape's western railway, the line which ran north to Rhodesia through Kimberley. By assembling an army on this railway, beyond the Orange River, Roberts was well placed to relieve Kimberley (where the beleaguered Cecil Rhodes was clamouring for action) before sending his main force eastwards across the sun-bleached grassland of the Orange Free State to cut the central railway line and capture the republican capital of Bloemfontein. From there the army was to push on to the Transvaal.

It was a plan which entailed punishingly long marches at the height of the southern summer, marches for which the unacclimatized British troops were ill-prepared and inadequately equipped. But it started well. First, on 15 February, soon after Roberts and Kitchener (his chief-of-staff) joined the troops in the northern Cape, Kimberley was relieved by General French; then came the surrender of some four thousand burgers, under General Piet Cronjé, at Paardeberg in the Orange Free State on 27 February – giving the British army its first great victory on the nineteenth anniversary of Majuba. These successes were followed by Boer routs at Poplar Grove, where the visiting President Kruger narrowly escaped capture, and Abraham's Kraal. Finally, on 13 March, Lord Roberts made his formal entry into undefended Bloemfontein. Riding at the head of his troops, the trim, grey-haired little Field Marshal (he was only five foot two) was cheered by a scattering of English-speaking inhabitants, mostly women, as he made his way through the town to the Boer Presidential residence. Here he entered the gates to the singing of the national anthem and then a small Union Jack, worked for the occasion by Lady Roberts, was hoisted on a flagpole in the garden. It was an extraordinary moment. With so much having happened in so short a time, who could doubt that the war was as good as won?

But Lord Roberts's progress had not been made without cost. At the battle of Paardeberg, before the Boers surrendered, there had been heavy British losses: 1270 casualties, with over 300 men and officers killed. Nor had the march been accomplished without serious mishaps. Before setting out for the Orange Free State, Roberts had suffered a blow to his ill-organized transport arrangements. On the same day that Kimberley was relieved, 15 February, Christiaan De Wet – soon to be a famous Boer guerrilla leader – had successfully attacked a convoy of supply wagons at the Riet River, cutting off nearly a third of Roberts's entire transport and depriving the army of essential forage, food and medical supplies. Instead of trying to make good the loss of some 200 wagons and an estimated 1600 oxen, Roberts had pressed on with the march, weakening both the health and the morale of his troops. His triumphant entry into Bloemfontein was at the head of a long procession of dust-begrimed soldiers 'worn with half-rations and whole-day marches . . . gaunt and haggard, with their clothes in such a state that decency demanded that some of the men should be discreetly packed away in the heart of the dense column.'[1]

Roberts was alive to the danger posed by the free-ranging commandos. He had tried to counter their activities with threats and promises. Shortly after invading the Orange Free State he had issued a proclamation warning all burgers to stop fighting. Those who did so and who remained at home 'pursuing their ordinary occupations' were promised that they would not suffer 'in their persons or property'. But those who continued to oppose the British forces, or who furnished the enemy with supplies or information, were to be dealt with according to the customs of war. Two days after entering Bloemfontein, Roberts issued another proclamation to the same effect. This time, though, the conditions imposed were more stringent. No amnesty was to be granted to burgers who had taken a prominent part in the policy which had led to war or had 'commandeered or used violence to any British subject'; and those who returned peacefully to their farms had first to bind themselves by taking an oath of neutrality.[2]

Roberts had little doubt that his edicts would prove effective. On the day his second proclamation was published he wrote to Queen Victoria assuring her that the Boers were daily laying down their arms and that he expected no more serious trouble in the Orange Free State. And, for a while, it seemed that he was right. Even after the fugitive President Steyn – who had transferred his government to Kroonstad, about 130 miles north of Bloemfontein – had emphatically denounced Roberts's proclamations, reports of Free State burgers surrendering continued to come in. But appearances were deceptive: the spirit of resistance was not so easily crushed. This was forcibly demonstrated at the end of March when the audacious Christiaan De Wet reassembled his commando and launched a surprise attack on a British force at Sannah's Post, twenty miles from Bloemfontein. As a result of this action the British lost over 600 men – killed, wounded or captured – 117 wagons, 7 guns and a huge quantity of stores and ammunition. Nor was De Wet alone; other commandos, if not so spectacularly successful, were also beginning to make their presence felt.

'I trust nothing will prevent my moving steadily on . . .' Roberts wrote to Sir George Forest on 7 April. 'Meanwhile we are being a good deal worried; the Boers are spreading over the country in small parties, cutting off supplies, turning the people against us, and threatening the line of the railway.'[3] The nature of the war was changing: the days of the great set battles were over and the guerrilla phase had begun.

'Before I had been many days in Bloemfontein,' wrote a young woman who arrived there shortly after the occupation, 'I realized it was a veritable city of hospitals. Every large building in the least suitable had been commandeered for the purpose – girls' schools, boys' schools, sisterhoods, colleges and public buildings – and there were besides the two large tent hospitals and two field hospitals.'[4] Soon she was to become acquainted with another grim feature of Bloemfontein life: the daily funeral processions which left from those hospitals and wound their way through the streets to the hillside cemetery. There was nothing stately about these cortèges: for the most part they consisted of nothing more than a creaking, mule-drawn cart carrying a blanket-wrapped body covered by a Union Jack. Beside the cart shuffled a handful of soldiers with arms reversed. This was the best the military could do for the hundreds of soldiers who were buried during Lord Roberts's stay in the Free State capital. They were victims of what has been described as the 'greatest misfortune of the campaign'.[5] This was the typhoid epidemic which devastated the British troops after the occupation of Bloemfontein.

Various explanations have been given for the rapid spread of the disease. Some claim the troops, weakened by their gruelling march on half-rations, were in no state to resist infection; others blame the insanitary conditions of the army camps, the overcrowding in and around Bloemfontein, where the arrival of the troops caused the population to rise from four thousand to forty thousand in a month. There was also an appalling shortage of medicines and medical equipment – resulting from the losses inflicted by De Wet and a later disruption of the railway line – which prevented effective hospital treatment. But while all these handicaps undoubtedly made things worse, the root cause appears to have stemmed from a lack of efficient organization.

The disease had first manifested itself during the march. Conan Doyle, who worked as a volunteer doctor at the converted Bloemfontein Club, was among the first to acknowledge this. 'There can be no doubt', he wrote, 'that this severe outbreak had its origins in the Paardeberg water.' That the military authorities had allowed men to drink that water was, in his opinion, inexcusable. 'If bad water can cost us more than all the bullets of the enemy,' he protested, 'then surely it is worth our while to make the drinking of unboiled water a stringent military offence . . . It is heartrending for the medical man who has emerged from a hospital full of water-borne pestilence to see a regimental water-cart being filled, without protest, at some polluted wayside pool. With precautions and with inoculation all those lives might have been saved.'[6] He was writing after the event, but what he says should have been known by army doctors. Typhoid, or enteric fever as it was more widely known, had a long history in South Africa. It was, as Doyle pointed out, endemic in the country.

By April there were an estimated 4500 soldiers in hospital in Bloemfontein and thousands more were being evacuated to the Cape. It was more than the makeshift, understaffed and ill-equipped hospitals could cope with. There were not enough beds, mattresses or stretchers to accommodate the never-ending stream of patients. In one general hospital with five hundred beds there were seventeen hundred sick, 'nearly all enterics', and those in the field hospitals fared even worse. Not only were the hospital tents shockingly overcrowded but, with an average of one doctor to every 100 patients, most of the fever-stricken men were left shivering on a waterproof sheet with little or no medical attention and cared for by 'a few ordinary private soldiers' who acted as orderlies. A visiting British MP, William Burdett-Coutts – husband of the philanthropic banking heiress, Angela Burdett-Coutts – was appalled by the hospital conditions in and around Bloemfontein. He had been sent out to investigate the hospitals by *The Times* and when he returned to England he fiercely denounced the neglect by the military authorities. He wrote of how he had seen hundreds of men in the worst stages of typhoid, 'their faces covered with flies in black clusters too weak to raise a hand to brush them off, trying in vain to dislodge them by a painful twitching of the features. There was no one to do it for them.' In some of the tents he visited 'there were ten typhoid cases lying closely packed together, the dying with the convalescent, the man in his "crisis" pressed against the man hastening to it. There was no room to step between them.' The patients were stretched out on the hard ground with 'hardly any medicines . . . without pillows, without linen of any kind, without a single nurse amongst them.'[7]

The outcry caused by Burdett-Coutts's report added to the alarm created by published lists of men dying from disease in South Africa. Even so the War Office failed to recognize the crisis, preferring instead to rely on the bland reports of two civilian surgeons, Sir William MacCormac and Mr (later Sir) Frederick Treves, who had left South Africa about the time Lord Roberts occupied Bloemfontein. These two distinguished medical men had been attached to the British army and, wanting to curry favour with the authorities, sprang to the defence of the medical corps. 'I left South Africa', Treves wrote in a letter to the *British Medical Journal*, 'with the impression that nothing more could have been done to mitigate the sufferings of the sick and wounded than had been done.' Lord Roberts was to cite Treves and MacCormac when answering his critics.

Later Frederick Treves was to admit that the army medical services were inadequate, but in his battle with Burdett-Coutts he refused to make any concessions. He had a weakness for playing to the gallery and many of his arguments were as flippant as they were irresponsible. Knowing his audience, he did not hesitate to have a swipe at the frivolous women who badgered their way to the front and whose meddling in hospital work was hampering the doctors and nurses. The typhoid crisis in South Africa, Treves quipped, was partly the result of 'a plague of flies and a plague of women'.

This is not how it appeared to those who battled in the hospitals. Dr Conan Doyle, who could hardly be described as an alarmist, had no doubts about the extent of the catastrophe. 'The total number of cases could not have been less than six or seven thousand', he says. 'How great was the strain only those who had to meet it can tell . . . At Bloemfontein alone as many as fifty men died in one day, and more than 1000 new graves in the cemetery testify to the severity of the epidemic.'[8]

It was only after the arrival of more trained nurses from England – by which time Lord Roberts had long since left Bloemfontein – and the onset of colder weather that the fever died down. But this was not to be the last that was heard of typhoid during the war. Not the least disturbing thing about the Bloemfontein outbreak is that no lessons were learned from its rapid spread. When faced with new epidemics, this time claiming more vulnerable victims, the military authorities not only failed to recognize the danger signals but, until they were shaken out of their complacency by a determined woman, refused to acknowledge their responsibility. Prolonged neglect resulted in an even greater death toll.

The epidemic, the need to rest his troops, to bring up reinforcements and to counter the activities of the commandos, kept Roberts at Bloemfontein for almost two months. Not until then was he ready to resume his march northwards to the Transvaal. It was early in the morning of 3 May 1900 that Roberts joined his troops assembled at Karee Siding, twenty miles north of Bloemfontein, to be greeted with the soon-to-be-famous refrain: *We are marching to Pretoria*. With the Commander-in-Chief travelling in a covered wagon, which acted as his mobile headquarters, the huge army of over thirty thousand men started on another punishing march.

They met with very little resistance. Within two weeks they had reached and captured Kroonstad – evacuated earlier by the Free State government – and so completed the first half of the march. Roberts was obliged to halt at Kroonstad for ten days. He needed time to recuperate. Once again his long, vulnerable supply line was bedevilling his every move. Roberts had hoped that by following the single-track railway between Bloemfontein and the Vaal river he could overcome his transport problems: he was soon disillusioned. Boer guerrillas had already been at work blowing up bridges and tearing up the railway line, creating such havoc that repair work could not keep pace with the steady march of the troops. Not only was the army again on short rations, but men were still collapsing from typhoid; medical equipment was as desperately needed as food.

It was during the Kroonstad stop-over that they heard the siege had been lifted at Mafeking. On 22 May Roberts led his troops out of Kroonstad and five days later splashed across the Vaal river in the wake of his advanced mounted infantry. The Boers put up a token resistance at the Transvaal border but, vastly outnumbered, they were forced to retreat after a brief skirmish. They left the field, not in panic, but with the same odd mixture of fatalism and defiance which they had shown throughout the British advance.

Shortly before crossing the Vaal, Roberts had, after consultation with Cape Town and London, drawn up a proclamation annexing the

Orange Free State as a crown colony. Then it was that the inhabitants of the Free State learned that their country was to be known as the Orange River Colony and that overnight they had become British subjects. A couple of days later the newly-named Orange River Colony was placed under martial law: the Queen's fledgling subjects were to be allowed little freedom.

After entering the Transvaal Roberts met with no serious opposition until he approached Johannesburg and encountered a Boer force which, under its new commandant-general, Louis Botha, made a valiant last-ditch stand before retreating to Pretoria. The following day, 31 May, British troops, watched by a mixed crowd of unimpressed foreigners and wide-eyed Africans, marched triumphantly into Johannesburg. At a short ceremony staged in the market square the Transvaal's republican flag, the *vierkleur* (four colour – red, white, blue and green) was solemnly hauled down and replaced by Lady Roberts's home-made Union Jack. Then, at the bidding of Lord Roberts, the assembled troops gave three cheers for the Queen.

No time was lost in advancing on Pretoria. There seemed no reason to delay when the Boer capital appeared to be there for the taking. For days Pretoria had been in a state of chaos. President Kruger, accompanied by some senior officials, had already fled to the eastern Transvaal and with his going – he hoped to establish a new seat of government – the situation in the capital had deteriorated. Wild rumours were spread, food stores were looted and the small force found it impossible to maintain order. When Louis Botha arrived, after his retreat from Johannesburg, he tried to restore calm by appointing a triumvirate to govern the town. He urged the burgers to assist the rearguard which was gathering to the south of Pretoria. Before he left to rejoin his commando, the women of the town presented him with a silk *vierkleur* embroidered with the words *Strijdt met Gods Help* (Fight with the help of God).

But even with God's help, Pretoria could not be defended. The Boers were hopelessly outnumbered and would have to give way. Botha was fully aware of this. At a Boer council-of-war it had been decided that the most honourable course to adopt was that of a 'fighting retreat' and Botha was instructed to impede the British advance, rather than defend the capital. The forts on the outskirts of the town – built after the Jameson raid – had been abandoned and, after a short exchange of fire, the Boers began to fall back. Later Botha as part of his delaying tactics put out peace feelers, but Roberts was in no mood to negotiate: sure of victory, the British commander demanded unconditional surrender. With that Botha, aware that Pretoria could be shelled if he continued to hold out, ordered his men to evacuate the capital and beat a tactical retreat.

On 5 June Lord Roberts entered Pretoria shortly after two o'clock in the afternoon. This was the moment he had waited for. That he had lost almost a quarter of his force, mostly from disease, on his march from Bloemfontein, that hundreds more had died in the Free State capital for want of proper medical attention and that his troops had endured untold privations because of his inadequate supply line was regrettable, but such were the fortunes of war. What could not be denied was the fact that he had taken possession of the enemy capital, scattered their forces and put their president to flight. All that now remained was to pacify the rest of the Transvaal and annex it to the British crown.

Only a scattering of Afrikaners turned out to witness the occupation of their capital. Apart from an occasional angry whisper, those Boers who were present looked on in silence. One young woman was far too distressed to speak. Years later she was to recall the humiliation of the occasion. 'One day to be full of hope that a beloved country and independence would be restored to its people,' she wrote with unappeased bitterness, 'the next with those hopes laid low in the dust, shattered, destroyed for ever, by the sight of a small, unfamiliar flag standing out against the blue sky . . . [it was] like some hideous nightmare.'[9]

She was torn by conflicting emotions, a mixture of sorrow and anger. When the British troops had first arrived, she had stood watching them sprawled out in Church Square where they had been given permission to rest before their victory parade. Some of the men had immediately fallen asleep from exhaustion, others sat idly chatting. One of them looked up and spoke to her. 'Thank God,' he sighed, 'the war is over.'

Her reply was every bit as heart-felt. 'Tommy Atkins,' she hissed, leaning towards him , *'the war has just begun.'*[10]

Pretoria now became the centre of British activity in South Africa. It was an attractive little town and one which, before the war, had been notable for its calm, relaxed atmosphere. Anthony Trollope, visiting the Boer capital some years earlier, had been charmed by its simple white-washed cottages, its leafy gardens with their rose-bush hedges and weeping willow trees and by the water-filled furrows that ran down many of its streets. He was equally impressed by the official and commercial buildings, the broad streets and the 'fine square'; in all of which he detected signs of a city 'struggling into birth'.

It was a protracted birth. Not until the discovery of gold in the Transvaal and the coming of the *uitlanders* did Pretoria outgrow its essentially rustic appearance. Within a very few years this newly-created wealth led to a surge of rebuilding: unpretentious government offices gave way to suitably imposing, typically late-nineteenth-century piles such as the Raadzaal and the Palace of Justice – all domes and pillars and pediments. The white-washed cottages which had so charmed Trollope were replaced by the ornate homes of the *nouveaux riches* merchants and professional men. Visiting Pretoria later, Alfred Milner admitted that it was 'a lovely little spot – of water, trees and gardens', but went on to complain of it being 'ruined by the most *horrible* vulgarities of the 10th rate continental villadom – German architecture of the Bismarckian era at its worst.'[11]

The troops, some thirty thousand of them, camped in or about the capital, many of them being cared for in field hospitals. There were so many sick men, in fact, that the hospitals were unable to accommodate them all and once again public buildings were converted into infirmaries. This was something that Lady Sarah Wilson, who arrived in Pretoria shortly after the occupation, found most disturbing. 'One specially sad feature [of the town] was', she wrote, 'the enormous number of sick in addition to wounded soldiers. Of the former, at that time, there were over 1500 and the recollection of the large numbers buried at Bloemfontein was still green in everyone's memory . . . As additional accommodation for these patients, the magnificent and recently finished Law Courts had been arranged to hold seven or eight hundred beds.'[12]

Sarah, her maid Metelka, and her friend Mrs Godley were the first women to enter occupied Pretoria. To do so they had had to ride through enemy territory without an escort: a feat which earned them special mention in the history of the Imperial Light Horse. 'These daring young ladies', it was observed, 'succeeded in driving from Mafeking to Pretoria, a distance of some 230 miles, and were not molested by anyone – a strange contrast between the powerful column, seeing an enemy behind every bush and the sprightly young ladies (well known in the fox-hunting world) caring nothing for all the Boers in Christendom.'[13] Their journey, in fact, had been relatively uneventful and Sarah made light of it in her own account.

She would have left Mafeking much earlier had it been possible. A few days after the relief of the town, Metelka had joined her from

Setlagole and there seemed no reason then to delay their departure. Writing her last despatch to the *Daily Mail*, on 18 May, Sarah had said: 'I am leaving for England when the line is open.' That, she thought, would not be long. But she was mistaken. By the end of May, although supply trains were arriving from Rhodesia, there seemed little hope of the disrupted rail to the Cape being repaired. Eventually Sarah decided that her best hope of reaching the coast was by travelling through the Orange Free State, by way of Pretoria and Johannesburg. Baden-Powell, however, would not hear of her travelling alone. Not until Mrs Godley, Sarah's erstwhile ally, arrived from Bulawayo and agreed to accompany her did she decide to take the risk. 'They were wise enough not to ask leave,' says Major Godley, 'which would almost certainly have been refused.'[14]

On arriving in Pretoria, the women almost despaired of finding accommodation, so crowded with troops was the centre of the town that it seemed to Sarah, after months of confinement, that all the inhabitants of England had been transported to the Boer capital. Nowhere was the congestion more apparent than in the hotels. When the two women drove up to the Grand Hotel, they found the place swarming with soldiers and the hotel manager in a state of jitters. The idea of accommodating two respectable women amid the crush of soldiers was almost too much for him. Hurrying along the corridors, with Sarah and Mrs Godley at his heels, he hunted desperately for a suitable room. Then an idea struck him. He conducted them to an apartment which, he explained, would be free in a few hours as the gentleman occupying it was due to leave that evening. He threw open the door to reveal a young man busily stowing away his clothes and papers. To Sarah's amazement, the startled guest was none other than her nephew Winston Churchill.

What Winston thought of this meeting with his aunt is not recorded. However, he played the dutiful nephew; not only did he give up his suite, but he postponed his departure for another twenty-four hours in order to give Sarah a guided tour of the town.

He had a great deal to show her. Having resumed his role as war-correspondent, he had accompanied the troops on their march from Bloemfontein to Pretoria. Together with his cousin the Duke of Marlborough he had attached himself, not to Lord Roberts's central column, but to a flanking detachment commanded by General Ian Hamilton. The two Churchill cousins had been among the first to enter Pretoria. Not surprisingly Winston Churchill's first thought had been for the prisoners he had left behind when he escaped from the

Staatsmodelskool and who he knew had since been transferred to a camp on the outskirts of the town. Unsure of exactly where the prisoners were 'caged', they persuaded a passing burger to guide them to the camp. As they approached the barbed-wire enclosure, Churchill let out a cheer and started waving his hat. He did not have long to wait for a response: the prisoners came rushing from their huts, shouting and waving to the two Churchills. The Duke of Marlborough demanded a surrender, the guards threw down their rifles and the gates were thrown open. Someone produced a camp-made Union Jack and then, says Churchill, the 'Transvaal emblem was torn down and, amid wild cheers, the first British flag was hoisted over Pretoria.'[15]

Churchill started his aunt's tour with a visit to the prison camp, or the 'Birdcage' as it was known. They then went to inspect the Staatsmodelskool. Sarah examined the building with an experienced eye. 'These quarters', she declared, 'must have been a particularly disagreeable and inadequate residence.' For once she had nothing but admiration for her nephew's audacity, and thoroughly approved of his escape. She was beginning to look at Winston with new eyes. When she attended a farewell dinner given for him that evening by a group of army officers, she was impressed by how popular he had become. 'The "bosses" doubtless disapproved of his free utterances,' she admitted somewhat grudgingly, 'but he was nevertheless most amusing to listen to, and a general favourite.' When, next morning, Churchill left Pretoria by train, Sarah and Mrs Godley were at the station to see him off.

With so many escorts available, Sarah continued to wander about Pretoria until she left for Johannesburg a few days later. A place of particular interest to her was the Sunnyside area where several of her officer friends were living. 'The surroundings of these dwellings', she wrote, 'were exceedingly pretty, with shady trees, many streams, and a background of high hills crowned with forts, which latter were just visible to the naked eye.'[16]

In her many strolls through this semi-wild area, Sarah must have passed the entrance to a house called Harmony. This former farmhouse, situated within a few minutes' walk of Lord Roberts's headquarters and surrounded now by army encampments, was one of the few dwellings in the neighbourhood that had not been commandeered by the military. The house stood in its own extensive grounds. It was the home of Mrs Maria van Warmelo and her young daughter, Johanna.

Why it had escaped the military's grasp was something of a mystery. It could have been the fact that Mrs Van Warmelo was known to have influential connections. In 1893 her elder daughter had married Mr Hendrik Cloete who, despite his Dutch-sounding name, was looked upon as a pillar of the English-speaking establishment in Cape Town and had recently acted as the British agent in the Transvaal, being appointed a Companion of the Order of St Michael and St George (CMG). On the other hand, it was also known that the Van Warmelos were intensely patriotic Transvaalers, that all three of Mrs Van Warmelo's sons had joined the commandos and that two of them were still serving with Louis Botha. The third boy had been captured in battle but the obliging Mr Cloete had stepped in and secured his release so that he could return to Holland to continue his studies. It was strange, this combination of Boer loyalty and British patronage. People who did not know the Van Warmelos well found it confusing.

There was no confusion in the minds of Mrs Van Warmelo and her daughter Johanna. They both fiercely resented the suggestion that they were indebted to the wire-pulling of Hendrik Cloete. 'All I can say', wrote Johanna, after explaining her brother-in-law's links with the British, 'is that if the Van Warmelos owed their security to these facts, we can only look upon that as one of the fortunate circumstances of war over which we had no control.'[17] She would never have set out intentionally to curry favour with men she regarded as enemies. Few women were more passionately devoted to the Boer cause than young Johanna van Warmelo. She it was who had hissed so menacingly at the soldier in Church Square before the victory parade.

The fact that she went to the square that afternoon, when so many of her compatriots stayed away, was evidence that she intended to defy the occupying army. How she would do this she did not then know. She was aware only of how bitter she felt. It was a bitterness that had been intensified by her recent experiences. Earlier that day she had said goodbye to her two brothers who, having retreated from Johannesburg, were then leaving Pretoria to rejoin their commando. Both Johanna and her mother had urged them to go, saying it was their duty to unite with those burgers who were still fighting. But the parting had not been easy. The boys had been at home for only a few days – their first visit for months – and there was no telling when they would return. Johanna was never to forget their departure on 'that dark and dreadful June 5th'.

When Johanna announced that she was going to town to see the British troops arrive, her mother refused to accompany her. Nothing could make Mrs Van Warmelo join in such an unseemly exploit. But she was unable to dissuade Johanna. She did not, she claimed, want to miss such an historical event. Jumping on her bicycle and calling to her black retriever dog, Carlo, to accompany her, she rode off towards the centre of town. Before leaving she took one precaution. Afraid that she might pass friends who would think she was going to welcome the troops, she wound a broad ribbon of the Transvaal colours round her hat to show her true allegiance. Not until she neared Church Square did she become aware of a change that had come over the town. The black and coloured population, she noticed, were behaving in a most unusual manner. Under the laws of the Boer republic only whites were allowed to walk on the pavements, and these laws were now being openly defied. Johanna, an obedient daughter of the republic, was appalled.

'They had come out in their thousands', she protested, '– the streets literally seethed with them, the remarkable part of this being that they were all on the pavements, while their "white brothers" walked in the middle of the road . . . This noisy, unlawful demonstration was an expression of joy on their part at the prospect of that day being set free from Boer restrictions.'[18]

But they were dancing too soon. The much-vaunted liberalism of the conquering army was extremely selective. Lord Roberts was intent on winning over the Boers. He did not hesitate to pander to their prejudices, and within a matter of days the degrading laws were reimposed in both Pretoria and Johannesburg. There was no more merry-making on the pavements of the Transvaal. Britain might have freed the slaves, but it had little to offer the serfs.

Returning home after the parade, Johanna received an even greater shock. All the open space around Harmony was occupied by troops; camps had been erected close to the front entrance to the house; the roads were jammed with soldiers unsaddling their horses. Even more alarming was the sight of Mrs Van Warmelo standing at the gate, wild-eyed and stony-faced, brandishing a loaded revolver. An officer had already assured the old lady that orders had been given that no man was to enter Harmony, but she was taking no chances. She stood her ground until her daughter returned. That night the two women barricaded all the windows and doors. Fresh from what she described as a 'soul-sickening display of imperial patriotism', Johanna thought it best to remain on guard. There was no escaping the fact that she was now living in enemy-occupied Pretoria.

8

The Ladies of Harmony

JOHANNA VAN WARMELO was known to her family and friends as Hansie. This pet name, a diminutive of Johanna, was given to her as a child and remained with her in her adult years: it was as Hansie that she preferred to be known. When war broke out she was in her early twenties, having been born in the little Transvaal town of Heidelberg in November 1876. She was a pretty young woman, round-faced, apple-cheeked and dark haired. But her somewhat Dutch-doll looks belied her force of personality. Hansie was a young woman of considerable daring and firmly-held convictions. Her parents came from solidly respectable, devoutly religious backgrounds and their strict adherence to the Calvinist doctrines of the Dutch Reformed Church, as well as their loyalty to the Transvaal, undoubtedly influenced Hansie's thinking and helped to fashion her ideals.

Her father, Nicolaas van Warmelo, was the minister of the Hervormde Kerk in Heidelberg. Born in Holland, where he trained as a theological student, he had arrived in South Africa as a young man intending to join the ministry of the Dutch Reformed Church in the Cape, but he ran into difficulties and decided instead to accept a call from a congregation in the Transvaal. This change of territory resulted in a shift in denominational allegiance, for the Hervormde Kerk of the Transvaal, although an offshoot of the Dutch Reformed Church, had earlier separated from the church in the Cape. Originally founded by the voortrekkers in their bid for independence, it had developed into an illiberal organization which not only differed from the Cape in its form of worship – there was a dispute, for instance, over public hymn singing – but also rejected any suggestion of equality between black and white Christians. Nicolaas van Warmelo, one of nature's conservatives, had no difficulty in adjusting to the demands of the Hervormde Kerk but he never ceased to regret the division in the Afrikaner church and spent most of his life trying to unify the opposing factions. He believed strongly in the virtues of working for harmony among minorities and instilled this belief in his children.

It was while serving in the northern Transvaal – in the then primitive Zoutpansberg region – that Van Warmelo met and married Hansie's mother. She was his second wife and came from a long-established and extremely prolific Afrikaner family. Her father, Dietlof Maré, was one of a family of seventeen children and, during the course of two marriages, produced no fewer than twenty-two children himself. Hansie liked to claim that her mother was a 'voortrekker pioneer' but in fact the Maré family did not reach the Transvaal until long after the voortrekkers, and Mrs Van Warmelo was still a small child when the Transvaal was declared a republic. But the Marés were indisputably pioneers in the northern Transvaal. There were very few white people living in the wild Zoutpansberg region when Dietlof Maré set up there as an ivory trader in the northern outpost of Schoemansdal. This was the town in which Mrs Van Warmelo and her husband met; her memories of life in the primitive settlement were vivid. She could speak from experience of the dangers that faced an isolated community surrounded by hostile tribes; she had witnessed the panic with which families fled to the nearest laager when their farms were threatened. Her hair-raising stories of encounters with 'savage foes and wild beasts' kept her children enthralled. One of her more dramatic accounts concerned an event which occurred in Schoemansdal two months after her marriage. In July 1867 the town was attacked by Bavenda warriors and the entire population had to be evacuated to escape the attackers, who proceeded to loot and set fire to their homes. All that was left of Schoemansdal the following day was a heap of smouldering rubble. Most of the townspeople fled south to the village of Marabasted where, for the next few months, Nicolaas van Warmelo continued to minister to his scattered congregation.

Hansie was immensely proud of her family's association with the northern Transvaal. For her the Zoutpansberg would always be 'the strange, rich, wild country' where her 'forefathers had fought and suffered'. Like her brothers and sister, she knew all her mother's stories by heart. They had an unnerving effect on her: the possibility of a mass rising among the blacks of South Africa was never far from Hansie's thoughts.

A year after the sacking of Schoemansdal, the Van Warmelos moved further south to Heidelberg after Nicolaas had accepted a call to minister there. In the more settled surroundings of Heidelberg the family was to live for the next twenty-five years. Hansie was born there eight years after the move. She was the Van Warmelos' fourth child. In time she was to have five brothers (two of whom died young) as well as an elder sister. Her childhood was a time of political strife for the Boers. She was only a year old when Lord Carnarvon embarked on his plan to federate South Africa and annexed the Transvaal. This high-handed move brought Nicolaas van Warmelo to the forefront of national affairs. Passionately opposed to British rule, he travelled the country preaching at meetings called to demand the restitution of the Transvaal's independence. At a huge, historic mass meeting held at Paardekraal in December 1880 and addressed by Paul Kruger and other Boer leaders, Nicolaas van Warmelo was the only ordained minister present. On this occasion he not only preached but played an important part in the proceedings, which ended with the republican flag being hoisted to signal the beginning of the first Anglo-Boer war. His influence was felt throughout the three-month war when Heidelberg acted as the Boer seat of government.

Little is known of Hansie's early years in Heidelberg, or of her later years at school in Cape Town. She was too young to appreciate fully the controversies which surrounded her father in his attempt to unify the Afrikaner churches. These disputes caused divisions in Nicolaas van Warmelo's home life – some of his wife's family were vehemently opposed to unification – as well as in his public life. So tormented was he by the endless wrangling that it affected his health and may even have contributed to his premature death. He was only fifty-six when, in 1892, he died a sad and disillusioned man.

A year after his death, his elder daughter married the middle-aged Hendrik Cloete, who was then a practising lawyer, and went to live in Pretoria. The newly married couple settled in the Sunnyside district where they were joined a few years later by the rest of the Van Warmelo family. Mrs Van Warmelo wanted to live near her daughter and looked for a house in Sunnyside which, according to Hansie, was then a 'wild romantic suburb' with only a scattering of old, isolated houses dotted about its grass-covered hills. Harmony was hardly a find. Of all the dilapidated houses in the neighbourhood, the run-down farmhouse was probably the most secluded, overgrown and neglected when Mrs

Van Warmelo bought it. Not that this worried her unduly. Having lived in primitive Schoemansdal, she knew all about making a home in the wilderness. She quickly set about clearing the ground, cutting down the willow trees which overshadowed the house and laying out a flower garden. Harmony, once a favourite picnic spot for the people of Pretoria, was completely transformed by the time the Cloetes left the Boer capital to live in Cape Town.

Hansie was full of praise for her mother's achievements, for the improvements she made to the house and gardens and for the orchard she cultivated in the outergrounds. But it is doubtful whether she assisted in this work. Hansie was hardly out of her teens when the family moved to Pretoria and shortly afterwards, in 1897, she left South Africa to study music in Europe. By the time she returned, two years later, not only was the restoration work almost complete but, within a few months, war was declared and all domestic concerns were swept aside.

The two of Hansie's brothers who were then at home, Dietlof and Fritz, were among the first volunteers to join a commando. They left Pretoria on 28 September 1899, almost two weeks before war was officially declared. For the first time in their lives, Hansie and her mother were left alone. But they had little time in which to feel sorry for themselves. Hansie was to say that she could have filled a three-volume book recording all her experiences in Pretoria before the British occupation. Like a great many other women in the Boer capital she kept busy nursing the wounded brought back from the battlefields in the Cape and Natal. She worked first in the Volks Hospital and later in the Girls' State School which was converted into a nursing home. But she left no record of this work: with the hospital trains arriving daily at Pretoria station, she had no time for writing.

But it was not nursing alone that kept the women of Pretoria occupied. Feelings were running high when Lord Roberts began his march into Boer territory and the tension mounted with each British victory. The thought of the Transvaal being invaded and its capital falling to the enemy appalled the burgers of Pretoria. They responded with a show of bravado: there was talk of a fight to the finish, of a do-or-die resistance. Nowhere was the spirit of defiance more apparent than among the women who, with their husbands, sons and brothers on commando, had little faith in the old men who were left. Henry Batts, a Baptist clergyman who was one of the few Englishmen allowed to remain in the capital, was startled to hear the women 'talk, very loudly of what they would do if their men ran away; they said they would go out and shoot – anyway they would do something to keep the arch-enemy from coming into the capital. They clamoured for the formation of an Amazon corps for fighting purposes.'[1]

The women's demands became more urgent after the fall of Bloemfontein. A meeting was called to protest against the lack of preparedness. Hundreds of angry women attended. There were passionate speeches and bitter denunciations, both of the British and of the cowardly men in their own ranks. One woman was loudly cheered when, in the course of a fiery harangue, she offered to lead any women who would join her into battle. Others, less bellicose, volunteered to work in offices, act as telegraphists or deliver the post so that more able-bodied men would be freed for military service. The meeting ended with a committee being formed under the presidency of Mrs Cornelia Reitz – wife of a former Orange Free State president – but it was overtaken by events.

A garbled account of the meeting reached England. In March 1900, a London newspaper reported that a women's commando had been mobilized. 'It is understood', the news item went on, 'they are being drilled, about 2000 of them at Pretoria and that all are first-class shots. They are said to be dressed in kilts like Highlanders and are known as the Amazon Corps.'[2] Whether this was meant to be taken seriously is not clear. This type of report often appeared in the Victorian press as a joke. The report was republished in a Transvaal newspaper but it could not have amused many readers in the Boer capital. Certainly Mrs Van Warmelo and Hansie would not have considered it funny. Hansie makes no mention of the meeting but, whether she attended it or not, she would have sympathized with its purpose.

Hansie quickly discovered that martial law in Pretoria was less intimidating than she had expected. Having the house surrounded by military camps – the Montmorency Scouts to the south, Kitchener's bodyguards to the west and the mounted military police to the east – was not pleasant but it was something that the ladies of Harmony learned to live with. More irritating was having the northern entrance blocked by the tent of the military post-office, making it extremely difficult to squeeze through the small opening at the side of the gate. This, and the thought of Lord Roberts a few minutes' walk away, heightened their sense of humiliation.

What most annoyed Hansie was not being able to show openly her contempt for the occupying army. The soldiers she met, or passed in the street, were all very friendly; those who spoke to her were every bit as courteous as the burgers at Snyman's laager had been to Lady

Sarah Wilson. Even though Hansie tended to bridle at the sight of a khaki uniform, she could not complain about the behaviour of the soldiers. She found few opportunities to give vent to the barbed remarks that were always on the tip of her tongue.

Occasionally, however, a passing remark or a tactless gesture seemed to invite a spirited response. One such occasion occurred shortly after the soldiers had settled in. Answering the door at Harmony one evening, Hansie found three sheepish-looking officers standing outside. One of them introduced himself as the commander of the Montmorency Scouts and asked whether there were any empty rooms in the house. 'Only three officers,' he explained, 'no men; we shall give no trouble.' Politely but firmly Hansie told him that she was unable to provide accommodation. She was surprised when he started to plead with her. 'Our tents are bitterly cold at night,' he implored. 'Let us at least sleep in the house.' That was too much for Hansie. 'My brothers in the field', she snapped back, 'have no tents, they sleep under the open sky. Do you think we are going to allow British officers to sleep in their beds? Allow me to tell you that we are red-hot Republicans.' With that, the would-be lodgers scurried away. Afterwards Hansie wondered whether she had been wise. She did not regret what she had said, but feared possible repercussions. Had she now given the military the excuse to take over Harmony? Her mother shared her misgivings. For the next few days the two women waited, expecting a requisition order to arrive at any moment. But nothing happened. They saw no more of the officers and the soldiers remained as friendly as they had always been.

For all that, Hansie was not won over. Like many of the young women in Pretoria she kept herself aloof from the army, even though she was constantly receiving invitations to social evenings and tennis parties organized by the officers. Before the British marched into Pretoria, she had solemnly vowed never to be seen with a 'khaki officer' while the men of the Transvaal were still in the field. This was a pledge she was determined to keep. Not only did she refuse all invitations but, she says, she found it 'necessary to give up riding and tennis altogether'.

More positively, she continued to cycle about Pretoria wearing her hat decorated with the Transvaal colours. This alarmed her mother, particularly after an order was issued forbidding the display of the *vierkleur*. But Hansie refused to listen to her mother's warnings. She intended, she declared, to wear the colours in her hat and 'see what happens'.

At first nothing happened; or, at least, nothing happened to Hansie. Stories began to circulate about women and girls who had been stopped in the street and marched to the charge office to have their colours forcibly removed. But for a long time, Hansie was allowed to go about unharmed. Then one day, as she was on her way to the Portuguese consulate, she was stopped by a junior officer and told to remove her hatband. She refused. This so angered the officer that he threatened to seize the ribbon himself. 'Take the Transvaal first,' scoffed Hansie, 'then you will be quite welcome to my bit of ribbon.' At a loss as to what to do next, the man rode off to get help. When Hansie saw him returning with two soldiers, she darted into the consulate garden shouting that she was being chased by three men. She was rescued by the Portuguese consul, Mr Cinatti, who was an old family friend. Taking her into the house he gave her a broad white ribbon to cover the Transvaal colours and escorted her to the gate. The soldiers were waiting outside but, seeing Mr Cinatti, they allowed her to pass. That night Hansie removed the Transvaal colours from her hat and replaced them with 'a black band in token of mourning and bereavement'. Her cycle rides through the town were never quite the same again.

Mrs Van Warmelo, loyal Transvaaler though she was, sighed with relief when the coloured ribbon was packed away. She was far more level-headed than her daughter and had repeatedly warned Hansie about drawing attention to herself. Her own attitude towards the authorities was one of guarded hostility. She realized that if two lone women wanted to help their country, they could only do so by appearing harmless. She was very circumspect in her dealings with the army. It took some time for the intrigues at Harmony to get under way.

Major-General John Maxwell, the military governor of Pretoria, was a seasoned soldier and a capable administrator. Then in his early forties, he had commanded the 14th Infantry Brigade on the march from Bloemfontein and had been appointed to his new post shortly after the Boer capital was occupied. A compassionate man with a strong sense of justice, he became surprisingly popular with the people he governed. Hansie, who first met him when she applied for permission to keep a pocket-pistol, described him as 'charming and affable'. Not only was she given the necessary permit, but Maxwell made it clear that she would be welcome in his office at any time. It was the beginning of an unexpected friendship. With the passing of time, says Hansie, she 'learnt more and more to admire and respect the Governor for his humanity and nobility of character.' Not for one moment, though, did she forget that she and General Maxwell were on opposite sides.

But it was not enmity that launched the ladies of Harmony on their espionage activities; it was irritation. The restrictions imposed on civilians during the British occupation of Pretoria infuriated both Hansie and her mother. Mrs Van Warmelo particularly objected to her family correspondence being subjected to military censorship; the thought of some unknown, unfriendly army inquisitor reading her letters to her daughter, Mrs Cloete, in Cape Town never failed to annoy her. This is what made her decide to outwit the censor. So began what Hansie calls 'an exciting period of smuggling and contriving which led to . . . a well-organized and exceedingly clever system of [secret] communication with friends in every part of the world.' It started almost by accident. A Boer sympathizer, who was about to leave the country for good, offered to arrange for any document Mrs Van Warmelo might like to send to be secretly delivered to Mrs Cloete. Unfortunately, neither Hansie nor her mother had anything ready but, not wanting to waste the opportunity, Mrs Van Warmelo wrote a message on a small piece of paper telling Mrs Cloete to examine closely anything sent to her marked with a small blue cross. That was the first step in an unsophisticated but, at the time, remarkably effective espionage venture.

The next time the services of a suitable courier were offered, Mrs Van Warmelo was better prepared. She had obtained a small morocco case, lined with maroon velvet, which had a tray-like bottom. This she used as a despatch-box: first prising the tray loose and pushing a letter written on tissue paper beneath it, then firmly replacing the tray before pasting a tiny blue cross on the bottom of the case. After sending this to Cape Town there was a long wait before the Van Warmelos learned that it had reached its destination. Confirmation came with the return of the case, carrying a gold antique bracelet for Hansie and, concealed beneath the tray, a long uncensored letter for Mrs Van Warmelo. Over the next few months the little morocco case travelled several times between Pretoria and Cape Town.

It was more of a game than a conspiracy. Life in Pretoria, cut off from friends and relatives and with few visitors, had become extremely boring. Like the inhabitants of besieged Mafeking, the Van Warmelos were in desperate need of diversion. The spying game answered that need. Thinking up new ways of smuggling messages to Mrs Cloete became an end in itself: it was some time before they realized it could be put to a more useful purpose.

Hansie was more adventurous than her mother. Her first experiment in message smuggling involved a woman whom she vaguely calls 'the English lady'. In fact she was not English: she was an English-speaking South African from the Cape, highly respectable and fervently loyal to the British cause. Hearing that this woman was about to return to Cape Town, and that she had expressed distrust of the Van Warmelo family, Hansie decided to use her as an unsuspecting courier. After talking her plan over with her mother, she dismissed the idea of using the morocco case and decided instead to buy three medium-sized dolls with hollow heads. This done, she wrote a long letter while her mother loosened the head of one of the dolls. The letter was then rolled up and pushed into the doll's head before it was replaced. Shortly afterwards the 'English lady' called at Harmony to say goodbye and was persuaded to take the dolls to Cape Town as presents for Mrs Cloete's daughters. The next day Hansie had the dolls professionally wrapped by a sympathetic shopkeeper and then delivered them to the woman herself, pretending that she had just bought them. It was all good cloak-and-dagger stuff, spoilt only by Hansie's admission that 'there were no dangerous communications in the doll's head'. Several other ruses were used and, for the most part, they proved successful. But sending concealed messages to Cape Town was only a start. The Van Warmelos later discovered another method of transmitting secret information, a method that resulted in them becoming serious espionage agents.

Like Mrs Van Warmelo, Hansie deeply resented her personal mail being read by the censors. She had good reason to object. The most intimate letters she received came from Holland, which meant there was no way they could reach her without being opened by the censors. This she found infuriating. The letters were sent by a young man she had met during her two years in Europe. She does not give his name but says he was 'a young minister of the Gospel' who lived in the north of Holland. This makes it fairly obvious that she is referring to Louis Ernst Brandt, the man she was later to marry and who had studied theology at the Rijks University in Utrecht before serving as secretary of the Dutch Christian Students' Union. According to Hansie, she and the young man had been separated for a couple of years by an unfortunate misunderstanding which they were then trying to correct, and 'had reached the delightfully unsettling stage of exchanging photographs'. It was a delicate business, made all the more delicate by having censors doctor their correspondence. A point was reached when the letters Hansie received were so mutilated that she stormed into the censor's office to demand why she had been subjected to 'such petty persecutions'.

She could not have chosen a worse time to complain. The head censor was away and she was interviewed by a man whose name and accent told her he was a Boer. This, for Hansie, was the final straw. To be confronted by a Boer collaborator made the situation intolerable. She had difficulty in choking down her anger and it was not until he promised that if she brought her letters to him personally, he would see that they were passed, that she calmed down. She could not, she realized, afford to make an enemy of a man in his position. All the same, she left the office muttering: 'Miserable Renegade'. That, from then on, became his name whenever she thought or spoke about him.

And she thought and spoke about him a great deal. Not only did she detest the man for working with the British but she was put off by his attempts to ingratiate himself with her. Even so, she felt that his obsequiousness might be turned to her advantage. Was there not, she asked her mother, some way in which they could make use of this 'hatefully affable' man without his being aware of it? Mrs Van Warmelo promised to think about it: eventually she came up with a scheme.

The idea came to her while she was pondering over an old method of secret writing: that of concealing a message in invisible ink between the lines of a letter. This she knew would be too risky. In any case, invisible ink was not easy to obtain. But she decided to experiment. One day she wrote a few words in lemon juice on a sheet of white paper and found, once the writing had dried, there was no trace of it until she passed a hot iron over the paper. This, however, did not solve the problem. Having dismissed the idea of writing between the lines of a letter, there seemed no way in which the invisible writing could be used without arousing suspicion. Her next move was more ingenious. Taking a thick white envelope, she carefully opened the glued flaps with a blade, flattened out the envelope, wrote in lemon juice on the inside and then glued it together again. This gave her the answer. Who, in those days of crude censorship, would think of looking on the inside of an envelope for a message written in invisible ink?

She had said nothing to her daughter about her experiments and waited until Hansie returned that afternoon to hand her the envelope. Hansie examined it on all sides and remained mystified, even when she was told to look closely inside. Delighted, Mrs Van Warmelo then opened the envelope out, ironed it, and handed it back to her astonished daughter. At first Hansie was speechless. Then 'she threw her arms round her mother and hugged her.' Now, she thought, they would be able to put 'Miserable Renegade' firmly in his place.

It was not that simple. First they had to instruct Hansie's clerical friend in Holland how to open the envelope and read the message. This could not be done by post and they had to wait several months before they found someone they could trust to deliver the instructions. By the time they were delivered, another problem had arisen. Some further experimenting with lemon juice showed that if certain paper was used the writing became visible after a few days. Holland had to be alerted to this danger immediately. For although it would not matter if messages became visible by the time they reached Europe, no risks could be taken with letters travelling in the opposite direction. Any letters arriving in Pretoria were bound to be opened by the censors. If a message was spotted on the inside of an envelope it would give the game away. Luckily Hansie was able to warn Holland about this before any harm was done.

Once this danger was overcome the exchange of secret messages went ahead. They were despatched in white envelopes only – all other correspondence was sent in grey or coloured envelopes – and 'the sign of the White Envelope', as Hansie puts it, became an understood thing between the conspirators. Very few others, even among the Van Warmelos' most intimate friends, were let into the secret.

Taking the first white envelope to the censor's office, tucked into a pile of ordinary mail, was a nerve-racking experience for Hansie. She was quaking when she handed the letters to the 'Miserable Renegade'. She need not have worried. Her accommodating friend, now an unwitting accomplice, scarcely glanced at the letters before stamping them with the censor's mark. They would, he assured her, be forwarded that day. There was then a seven weeks' wait before the reply came from Holland. No seven weeks, says Hansie, could have been longer or more full of suspense. When at last a square white envelope addressed in a 'well-known hand' arrived, the relief and rejoicing at Harmony was indescribable.

So began an espionage service which, in time, was to be used by Boer agents in South Africa and Europe. The distinctive white envelopes containing vital information were to be sent to commandos in the field as well as to political contacts abroad. A great many risks were run and sometimes exposure was narrowly averted, but this did not daunt the ladies of Harmony. They kept up their undercover activities throughout the war and, as Hansie later boasted, were 'never found out by the enemy'.

It was as well that they were not. Some of the information sent to England by Mrs Van Warmelo was of considerable significance. One of her reports was intended to supply W. T. Stead, the crusading pro-Boer journalist, with ammunition for his campaign against the British government. Stead was an unrelenting critic of the war. He was editor of the popular weekly *Review of Reviews* but had brought out a separate magazine, *War Against War*, to widen his attack, and in January 1900 had helped to launch the Stop-the-War movement. A few months later he became one of the leading opponents of the so-called 'scorched earth' policy, initiated by Lord Roberts, which started with the burning of Boer farms and resulted later in the herding of women and children into concentration camps. This is what prompted Mrs Van Warmelo to contact him.

Hansie knew all about the concentration camps. She had personal experience of the appalling conditions in the Irene camp, south of Pretoria. Her description of the overcrowded, ill-equipped and disease-ridden camp had been included in the report her mother sent to Stead. This was not something which either the military or the political authorities wanted published. Already there was growing concern about the turn the war had taken in South Africa.

The burning of Boer farms was not a new development. As early as the beginning of January 1900, before Roberts and Kitchener arrived at the Cape, it was reported that a party of British soldiers, under Major-General J. M. Babington, had ridden twelve miles into the Orange Free State and destroyed three Boer farmsteads 'with dynamite and fire'. In fact, one of the first communications Lord Roberts received from the Boer authorities was a telegram signed by President Kruger and President Steyn protesting about this wanton destruction by 'white brigands' which left 'unprotected women and children . . . deprived of food and cover'.[3] Roberts replied saying that the accusations against the British army were vague – the Presidents had not mentioned specific incidents – and insisting that the most stringent instructions had been issued to his troops 'to respect private property, as far as is compatible with the conduct of military operations'. A few days later he sent another telegram giving details of Boer vandalism and the looting of British farms in Natal. The Presidents then replied listing, at great length, the farms that had been burnt or destroyed in the Orange Free State.

This sort of tit-for-tat correspondence, couched in polite language, was typical of what became known as the 'last gentlemen's war'. Each side was careful to address their opponents respectfully as 'Your Honour' or 'Your Excellency' when accusing them of uncivilized behaviour, of breaches of the Hague Convention or, as repeatedly happened, of arming Africans and inciting them to violence in a 'white man's war'. In the same way each side justified any atrocity as a 'military necessity' and blandly refused to admit to the most obvious transgressions. So routine were these exchanges, so predictable were the accusations and responses, that they failed at first to make any impact. Consequently the incidents complained about were either ignored or dismissed. Not until the burning of farms became more widespread and the sufferings of civilians more serious did the subject become a matter of international concern.

It was after Lord Roberts's capture of Bloemfontein that stories about the wholesale destruction of Boer homes began to appear in London newspapers. One of the first accounts was published in the liberal *Morning Leader* which, at the end of April, reported that British troops in the Orange Free State were 'marching in, burning practically everything on the road'. The paper's war-correspondent, E. W. Smith, went on to describe the burning in graphic detail.

At one farm only women were left. Still rifles were found under the mattresses. Orders were inexorable. The woman threw her arms round the officer's neck, and begged that the homestead might be spared. When the flames burst from the doomed place, the poor woman threw herself on her knees, tore open her bodice, and bared her breasts, screaming, 'Shoot me, shoot me! I've nothing more to live for, now that my husband is gone, and our farm is burnt, and our cattle taken.'

This was the first of many such reports to appear over the next few months. They were not all as lurid, but they all told the same story of women and children, huddled together, surrounded by a few sticks of salvaged furniture, watching the smoke spiralling from the thatched roof of a farmhouse before the entire building burst into flames. Ostensibly it was only the houses of insurgents – those who refused to surrender their arms and take the oath of neutrality – that were burnt, but all too often mistakes were made and the torch was put to the homes of perfectly harmless families. But, whether done for a reason or on a whim, the meaningless destruction of so many farms seemed unwarranted. 'I cannot think', wrote Filson Young of the *Manchester Guardian*, 'that punishment need take this wild form; it seems as though a kind of domestic murder were being committed while one watches the roof and furniture of a house blazing . . . The ends achieved are so small – simply an exhibition.'[4]

Reports of farm-burning continued to appear in the British press throughout Lord Roberts's march to the Transvaal. Action was usually taken against known insurgents, but there were occasions when British soldiers were deliberately shot at on approaching a house which was displaying a white flag: this invariably resulted in the destruction of the house. Later, doubt was expressed about the culpability of the occupants of some of these houses; they were said to be pawns of the commandos, who surrounded the farm and shot at the soldiers from concealed vantage points. But these were exceptions and there can be little doubt that most incidents of 'white flag abuse' were deliberately planned and executed by the Boer occupants.

Protests continued to be made by the Boer leaders and Lord Roberts repeatedly claimed that he had ordered his troops to respect private property and to punish only those who actively opposed the British army. It was not until after the occupation of Pretoria, at the beginning of June, that farm-burning became openly declared policy. Then it was that Roberts decided to take retaliatory action against the Boer guerrillas and their accomplices who had played havoc with his supply line by tearing up the railway lines, destroying bridges and cutting telegraph wires. This, he claimed in a proclamation dated 16 June, could not have been done without the connivance of the local populace. He warned the 'inhabitants and the principal residents' of districts in which public property was destroyed that they would be held responsible for aiding the offenders, and that houses in the vicinity of the place where damage was done would 'be burnt and the principal civil residents will be made prisoners of war'. Three days later another proclamation reiterated these threats and reinforced them by announcing the imposition of heavy fines on the community in or near places where public property had been destroyed. In an attempt to counter the growing number of guerrilla attacks on trains, it was also announced that the director of military railways had been authorized to select one or more of the principal local residents and order them, from time to time, 'to accompany the trains while travelling through their districts'.

No time was lost in carrying out these threats. It was necessary, Roberts told his senior officers, to set a few examples, and he decided to start by burning the farm of his old antagonist, General Christiaan De Wet. At that time De Wet was humiliating the British with his spectacular, highly successful raids. He had recently blown up a railway bridge, damaged ten miles of line and destroyed an ammunition dump and stores estimated to be worth over £100,000 – all of which made him a prime target for punishment. The De Wet farm, in fact, was demolished on the day Roberts issued his first proclamation.

But if De Wet was singled out as an example, he was not representative of the many families who were to suffer from the retaliatory measures. Few of these families were shown to be as guilty as Christiaan De Wet. Farm-burning had always been a hit-and-miss punishment and now, with officers in the field given a free hand, it became increasingly indiscriminate, often vindictive. Lord Roberts's attitude towards non-combatants had hardened. The change became apparent after he left Bloemfontein. Until then his approach to the civilian population had, for the most part, been conciliatory. In his early proclamations he had – at Alfred Milner's prompting – urged the inhabitants of the Orange Free State to lay down their arms and return to their farms, promising those who did so that they would not 'be made to suffer in their persons or property'. By the time he reached Pretoria the tone of his proclamations was very different. Not only had a great many Boer families suffered in their persons and property but they were now being threatened with punishment simply for living in an area where train wreckers had been active. How had this come about?

The most obvious explanation for the change was the frustration Roberts felt at not being able to claim an outright victory. Far from his invasion of the Transvaal ending the war, it had merely marked a new phase: the British army was no longer confronted by the Boers, but harassed by them. It was evident that the fighting would continue as long as the Boer commandos were in the field. Only by isolating these commandos, by cutting them off from the farms which kept them supplied with food, shelter and information, could the war be brought to an end. It was this which made Roberts, who was not naturally ruthless, prepared to go to any lengths – even allowing his officers to punish civilians on suspicion of wrongdoing – in order to defeat the guerrilla force. He knew that his reputation depended on bringing the war to a speedy end. He was also aware that his old rival, Lord Wolseley, was due to retire as Commander-in-Chief of the British army at the end of the year and he was anxious to be back in England by then so that his claim to the vacant post could be recognized.

There may have also been a more personal influence which helped to harden Lord Roberts's attitude. According to Thomas Pakenham, at least one of Roberts's senior officers was convinced it was the arrival at Bloemfontein of Lady Roberts that had caused his chief to take a tougher line with Boer women and children. There may well have been truth in this. Rumours that Lord Roberts was influenced by his wife in these matters were already current in London.

Nora Roberts was a formidable woman. So imperious, so sharp-tongued was she that she was universally feared: jokes about her bossiness were part of a popular parlour game. Although only slightly taller than her diminutive husband, she gave the impression of being a much larger woman, a woman whose heavy masculine features, set in a perpetual glower, were as intimidating as her personality. For all that, Lord Roberts was devoted to his wife. He was proud of the fact that during their forty years of marriage, spent mostly abroad, they had rarely been parted. That record was not broken by the South African campaign. Knowing full well how strongly Queen Victoria objected to women following the army, Roberts had not only insisted that his wife join him in Bloemfontein but had allowed his two daughters, Aileen and Edwina, to accompany her. His wife and daughters, he explained to the Queen, were needed for hospital work. To prove her worth, his wife had indeed busied herself attending hospitals and opening recreational rooms for troops in Bloemfontein, but this had not increased her popularity. Her efforts were more often deplored than appreciated. Once Pretoria had been occupied, a special armoured train was authorized to transport Nora Roberts to her husband's side. 'Lady Roberts has arrived here', General Maxwell wrote to his wife, 'and, as Kitchener says, she had represented nearly 500 tons of supplies, for her ladyship . . . upset all arrangements.'[5]

What fostered the belief that Lord Roberts's harshness towards Boer civilians was encouraged by his wife was her rabid hostility towards Afrikaners. The death of her only son at the battle of Colenso had left her bitter, unforgiving and vengeful. It was inevitable that as Lord Roberts stepped up his campaign, as more farms were burnt and more people were made homeless, his wife should be suspected of goading him on. How true these accusations of 'petticoat government' were, it is impossible to say, but there is no escaping the fact that the campaign began after Bloemfontein and was intensified about the time Nora Roberts arrived in Pretoria.

Following Roberts's two July proclamations, reports of farm-burning began to appear regularly in the British and South African press. Damning letters written by disenchanted British soldiers who had reluctantly taken part in the demolitions were published in radical newspapers, and detailed protests from Boer officials multiplied. Of all that was written about the burnings, few descriptions equal the heart-felt honesty of those by Captain March Phillipps, an officer serving under Major M. F. Rimington in the newly-named Orange River Colony. He wrote, in an account dated 6 September 1900,

> I had to go myself the other day, at the General's bidding, to burn a farm near the line of march. We got to the place and I gave the inmates, three women and some children, ten minutes to clear their clothes and things out of the house, and my men fetched bundles of straw and we proceeded to burn it down. The old grandmother was very angry . . . Most of them, however, were too miserable to curse. The women cried, and the children stood by holding on to them and looking with large frightened eyes at the burning house . . . We rode away and left them, a forlorn little group, standing among their household goods – beds, furniture, and gim-cracks strewn about the veld; the crackling of the fire in their ears, and the smoke and flame streaming overhead. The worst moment is when you first come to the house. The people thought we had called for refreshments and one of the women went to get milk. Then we had to tell them that we had come to burn the place down. I simply didn't know which way to look . . . Our troops are everywhere at work burning and laying waste, and enormous re-serves of famine and misery are being laid up for these countries in the future.[6]

The indiscriminate fire-raising went on. Two months later Captain Phillipps was reporting that his men usually burnt six to a dozen farms a day and that their course through the country was marked by pillars of smoke by day and fire by night.

> I do not gather that any special reason or cause is alleged or proved against the farms burnt. If the Boers have used the farms; if the owner is on commando; if the line within a certain distance has been blown up; or even if there are Boers in the neighbourhood who persist in fighting – these are some of the reasons . . . Anyway, we find that one reason or other generally covers pretty nearly every farm we come to, and so to save trouble we burn the lot without enquiry; unless indeed, which sometimes happens, some names are given in before marching in the morning of the farms to be spared.[7]

But Phillipps was far from sure that these terror tactics would frighten the Boers into surrender.

With more and more families becoming homeless, the problem of what to do with them became more pressing. It was a problem that Roberts had tried to solve shortly after issuing his proclamations. At that time the homeless and destitute families seeking shelter in the Transvaal towns were more of an embarrassment than a burden. They were merely following a custom which had existed before the coming of the British army, a custom which required townspeople to care for those who had been forced to leave their farms because of food shortages or fear of attacks by African tribesmen. Roberts at first had encouraged this, but when his officers objected to feeding the dependants of fighting commandos and supplies began to run low, he was obliged to change his mind. Then it was that he gave instructions for any women and children who had been 'deserted' by a man on commando and who were living in Pretoria to be deported to 'a place or places beyond the British lines'. In other words, they were to be sent to join the commandos in the field. The Boers were given little warning of their coming and, being in no position to accommodate hundreds of refugees, protested strongly. Roberts, who was hoping to demoralize the commandos, replied that it was their duty to support their dependants and pointed out that British families in the Transvaal at the outbreak of war had been similarly expelled.

Families chosen for despatch to the Boer lines were ordered to report to Pretoria station on 19 July. The operation was not a resounding success. Of the estimated 600 people who were given their marching orders, little more than 100 women and 300 children turned up, and some of these were sent home after being found too ill to travel. But there was no panic. According to British officials, the women did not seem to resent being deported in open railway trucks, their only complaint being that the train was five hours late in leaving. The journey to the Boer headquarters in the eastern Transvaal was long, wearisome and extremely uncomfortable. Some of the women were reported to be exhausted and ill by the time they reached their destination. They were met by helpers from the hastily formed welfare committees and housed in the little mining town of Barberton.

There was a flood of protests from the Boer leaders. High on their list was the accusation – apparently well-founded – that the British had used the transfer of the women as a cover for the forward movement of their troops in the eastern Transvaal. Louis Botha also strongly objected to being made responsible for all the women and children.

Many of these families, he claimed, had been turned out of their homes and left unprovided for by the British; not all of them were dependants of men on commando and in some cases the stock looted from their farms had been used to supply the British troops; this, in his opinion, made them the responsibility of Lord Roberts. But Roberts refused to accept responsibility. He maintained that the destitute people who flocked to the towns had not been robbed by his troops but by Boer marauders who descended on farms and forced families of men who had taken the oath of neutrality to supply them with food. There may have been some truth in this, but it was ridiculous to pretend that the huge influx to the towns had been caused solely by avenging Boers.

Later attempts to send women and children to the eastern Transvaal met with varying success. Some of these efforts had, for one reason or another, to be abandoned entirely; others were better organized and more easily accomplished. At the beginning of August, for instance, about 2000 women and children were despatched from Johannesburg and arrived at the Boer lines displaying *vierkleurs* and singing patriotic songs. This was the sort of operation that pleased the British authorities. Not only did it allow them to shift an unwanted burden but, as they were aware, it added to the demands that were being made on their already hard-pressed opponents. For a while it looked as if threats to lumber the Boers with their own destitute families would develop into a form of psychological warfare.

The most serious of these threats was made on 2 September, the day after the Transvaal was declared a British colony, when Lord Roberts announced that he intended to send *all* the families of fighting burgers to the commandos, irrespective of their circumstances. The reason given for this was that Boer women were suspected of sending 'intelligence' to their men in the field. Among the highly-placed suspects was Louis Botha's own English-speaking wife, Annie, who was known to be in secret contact with her husband. It was made quite clear that both she and President Kruger's elderly wife, who had not accompanied her fugitive husband, would be among the women deported from Pretoria. The only concession made to these two women was that, unlike their less fortunate sisters, they would not be forced to travel in open railway trucks but could leave in any 'suitable carriage' the Boers sent for them. This, thought Lord Lansdowne, was a wise precaution. 'If some zealous officer', he observed in a private letter to Roberts, 'were to put Mrs Kruger into a cattle truck, we should never hear the last of it.'[8]

To the Boers, Roberts's proposal was outrageous. Replying three days later, Louis Botha denounced it as being contrary to all principles of civilized warfare, cruel to women and children, and as far as he knew completely without precedent. To subject the frail Mrs Kruger to such a journey would, he claimed, be tantamount to murder. He also informed Roberts that it had been decided to send families arriving at the Boer lines to Europe, and warned him that no action taken against commandos' families would deter them from continuing their fight for independence.

There was no mistaking Louis Botha's determination. How much this influenced Lord Roberts it is not possible to say but, after bemoaning Botha's decision to continue a war which would increase 'the suffering of helpless women and children', he let the matter drop. He was, in any case, contemplating other ways of dealing with the displaced families. A few weeks later it was announced that camps were being formed in Pretoria and Bloemfontein for men who surrendered voluntarily and were in need of shelter. No mention was made of women and children but it was assumed that accommodation would be provided at the camps for the surrendered burgers' families. It was soon to become apparent that the dependants of men who were absent on commando would also be taken to these, or similar, camps. This was not intended to be a long-term solution to the refugee problem, but that is what it became.

The idea was not new. Some of Roberts's senior officers had been advocating the concentration of homeless families in camps for some time. Alfred Milner was also in favour of the scheme, insisting that the camps be located near running water, accessible to railway supplies and out of reach of roving commandos. Somewhat more sinisterly, a Tory newspaper, the *St James's Gazette*, had recommended in August that Roberts follow the methods employed by the Spanish general, Valeriano Weyler, when trying to stamp out a recent rebellion in Cuba. This suggestion may have shocked some of the paper's readers. For Weyler's ruthlessness in burning the houses of non-combatants and then imprisoning them in fortified camps had earned him an evil reputation. The appalling conditions under which the inmates existed, the widespread suffering and ever-rising death toll had horrified civilized opinion throughout the world and had been used in America as propaganda against Spanish rule in Cuba. Weyler had become known as 'the Butcher'. It is doubtful whether Lord Roberts was aware of the macabre advice offered to him by the *St James's Gazette*, but his successor was to be repeatedly reminded of General Weyler's infamy.

No time was lost in getting the Bloemfontein camp established. In the second week of September it was already being hailed as a 'great success'. It also quickly became apparent that the camp was not meant to accommodate only surrendered burgers and their families. On 17 October, a few weeks after the formation of the camp, a Boer woman wrote to her prisoner-of-war son to say that she and the rest of the family had been moved to Bloemfontein.

> We were taken out of our house and the house was burnt . . . to punish us we were sent to this place. We were not allowed to take anything with us but our clothes; we get rations (chilled meat and baker's bread). It is hard to be beggars, but I hope everything will come right. We are half an hour from Bloemfontein, in a camp; they call it the Refugee Camp. There are 13 families in the camp. We are placed 12 in one tent . . . You can imagine what it is like to wash clothes, etc. in a small bath. They cart water here in two vats for the use of all the people. You can fancy what things look like . . .[9]

Less is known about the beginnings of the camp at Pretoria. At first it was known euphemistically as a 'rest camp', situated on the banks of the Apies River which flows through the town, and it was not until it was moved to Irene – about 13 miles south-west of Pretoria – that its purpose was fully recognized. The origins of yet another camp, said to have been started as early as July, are even more obscure. This was the so-called 'laager' near Mafeking, which appears to have been occupied solely by women 'whose husbands were still fighting'. Later reports were to confirm that conditions in this early Mafeking camp were primitive in the extreme.

Other camps seemed to spring up overnight. Sometime between October and November a camp was started at Port Elizabeth, in the Cape Colony, to accommodate women described as 'undesirables'. These women came from the Orange River Colony, were known to have supplied a commando with food and were rumoured to have fired on British troops. Whether, in fact, they did take up arms is doubtful – recent investigations tend to disprove the accusation – but it served as an excuse to pack the women and children off to Port Elizabeth. Another group of 'undesirables' was sent to Pietermaritzburg in Natal, where a camp was formed early in November. By the end of 1900 there were at least eight camps in the Transvaal and four in the Orange River Colony.

Exaggerated reports of women being banished to Port Elizabeth became news, but otherwise nothing was known in Britain about the concentration camps. When Lord Roberts finally handed over command to Lord Kitchener, on 29 November 1900, he was able to do so without the accusation of having incarcerated large numbers of women and children sullying his leave-taking. Later, when it became necessary to defend the need for the camps, it was argued that they had been instituted to succour the helpless and the homeless. The British authorities, it was said, had displayed great humanity in caring for the enemy's abandoned women and children at the British taxpayers' expense. Why then was the creation of the camp system kept so secret? If it was intended purely as a humanitarian act, there was no reason why it should not have been spoken about openly, and used as propaganda to counter international criticism of Britain's conduct throughout the war. But no mention was made of the camps until they were visited by a singularly determined Englishwoman.

It was the dedication of this woman which led to the true nature of the concentration camps being brought to the notice of the world. Her name was Emily Hobhouse. By an odd coincidence, the ship taking her to South Africa in December 1900 passed that taking Lord Roberts back to England where he was to be met with a hero's welcome.

9

The Archdeacon's Daughter

ON 13 JUNE 1900, eight days after British troops entered Pretoria, a huge gathering of women crowded into the Queen's Hall in London to express concern over recent developments in South Africa. The meeting was organized by the women's branch of the South African Conciliation Committee, a body formed shortly after the outbreak of war to counter the ill-informed jingoism then rampant in Britain. The women's branch was started two months later. At first it was expected that members of this auxiliary body would do little more than initiate discussion groups and help with the fund-raising. It was their honorary secretary, Miss Emily Hobhouse, who jolted them into more purposeful action. The meeting in the Queen's Hall was held at her request.

Organizing such a large assembly of women was not easy. Few were experienced in this type of voluntary work and things were not helped when, at the last minute, it was decided to extend the scope of the meeting. Originally it had been intended that the women should protest about the proposed annexation of the two Boer republics by Britain. This was in line with the stated aims of the parent Conciliation Committee, which was pledged to work for a just settlement of the war, a settlement which would allow the republics to retain their independence. But as news of the farm-burnings began to trickle in, the need for protest assumed a greater urgency: it was considered essential to highlight the sufferings of Boer women and children.

There were other problems. Not least was the possibility, as had happened at similar meetings, that the Queen's Hall would be invaded by hooligans. The fact that it was to be an all-women affair did not lessen the apprehension. The 'war-party' could produce hecklers of either sex. So, to lessen the chances of the meeting being disrupted, it was decided that only ticket holders should be admitted and that all tickets would be issued personally by Miss Hobhouse. This caused Emily some embarrassment. She had to fend off men who wanted to attend and to guard against tickets going astray. One of the most persistent male ticket seekers was her friend Leonard Courtney, the distinguished president of the Conciliation Committee. He was so persistent that, as he had encouraged her to hold the meeting, Emily was forced to compromise. 'I was adamant as regards allowing him into the hall,' she said, 'but on his solemn promise that he would come no further than the corridor and be content to listen behind the curtain, I eventually gave way.' The only man to remain visible in the hall was the 'organ blower'.

But, for all its uncertainties, the meeting was a great success. The hall was packed with delegates from all over the country, some invigorating speeches were made, and a Madame San Carlo recited a poem written for the occasion by the popular poet William Walton. It fell to Emily to propose the last, the most emotive of four resolutions, which read: 'This meeting desires to express its sympathy with the women of the Transvaal and Orange Free State, and begs them remember that thousands of English women are filled with profound sorrow at the thought of their sufferings, and with deep regret for the action of their own Government.'

The reading of this resolution was not Emily's first appearance on a public platform, but it was one of the most important. She found addressing the large audience daunting. What most unsettled her was the glimpse she caught of Leonard Courtney's 'fine dome' of a head, popping out from a curtain at the side of the stage, just as she was about to speak. This, she admitted, had made her extremely nervous. Soon, however, she was to be forced to brave far more than alarming sights.

One such occasion came a month later when a meeting was organized for the Conciliation Committee by a group of Quakers at Liskeard in Cornwall. This time the general public was invited. The chairman was the well-known novelist Arthur Quiller-Couch, and the main speaker was a fiery young Liberal MP named David Lloyd George. Emily, who was also billed to speak, travelled to Liskeard with Lloyd George. They must both have known what to expect. Reports of anti-war speakers being howled down, manhandled, and sometimes seriously beaten up, were often featured in the press. Only two months earlier, Lloyd George had been hit over the head with a bludgeon and stunned, after a meeting in Bangor. He had also been burnt in effigy in his own parliamentary constituency. The mere announcement that he would be speaking at Liskeard guaranteed that the audience would be boisterous.

And boisterous it certainly was. Even before the chairman and speakers appeared on the platform, a crowd of youths started yelling, stamping and demanding cheers for Lord Roberts and General Buller. Quiller-Couch had to cut short his opening speech when the rowdies started whistling, cat-calling and blowing a tin trumpet. The first speaker, a young woman from Liverpool, was given the same treatment and forced to return to her seat. The youths then began to parade about the hall, breaking chairs, shouldering a soldier in khaki and cheering for 'Tommy Atkins'. Women sitting in the front row made a dash for the nearest exit. But Emily, whose turn it was to speak, marched boldly to the front of the platform, defying the mob to silence her.

'It seems strange', she bellowed, 'that the people of Liskeard should allow a few thoughtless and ill-mannered boys to spoil a meeting . . . But this kind of behaviour will do more to advance our cause than the most eloquent speeches we could deliver. The account of this meeting will be printed far and wide through England, and Cornish people will be held up to shame because they would not give a fair hearing, especially to a lady . . .' Her voice was drowned in the uproar that followed. Refusing to be intimidated, Emily carried on trying to make herself heard. Finally three men in the audience stood on chairs and demanded that she be given a hearing. For about ten minutes the noise subsided. Emily, somewhat surprisingly, went on to praise the defenders of recently-relieved Mafeking. It was a pity, she said, that the rowdies in the hall did not follow 'the noble example which has been set by the people of Mafeking'. This set the young hooligans off again. They kept up their barracking until they forced Emily to give up.[1]

Then it was Lloyd George's turn. This was the moment for which the trouble-makers had been waiting. According to one of the mob, who later became Major-General Sir Wyndham Childs, a plan had been devised by which the lights would be turned out, and Lloyd George captured and dragged off to be ducked in a cattle-trough. 'At a given moment,' he says, 'a little Union Jack was to be run up to the rafters of the building on a piece of cotton connected to a very thin piece of string. This was to be the signal for the assault.' In fact, the gas lighting was not put out and, after storming the platform, the not-so-brave attackers were at a loss as to what to do next. Lloyd George stood unruffled and smiling; Quiller-Couch remained firmly seated. The ladies from the platform began distributing leaflets among the audience. Not until the thwarted youngsters decided to erect a barricade of chairs on the platform and some 'pro-Boer sympathizers' tried to dismantle it, did it look as if a real fight would break out. Fortunately the police intervened. Quiller-Couch and his supporters were persuaded to retire to an ante-room. 'Lloyd George', says the disappointed Wyndham Childs, 'disappeared through the door leading to the platform, but Miss Hobhouse stood guard over the door, so naturally there was nothing more to be done.'[2]

For Emily it had been a particularly unhappy experience. She could not but regard the hostility at Liskeard as a personal humiliation. This is something she had tried to explain when pleading for silence in the hall. She said she was puzzled to find that Cornishmen would not listen to a Cornish woman. 'It is very strange to me,' she went on, 'after so many years of absence, to come again into the old familiar town and see around me so many familiar faces and be thus treated. It is a sad thought that I should be advocating what I am told are unpopular views in the town.' There could have been few in the audience who did not appreciate her deep disappointment.

For Emily Hobhouse was no stranger to Liskeard. Not only had she been born in the nearby village of St Ive but she had spent the first thirty-five years of her life there as the highly respected daughter of the rector. During the meeting she had been greeted by several of her former village friends who had walked four miles to town to hear her speak.

The village of St Ive – named after a long-forgotten Celtic saint, Ivo – straggles along the main road between Callington and Liskeard in south-east Cornwall. At the Liskeard end of the village stands the ancient parish church, an attractive but unremarkable building which has been extensively altered over the years, giving it a distinct nineteenth-century appearance. On the opposite side of the road stands another, undeniably 'Victorian ecclesiastical' building, a narrow granite house with a steeply pitched roof and pointed gables, which was once the St Ive rectory. Both the restoration of the church and the building of the rectory were the work of Emily's father, Reginald Hobhouse, who was the thirty-fifth Rector of St Ive and the first Archdeacon of Bodmin.

The Hobhouse family had been long established in the west of

England. In the seventeenth century a John Hobhouse was in business as a master mariner in Minehead and his descendants later became prosperous merchants in Bristol. Emily's grandfather, the third Henry Hobhouse, held a number of public offices, eventually becoming a Privy Councillor and Under-Secretary of State for Home Affairs. His four sons were educated at Eton and Oxford and it was largely through his influential contacts in the Tory party that Emily's father was offered, in 1841, the Crown living of St Ive. Four years after graduating from Balliol College, Reginald Hobhouse moved to Cornwall, where he served in the same parish for the next fifty years. He was thirty-three before he married Caroline Salusbury Trelawney, the third daughter of Sir William Trelawney, baronet, of Harewood House, Calstock. The new Mrs Hobhouse was not, as her daughter freely admits, a handsome woman; but what she lacked in looks she more than made up for in vivacity and intelligence. As one of the oldest, most distinguished families in Cornwall, the Trelawneys were regarded as local aristocracy. Emily, however, was prouder of the fact that her mother's ancestor, Jonathan Trelawney, was one of the seven Bishops imprisoned for defying the Catholic enactments of James II.

Reginald Hobhouse was very conscious of his family's social standing. In St Ive he was remembered as an energetic, hard-working minister who was also something of a snob. Narrowly conservative in his religious and political views, he seemed incapable of fraternizing with the villagers and the tin miners of his parish. 'He lived too much apart from ordinary humanity', admits Emily, 'to understand it well and strictly ruled out all that was modern in thought and science from his reading.' It was left to his cheery, outgoing wife to attend to the charitable work of the parish, visiting the sick and helping the poor. This she did with such friendliness, sympathy and understanding that she earned the love and respect of the St Ive churchgoers. Mrs Hobhouse was the pivot around which her family revolved. She was, says Emily, 'the medium between us [children] and our reserved and silent father . . . My mother did her duty well and her sense of humour was the salvation of our home and kept a continuous sparkle.'

Emily was born on 9 April 1860. She was the fifth surviving child of the family, having an elder brother, Alfred, and three elder sisters, Caroline, Blanche and Maud. Two other children, born earlier, had died in infancy and a younger son, Leonard, was born four years after Emily. In her early years Emily seems to have been closest to her sister Blanche, but later she was to have more in common with her younger brother, the intellectually gifted Leonard.

There was nothing remarkable about Emily's childhood. Her father's snobbishness made it difficult for his daughters to form friendships in the village, where only the privileged Wrey family were considered their equals, and they had to rely largely on each other for companionship. Emily had little time for her governesses, whom she thought 'shallow and incompetent'; she envied boys, who could pick the brains of their tutors. 'I never had anyone to cut my mental teeth upon', she complained. Things did not improve when she was sent to school. Here she was bored by lessons which she considered were badly taught and superficial, and she deeply resented being told 'little girls should not ask questions'. She only lasted two terms at the school.

There is a sadness about most of Emily's recorded childhood memories. They reflect feelings of isolation and frustration which surprised her brother Leonard when he read them. 'Our childhood', he says, 'was extremely happy, happy for us all and not the least for her, who all through life had an astonishing zest for the object in hand.' This is puzzling, coming as it does from a man who was fully aware of the disadvantages experienced by Victorian women. He seems not to appreciate the advantage he had over his sister. At an early age he had been sent to prep. school; when he was twelve he entered Marlborough College and then went to Oxford before starting his distinguished career as a philosopher and journalist. There was no such escape for Emily. In fact, it was being denied an outlet for her 'astonishing zest' that seems to have soured her early years. The one occasion when she tried to assert her independence, she was quickly crushed.

It happened when she became friendly, if nothing more, with the son of a local farmer. The boy was apparently in the church choir and attended practice at the rectory. This is said to be how he and Emily first met. Their meetings were not, however, confined to musical evenings at the rectory. They were seen out together, and the villagers began to talk. Emily was slightly the older of the two and for her to be seen with a local boy – whose sister-in-law had once worked as a maid at the rectory – delighted the gossips. How Emily's father came to hear about the affair is not clear, but hear about it he did and reacted with a display of controlled, but deadly, anger. Emily was summoned to his study and emerged two hours later, defeated, after promising to end the friendship. The rejected young man left for America shortly afterwards, his fare, it is said, paid by the Reverend Reginald Hobhouse.

Emily's eldest sister, Caroline, was more fortunate. In 1876 she was allowed to marry August Thornton, a deacon, whose father was the rector of nearby Callington. Her departure from St Ive heralded an unhappy period in the lives of the Hobhouse family. The following year the second daughter, Blanche, who had long suffered the debilitating effects of tuberculosis, died at the age of twenty. Emily, who had been close to Blanche, felt even more isolated after her death. Her mind, she says, 'turned in upon itself, and a natural mysticism and romance was unhealthily stimulated. I lived with heroes in this imaginary world and fell ardently in love with these fabulous beings.'

But it was not all day-dreaming for Emily. After Blanche's death, her mother's health began to decline and this, together with her father's elevation as the Archdeacon of Bodmin, made it necessary for Emily and her one remaining sister, Maud, to undertake the parochial duties. Maud, who was shy, confined her work to the village but Emily, who loved exercise, strode across country to the parish limits, visiting outlying farms and isolated cottages. She was a natural organizer, down-to-earth and self-assured; from her earliest years she had been known to her family as 'the missus' and this nickname was to stick to her throughout her life. She saw her parish work as a crusade, a force for good, which would bring dissenters as well as her father's parishioners into a close and loving community. Later she was to laugh at her youthful naïvety, but it was during this period of her life that she first widened her horizons. There can be little doubt that her experiences jolted her social conscience and inspired her life-long sympathy for the underprivileged.

Soon another death in the family added to her burdens. In June 1880, after a long and painful illness, her mother died of a brain tumour. The loss of his wife was a blow from which Emily's father never fully recovered. A year later he became dangerously ill and the strain of nursing him was shared by his two inexperienced daughters. Emily and Maud were now the only members of the family left at home. Their elder brother, Alfred, had emigrated to New Zealand and Leonard, the younger brother, was at Marlborough College.

For almost nine years Emily and her sister acted out their roles as dutiful daughters. Neither of them was happy. Emily suffered bouts of ill-health which required long periods of recuperation, either with relatives in England or with a companion abroad. But the greatest enemy was boredom. St Ive offered few distractions and, to keep herself occupied, Emily had to devise her own amusements. She dabbled in painting, took piano and singing lessons, read the only books available – mostly religious works and what she calls 'goody-goody' novels – and of course continued her parish visiting. Maud sought a different kind of solace and found it in the arms of her father's curate, Ernest Hebblethwaite. Needless to say this did not please Archdeacon Hobhouse, who did his best to stamp out the romance by forcing the lovers to part for almost a year. Not until Ernest Hebblethwaite was transferred to another living, in 1889, were the couple able to marry.

Once Maud had left home, Emily was trapped. 'I experienced', she says, 'a period of fresh and unusual trial and loneliness. I find but few records of these years, which left their scorching marks upon me . . . They are recorded only on my spirit, and fortunately will die with me. It was in a word a period of torture quite unrealizable for anyone, even for those who knew the outward circumstances, and none but myself could be aware of the inward circumstances.' She no longer had the energy for her parish work because of 'the fearful strain of the home life' which, she says, 'produced hysteria'. Five unhappy years were to pass before she was set free.

Archdeacon Hobhouse died on 27 January 1895, aged seventy-six. He was buried in the St Ive churchyard next to his wife: two very modest headstones mark their graves. These are not the only Hobhouse memorials in the parish. In the old mining village of Pensilva – part of the St Ive parish – is the humble 'Tin Tabernacle' built from funds bequeathed by Archdeacon Hobhouse. Having stood aloof from dissenting chapel-goers all his life, he had hoped to stem the drift to Methodism with this belated gesture, but by then it was too late. His successor, the last Victorian rector of St Ive, could claim few converts among the mining community.

The bulk of the Archdeacon's £33,000 fortune was divided among his five children. This meant that Emily inherited over £6000 from her father which, together with a legacy she had earlier received from an aunt, would have – in the 1890s – provided her with a modest, but comfortable, income. There would have been no need for her to work. She was thirty-five and could have settled for a life of water-colour painting, *petit point* and good works. But such a prospect would have appalled her. Emily was far too single minded, too strong willed, and had waited too long for her independence, to be sidetracked into conformity. A fortnight after her father's death she left St Ive for good. 'I was free,' she wrote, 'but also I knew that I was uneducated, and unfit to find any useful place in the world.'

She did, however, have a few contacts. Chief among these were her uncle and aunt, Lord and Lady Hobhouse, who had always been pillars of support for Emily and her sisters. Lord Hobhouse was the younger brother of Emily's father and, as Arthur Hobhouse, had served on various government commissions for which, in 1885, he had been created a baron. Both he and his wife Mary were staunch Liberals and their influence on Emily undoubtedly acted as a corrective to her father's narrow conservatism. She had spent several of her childhood holidays at her uncle Arthur's house near Bristol and her aunt had nursed her through the recuperation periods of her illnesses. It was to Lord and Lady Hobhouse that she fled on leaving St Ive, and they offered her advice and guidance. She toyed with the idea of going to university or training as a nurse, but it was her links with the Cornish church that gave her the practical help she needed. The Archdeacon of Truro, acting on Emily's behalf, contacted the ecclesiastical authorities in the American state of Minnesota and this led to her being invited to become a social worker in the Minnesotan diocese.

So it was that within six months of leaving St Ive Emily, accompanied by a young Cornish girl who was to be her maid, found herself on board a ship sailing for the United States. In the course of the following year Emily lived in the lawless little mining town of Virginia, Minnesota. There she flung herself into various good causes: a temperance crusade, the establishment of a public library and hospital visiting. She returned to England in the spring of 1896 for a short holiday. There is reason to believe that on this holiday she was joined by the owner of a Virginia grocery store, a man of her own age, who had recently been elected as the town's mayor. His name was John C. Jackson. Emily appears to have met him shortly after she arrived in Virginia when he helped her in some charity work, but little else is known about their relationship except that it blossomed into a romance which led to an engagement. That they should have been drawn to each other is understandable. The fair-haired, blue-eyed Emily, with her refined, piquant good looks, her ready sense of humour and her vibrant personality, was a very attractive woman. John Jackson, dashingly mustachio'd and seemingly prosperous, must have ranked as one of Virginia's most eligible bachelors. They appeared eminently well-suited.

Their engagement was not made public, but shortly after she returned to Minnesota Emily announced that she was leaving for Cleveland, Ohio. In fact she spent little time in Ohio, and was next heard of in Mexico City. This is where, or so it is said, she and John Jackson intended to start their married life. What is more certain is that Emily invested in a ranch, built a new house, and put money into a 'speculative concession'. Most of her time was spent in learning Spanish, studying the history of Mexico and exploring the prospects of making a living there. Over a year was to pass before she was joined by Mr Jackson.

What kept the couple apart is not clear. Admittedly Jackson still had to complete his term as mayor, but later disclosures make it doubtful that this would have weighed heavily with him. When he did leave Virginia, in April 1897, he did so in a hurry, after selling his grocery business. His prosperity was apparently a façade, for he left behind him a mass of 'legal complications' and was later alleged to be insolvent. He also appears to have left a large question mark hanging over his handling of the town's finances. How much Emily knew of all this is uncertain. She travelled to Chicago to meet Jackson and it was reported that they were to be married there. This proved untrue. A week or so later the resilient Mr Jackson wrote to a friend to announce his safe arrival in sunny Mexico.[3]

What happened after that is a complete mystery. Later in the year Emily again visited England, and returned to Mexico in the spring of 1898. She was accompanied by a cousin, but no mention is made of John Jackson. 'The result of her journey', says her biographer, Ruth Fry, 'was that her engagement was finally ended, and instead of a home of her own in the fascinating surroundings of Mexico, Emily Hobhouse returned to England . . . As was natural in a woman of such a highly emotional temperament, this grave disappointment left an indelible mark.'

The emotional trauma of her broken engagement was not the only wound Emily bore as a result of her American venture. On a more mundane level, she returned to England a great deal poorer, having lost a sizeable chunk of her capital in ill-advised investments. Although not destitute – she could afford to move into a Chelsea flat – she could no longer count on a comfortable income and had to watch her spending. Every bit as serious was the blow to her illusions.

For Emily had gone to Minnesota in the hope of finding an outlet for her frustrated idealism. She had been sadly disappointed. In her letters home she tended to make light of the petty-mindedness she encountered but it became obvious that, even had John Jackson not entered her life, she saw little future for herself in Virginia. Rescuing self-indulgent backwoodsmen from their excesses had not proved the noble, all-absorbing cause she was seeking. This, and her shattered romance, had made Emily more critical of human failings. While it would be wrong to think of her as embittered, she no longer trusted people unreservedly, and was certainly not the 'naïve do-gooder' that some of her opponents imagined her to be.

Yet she was still determined to be of use. Never one to sit around moping, she went to work for the Women's Industrial Committee as a researcher. She spent hours in the British Museum reading room studying the conditions under which children were employed before the passing of the Factory Acts, and decided to write a novel based on her findings. Unfortunately, she had second thoughts and later burnt the completed manuscript. This was also the period when Emily first met Leonard Courtney and his wife, or so it is said. But as Courtney, a Liberal MP, had for twenty-two years represented a Cornish constituency which included St Ive, it would be strange if he and Emily had not met before. Certainly Emily became intimate with the Courtneys, who lived near her in Chelsea, and so started a friendship which she was to value greatly. Then in his mid-sixties, Leonard Courtney – who was known as an 'advanced Liberal' – and his wife Kate (*née* Potter, a sister of Mrs Sidney Webb) were almost as influential in shaping Emily's political views as were her uncle and aunt and her younger brother Leonard.

It was Leonard Courtney who, on the outbreak of war, invited Emily to join the South African Conciliation Committee, of which he was president. She needed little persuasion. A month or so earlier she had been staying with Lord and Lady Hobhouse at their country house, and the South African crisis had been the main topic of conversation. Emily's uncle and aunt had been in full agreement with the Courtneys in opposing the war. For years Emily was to treasure the maxims expressed by her uncle in a press interview which was published about this time. Among other things, he maintained that 'a nation does not become great by increasing the number of its subjects without regard to quality or proximity; that extension of dominion by military force brings weakness and not strength . . . that the truest and bravest patriots are those who dare to warn their countrymen when hurrying in ignorance or passion to do wrong.' War hysteria prevented Lord Hobhouse's voice from being widely heard, but it was listened to and revered by his niece.

Emily's work as secretary of the women's branch of the Conciliation Committee was confined at first to arranging meetings in private houses, often her aunt's London drawing room, and answering correspondence from her Chelsea flat. A few months were to pass before she thought of organizing the women's meeting in the Queen's Hall and then went on to speak at other meetings, including the disastrous one at Liskeard.

Distressed as she was by the loutish behaviour in Cornwall, Emily did not allow it to discourage her. Within days she was trying to arrange meetings for a group of Dutch Reformed Church ministers who had arrived from South Africa to plead their people's cause. These were the first Afrikaners Emily had met, and she was deeply impressed by their 'old-world dignity'. But it was not easy to find them an audience. Few 'were the people who would lend them an ear', she reported. This, by then, had become an all-too-familiar difficulty. So inpenetrable was the wall of hostility that Emily finally decided to branch out in a new direction. As reports of farm-burnings continued to pour in, it became increasingly clear that help of a more practical nature was needed and so, after consulting with her family and the Courtneys, Emily started a fund to help the homeless.

The 'South African Women and Children Distress Fund' was nominally non-political and non-sectarian and it was founded to care for civilian victims of the war, be they Boer or British. A national committee was formed, money was appealed for and subscriptions sought from all over the country. Only then did Emily announce to her family that she intended to go to South Africa and supervise the distribution of the fund. Her uncle and aunt, she says, were 'interested but dubious'. They eventually agreed that she should go, but were not sufficiently impressed with the idea to give her 'material help'. In other words, she had to pay her own fare.

But this much Emily had expected. She had never asked her family for financial help and had, in fact, been saving up for the journey. Nevertheless, she was pleased to have Lord and Lady Hobhouse's approval. Her brother's objections – he was afraid she might catch a disease or be vilified – she brushed aside. Then she booked a second-class passage on one of the cheaper steamers. She delayed her departure long enough to attend the first meeting of the Distress Fund committee, where she handed over £300 (roughly £5000 today) which she had collected privately. The money was to be forwarded to a Cape Town bank for her use in South Africa.

She eventually sailed from Southampton on 7 December 1900, four days before Lord Roberts left Cape Town on his return home.

Emily Hobhouse arrived in Cape Town towards the end of December on a glorious midsummer's day. Like most new visitors to the Cape, she was completely bowled over by the grandeur of Table Mountain, which she first saw from the ship at sunrise, and was no less impressed by the jagged blue peaks of the Hottentot Holland range to the east.

So majestic did the mountains seem in the early morning light that, on coming ashore, she was surprised to find the Cape Town streets jammed with military trucks and the pavements teeming with soldiers. It was her first glimpse of a country at war.

But the warmth of the welcome she received quickly dispelled her gloomy thoughts. She stayed at first with Mrs Charles Murray, whom she had met earlier in London. Mrs Murray, a handsome woman of great dignity, was a daughter of Sir John Molteno, the first prime minister of the Cape Colony and, like the rest of her family, was openly a Boer sympathizer. Her London-based brother, Percy Molteno, was a founder-member of the Conciliation Committee and it was probably through him that Emily had met Mrs Murray. It was another of those friendships she was to prize.

Married to a prominent Cape Town doctor, Mrs Murray lived with her family in the suburb of Kenilworth. It was at her house that Emily met many of the men and women who were to become her supporters. Included among them were senior politicians such as J. X. Merriman and J. W. Sauer, both of whom had been cabinet ministers in Cecil Rhodes's government; Harry Currey, a former secretary of Rhodes's; and Lord De Villiers, the Chief Justice of the Cape. All these men, and more particularly their wives, went out of their way to make Emily welcome. She was surprised that they seemed to know all about her, and touched by their offers of hospitality; she was invited to stay with four different families during her first week in Cape Town. Yet, for all their friendliness, Emily was aware of a feeling of bitterness among the people she met.

'I was struck, for instance,' she wrote, 'by the intense devotion to England, a devotion which had received a severe blow . . . The Cape people had seen England through a veil of idealism which had small relation to reality. The Tory Government's war policy had torn asunder this veil with disastrous results. The effects were deep. Something life-long had snapped within them – their bearings were lost.'

She was speaking of course of those colonists opposed to the war; she seems not to have met any Cape 'loyalists' who were wholehearted in their support for Britain. The pro-Boers with whom Emily mixed in Cape Town were fewer in numbers than their counterparts in London. Many of them had relatives living in the former Boer republics and some had given refuge to women and children who, after seeing their homes burnt, had been deported by the military authorities. Emily met some of these refugees, who told her of the hardships they had endured. From them also she learned for the first time of the so-called 'refugee camps' that had been set up to accommodate destitute civilians. This was something for which Emily had not bargained. 'Port Elizabeth was the only camp known in England when I left,' she later explained, 'but in Cape Town I heard at once of the large camps at Johannesburg, Bloemfontein, Potchefstroom, Norval's Pont, Kroonstad, Irene and other places.'[4] Having arrived intending to distribute blankets, clothes and food among the homeless, Emily now had to revise her plans: she felt a visit to the camps was imperative.

Her chances of travelling north were not good. Martial law had recently been declared over parts of the Cape Colony and now extended almost to the coast. Permission from the highest authorities was needed for journeys up-country. Here, though, Emily had a slight advantage. When the 'South African Women and Children Distress Fund' was about to be launched her aunt had pulled a few political strings. She had written to Lord Lansdowne and Joseph Chamberlain – whom she had known in his radical days – asking for the fund to be given official sanction. Both ministers had sympathized with the object of the fund and promised to inform Sir Alfred Milner of its purpose. This had inspired Lady Hobhouse to give Emily a note of introduction to Milner, whom she also knew from earlier days. Now, urged on by her new Cape friends, Emily decided to make use of her aunt's contacts. She was suitably rewarded. Within a matter of days she was invited to lunch at Government House.

The thought of meeting Alfred Milner terrified Emily. It was not because he was governor of the Cape but, knowing how much depended on the interview, she was afraid she would fail to convince him when pleading her cause. Her nerves were not calmed on finding she was the only woman at a lunch with eight men. Cowed by the military talk, she was unable to say a word. When Milner tried to bring up the subject of her visit, she cut him short. She said it was not something she could talk about at a luncheon, and asked for a short interview afterwards. Reluctantly he promised her fifteen minutes. In the event, they were 'at it hammer and tongs for an hour'.

Sitting on a sofa in the drawing room, Emily recovered her nerve. She cross-questioned Sir Alfred, who responded with 'singular charm'. He admitted that the farm-burning was a 'mistake' and agreed that something should be done to help the Boer women and children. He also confessed to having seen 'truckloads of women' on the up-country railway, which he found 'rather terrible'. Emily did not mince her words when telling him what she had heard from the deported women to whom she had spoken. She described them as spirited and defiant.

How, she asked him, 'was he going to govern thousands of Joans of Arc?' Britain's honour was at stake, she said; people in England were uneasy about the mounting civilian war casualties.

The interview ended with Milner promising to do all he could to assist Emily in her mission to the refugee camps. He agreed that she should take an Afrikaans-speaking woman with her – she had in mind the wife of a Dutch Reformed Church minister – and that she should be provided with two railway trucks for her relief supplies. But he warned her that he could only make recommendations: the last word, he explained, rested with Lord Kitchener, the military commander.

Emily came away from the meeting treading air. She was pleased with her performance, confident that she had made a good impression. She had not succumbed completely to the governor's undoubted charm, but she felt she had touched his heart. She was not unduly worried about Sir Alfred's reservations, even knowing of Kitchener's reputation as a 'woman hater'. She was prepared to wait and hope for the best.

Almost two weeks passed before Kitchener replied. Emily filled in the time by interviewing more refugees, visiting Boer prisoners at a local camp and accepting invitations from her new friends. Kitchener's answer, when it eventually arrived, was disappointing. Permission was given for Emily to visit the refugee camps. She was also allowed to load a bogie-truck, capable of holding twelve tons of goods, with her relief supplies and send it on ahead of her. But her request for a 'Dutch' woman companion was turned down. There would, said Kitchener, be women in Bloemfontein who could assist her. And Bloemfontein was as far as she was permitted to go: she was strictly forbidden to visit any of the camps further north. This came as a blow, as Emily was extremely anxious to inspect the Transvaal camps which, she had been told, were indescribably squalid. She immediately went to Government House to consult Milner. He suggested that Emily should wait until she reached Bloemfontein and then write to Kitchener again; he supplied her with his own letter of authorization. Emily decided to accept what she had been granted. After all, she reasoned, 'half a loaf is better than no bread' and it would be foolish to demand all or nothing. On the night of 22 January, in 'glorious moonlight', Emily boarded the train that was to take her to Bloemfontein. Her friends had given her food for the journey and a kettle for making tea and cocoa; and a few of them came to wave her goodbye. As the train pulled out of the station, Emily suddenly felt lonely. 'I must own', she admitted, 'that my heart sank a little and I faced the unknown with great trepidation.'

Before leaving Cape Town Emily had met Charles Fichardt, the eldest son of a well-known Bloemfontein family. Although the Fichardts were of German descent their home language was English, and Charles himself had been partly educated in Scotland. He was a remarkable young man – at twenty-four he was mayor of Bloemfontein – with deeply-held republican sympathies. He had joined the Boer forces at the outbreak of war. After fighting in several major engagements, he was badly injured at Paardeberg, captured, and deported to Cape Town with his wife and son. Emily had found him charming and he had warmed to her. So much so that, on hearing she was leaving for Bloemfontein, he had written to his mother asking her to put Emily up.

This proved more difficult than he could have imagined. On reaching Bloemfontein, Emily discovered that life in the town was severely restricted by martial law. There were soldiers everywhere. 'You can't stir without their sanction,' she complained, 'a great ring of camps all round and pickets continually demanding your pass. It is a perfect terror.' That night she slept at an inn and the following morning a carriage arrived to take her to the Fichardts' house. Here she was given a hearty, but qualified, welcome. Mrs Fichardt was anxious to have her as a guest, but afraid to receive her without permission from General Pretyman, the military governor. An infringement of martial law, she explained, could mean trouble for her younger sons.

Emily decided to set things straight immediately. She drove to Government House, where she was surprised to be welcomed. General Pretyman was a friend of the Hobhouse family and remembered meeting Emily at her aunt's in Bournemouth. He said he had wanted to invite her to stay at Government House, but the town had not yet recovered from the typhoid epidemic and they were overrun by doctors and nurses. However, he gave her a general invitation to meals whenever she was free to come. Unfortunately, this happy exchange did not last long. When Emily told the General that she wanted to stay with Mrs Fichardt, he nearly, she says, 'jumped out of his skin'. He knew all about Mrs Fichardt and considered her 'very bitter'. Emily agreed. 'Just so,' she said sweetly, 'but my visit may have a softening effect upon her.' Poor Pretyman, who was notoriously pliable and easily hoodwinked, greeted this as a novel idea and quickly capitulated. 'I stood over him', the triumphant Emily wrote to her aunt, 'while he wrote me a permit, stating his approval.'

Settled in Mrs Fichardt's large, cool house, Emily had an ideal base from which to work. She lost no time in getting started. Pretyman, besides giving her permission to live with the Fichardts, also provided her with a permanent pass to the Bloemfontein 'refugee camp' and introduced her to army officers who could help her. This boosted Emily's confidence but, from the very outset, she insisted on being allowed a free hand when visiting the camp. She had no wish to be closely tied to officialdom.

The camp was two miles from the town: 'dumped down' as Emily put it, 'on the southern slope of a koppie [hillock] right out on the bare brown veld.' She first saw it at four o'clock on a scorchingly hot summer's afternoon. As she approached, the sight of rows of white bell-tents against the barren hillside – there were no trees, no shade of any kind – so numbed her that she found it impossible to describe her feelings. Her heart sank even further when she entered the camp.

There were then almost two thousand people living in the Bloemfontein camp: the majority were women but there were a few men – surrendered Boers known as 'hands-uppers' – and over nine hundred children. Emily started by looking for a Mrs Philip Botha, whose sister she had met in Cape Town. Such was the maze of tents, without names to the rows or numbers for the tents, that she became utterly confused. When she eventually tracked down Mrs Botha, she found her living in a small bell-tent with her five children and a little African girl servant in miserable circumstances. The tent was shockingly overcrowded, the heat stifling; flies lay thick and black on everything, there were no chairs and no table, the only furniture being a small deal box which served as larder. But Emily was welcomed and it was here, seated on a rolled-up khaki blanket, that she first met the women she had come to help. They called in, or were sent for by Mrs Botha, and stayed to talk. They 'told me their stories', reported the deeply touched Emily, 'and we cried together and even laughed together and chatted bad Dutch and bad English all afternoon.'

The stories the women had to tell were to become all too familiar in the weeks ahead. They spoke of seeing their homes destroyed, of being transported to the camp in wagons or open rail trucks, of their families being broken up (a mother of six said she had no idea what had happened to one of her children) and of their husbands who were either on commando or prisoners-of-war, deported to Ceylon or St Helena. According to Emily they cried very little and did not complain, but there was no mistaking their bitterness when they described conditions in the camp. Emily was told of the starvation rations issued to the women, the unsuitable food provided for the children. There was a serious shortage of water for washing and cooking, as well as for drinking, and essentials such as soap had become unobtainable. All the tents were overcrowded – some housed as many as twelve – smelly and unhygienic; during the day the sun blazed through the single canvas, making the heat unbearable, and on rainy nights water not only poured through the roof but flowed under the tent flaps, soaking the blankets of the sleepers. There were no beds, few mattresses and everyone, including sick children and pregnant women, had to sleep on the ground. As if to demonstrate the dangers involved, a puff-adder wriggled into Mrs Botha's tent while the women were talking, and they all rushed outside. Emily was left to deal with the intruder. Fearlessly she jabbed at the snake with her parasol and wounded it before a man arrived with a mallet to finish it off.

What most distressed the women were the sufferings of their under-nourished children. The sicknesses such as measles, bronchitis, pneumonia, dysentery and, inevitably, typhoid, which were to increase alarmingly over the next few months, had already invaded the camp, with fatal results. There were few tents which did not house one or more sick persons, a disproportionate number of whom were children. One woman whom Emily met was by no means untypical in having six children ill, 'two in hospital with typhoid and four sick in the tent'. Even so she had been refused permission to take her family to the Cape where she had relatives. Although she was expecting another child, she was forced to stay where she was and watch 'her children droop and sicken'.

This seemingly inflexible, senseless, inhumane treatment of helpless women added to Emily's growing anger. She was to encounter many more such cases. Even so, she was reluctant to blame the army officers in charge of the camp. They were not responsible for the system which herded women and children into the unhealthy, under-staffed camps, nor could they halt the stream of displaced families which arrived daily and had to be accommodated. Emily was aware of the difficulties involved in obtaining supplies from the coast on a railway line which was constantly threatened and disrupted, and of the shortage of doctors and nurses, most of whom were needed to attend men on active service. But she could not forgive what she called: 'Crass male ignorance, stupidity, helplessness and muddling.' This resulted from inexperience and lack of imagination, which made the officers obey orders blindly when dealing with the women, without a thought to the consequences. She reported,

I rub as much salt into the sore places of their minds as I possibly can because it is good for them; but I can't help melting a little when they are very humble and confess that the whole thing is a grievous and gigantic blunder and presents an almost insoluble problem, and they don't know *how* to face it . . . Major Cray now in charge not only of this camp but of everyone in the once Free State told me how he was curtailed – no money, no trucks in sufficient quantity – no power to do what he would like to have done. He begs me to go to all the camps . . .

Emily had every intention of visiting as many camps as possible. First, though, she had to do what she could at Bloemfontein. For the next week or so she was kept busy unpacking and distributing clothes, supplying pregnant women with mattresses and applying for more nurses and medical equipment. The spread of disease alarmed her: she dreaded another typhoid epidemic. On finding that the drinking water came from the polluted Modder river, she started a drive to have all the water boiled, only to discover that there was scarcely enough fuel to cook a daily meal and the women had no spare utensils to hold boiled water. Emily could do nothing about the fuel, but she quickly arranged for each tent to be given an additional pail, at government expense, and for the order that all water be boiled to be enforced. Later she got the army to agree that the camp's supply of water should be sterilized in a 'big railway boiler'.

Everywhere she was confronted by sickness and death. Returning to the camp one day she found a nurse collapsed on her bed after trying to attend to some 'thirty typhoid and other patients'. Emily later visited some of these patients. They ranged from a near-naked woman panting on her bed with labour pains to a six-month-old baby 'gasping its life out on its mother's knee watched by three other sick children'. In almost every tent she entered there were two or three white-faced, listless children stretched out on the ground, some of them too weak to walk. But the most pathetic sight was that of a distressed father kneeling beside a stretcher on which his twenty-four-year-old daughter lay dying while, in the next tent, his wife kept vigil over their two other children aged six and five. At a loss to know what to do, Emily turned on the army officer who had joined her and demanded he get brandy for the older girl. 'But', she sighed, 'for the most part you must stand and look on helpless to *do* anything, because there is nothing to do anything with.'

The officer with her was Captain Albert Hume who, as Major Cray was sick, was temporarily in command of the camp. He was the type of military man Emily most disliked. Ignoring the fact that the 'refugees' were prisoners in all but name Hume, and a few others, insisted that the women and their families had come to the camp for protection and should be grateful to be there. They were oblivious of the widespread suffering, often refusing to enter the tents. This Emily found intolerable. She was determined that Captain Hume should face up to his responsibilities. Having made him fetch brandy for the dying girl, she quickly found another tragic case. This was an emaciated four-year-old boy who had 'nothing left of him except his great brown eyes and white teeth from which his lips were drawn back too thin to close.' Emily immediately went in search of Hume. 'You shall look,' she exploded before propelling him into the tent to see the 'complete child-skeleton'. Then at last, she says, he was forced to admit 'it was awful to see children suffering so'.[5]

But it made no difference. The following day Emily was again complaining about Hume's callous indifference. He was among those, she said, who refused to acknowledge that a Boer had feelings. She wanted nothing more to do with him. From now on, she vowed, she would ignore 'subordinate officers' and take orders only from the High Commissioner and Lord Kitchener. If Hume tried to interfere with her work, she promised she would report him to Sir Alfred Milner. 'The missus' was getting into her stride, and woebetide anyone who got in her way.

The one Boer of whom Captain Hume fully approved was the Reverend Adriaan Hofmeyer. This somewhat suspect Dutch Reformed clergyman was touring the camps as Lord Kitchener's agent, trying to undermine support for the fighting Boers. It was a mission for which he was most unsuited. A few months before the outbreak of war Hofmeyer had been suspended as a minister of the church for his immoral conduct with a member of his congregation, and was now regarded as a 'disgraced character'. His renegade activities had increased his unpopularity. When Captain Hume asked Emily to meet the visiting clergyman she was adamant in her refusal. It was a slight which Hofmeyer was not to forget.

A person more to Emily's liking was Mrs 'Tibbie' Steyn, wife of the former Orange Free State President. Mrs Steyn was the daughter of a Scots missionary and had remained in the Free State capital until shortly before the British occupation. She had then left with her four young children to wander about the veld until she was finally arrested and brought back to Bloemfontein where she was placed under guard.

Emily had earlier seen her walking in the street, followed wherever she went by a soldier with a bayonet. It was inevitable that the two of them should meet, and when they did Emily discovered a soul mate. Over tea, Mrs Steyn spoke of her own experiences in the veld and of how saddened she was at having her father arrested and her sister marched through the streets to the concentration camp. Her calm dignity greatly impressed Emily. A lasting friendship was formed between the two women.

One of the first camps Emily visited outside Bloemfontein was Norval's Pont, on the south bank of the Orange River. Travelling there was uncomfortable and fraught with uncertainties. At that time Christiaan De Wet was expected to make a foray into the Cape, and there were fears that the railway line would be attacked – as indeed it was in places – and the type of troop train in which Emily was obliged to travel would come under fire. Luckily she escaped the guerrilla attacks, but was subjected to endless delays and bone-shaking discomfort as a result of the chaos on the line. On one occasion she was forced to sit bolt upright for fifteen hours in a guard's van while it shunted to and fro throughout the night and part of the next day. Experiences like this, combined with the sweltering heat and dust, left her totally exhausted.

Her decision to tour the camps had been reinforced by news that many more women and children were to be interned and that the military intended to 'sweep up' the entire population. Knowing how inadequate her supplies were to meet the needs of Bloemfontein, she was anxious to find out what was wanted elsewhere before reporting back to the Distress Fund. She was dreading what she might find.

At Norval's Pont she was agreeably surprised. The camp, she admitted, was far superior to that at Bloemfontein. Situated on a slope overlooking the Orange River and surrounded by flat-topped hills, it was well laid out with neat rows of tents, most of which were furnished with low wooden beds and mattresses. The rations were slightly better and the drinking water came from a pure spring on a nearby farm. There had been no violent outbreak of sickness, but most of the patients taken to hospital had died. A great curse of the camp was boredom, and Emily was pleased to hear that Milner was 'sending round the Education Commissioner' to arrange schooling for the children. This was something she had been demanding for Bloemfontein. Credit for the efficient organization at Norval's Pont was due to two army officers who, in turn, had supervised the camp from its beginnings. They both had a healthy disregard for 'red tapeism' and had been prepared to act on their own initiative. This tradition was to continue at Norval's Pont. On a later visit Emily was to meet the camp's third superintendent, Mr Cole Bowen, an Irishman whose tact and resourcefulness so impressed her that in her report back she suggested that he 'should be asked to visit other camps in order to inaugurate his superior methods, and so obviate needless sufferings.'[6]

Her next stop was at Aliwal North, another camp on the banks of the Orange River but further east, where she received an even greater surprise. Not only was the camp 'beautifully arranged' and well supplied, the tents capable of being extended and the rations better – although potatoes were eight times dearer than in London – but, staggeringly, there were no soldiers or sentries to be seen and the inmates were free to walk into town and receive visitors without the bother of passes. Again, it was the enlightened officer in charge who had made all this possible. The only real shortage, both here and at Norval's Pont, was in children's clothes and soap, both of which Emily did her best to supply. Such things, she grumbled, were bound to be overlooked by the witless men at headquarters.

She left Aliwal North in a more optimistic mood. Even though she was told the camp would soon be receiving an influx which would increase its population of eight hundred to over two thousand, she was not unduly worried. Having seen what could be done by efficient administration, she now had examples to hold up to the Bloemfontein authorities. She felt in a position to make realistic comparisons.

Once back at Bloemfontein she was quickly brought down to earth. She found that the three hospitals there were now full of typhoid cases, that sickness was increasing in the tents and the camp's population was 'rapidly doubling'. Almost as disturbing was the discovery that General Pretyman had been replaced by the former Major Goold-Adams, the man who had narrowly escaped death with Lady Sarah Wilson in the Mafeking convent. He had resigned from the army, and was the first civilian Lieutenant-Governor of the Orange River Colony. Alarming stories of the clamp-downs and wholesale arrests which had followed his appointment made Emily suspicious of Goold-Adams at first, but on meeting him she found him both sympathetic and helpful. She was not alone in her judgement: in time Goold-Adams was to earn the widespread trust and respect of the Boers.

Emily was kept busy in the camp for the next three weeks. After desperately hunting for suitable materials, she organized the men into making shoes and, encouraged by Goold-Adams, employed the women to make mattresses. She was helped by three Boer women from the town. Less pleasing was the discovery that four nurses sent to the camp after her urgent pleading were British refugees from the Transvaal, who could hardly be expected to sympathize with the Boer women, and she continued to badger her friend Mrs Murray in Cape Town to find more suitable recruits. With people dying at the rate of twenty to twenty-five a day – a death rate, claimed Emily, unknown 'except in the times of the Great Plagues' – the need for trained nurses was a high priority, although all they could be offered was five shillings a day, their rations and a tent. This was in strange contrast to another scheme Emily tried to initiate. Worried about the lack of schooling in the camp, she asked to be allowed to spend part of the Distress Fund money on sending 'some of the highest-class girls' to the smartest school in Bloemfontein. Wisely this idea – worthy of Emily's father – was knocked on the head by the Distress Fund committee, but not before four girls had been placed at the school, where they were then allowed to stay. Emily later claimed that she acted out of frustration when she found that nothing was being done by the authorities and the girls were becoming demoralized.

At the beginning of March she set off to visit two more camps: one at Springfontein, about a hundred miles south-west of Bloemfontein, and the other at Kimberley in the northern Cape. It entailed a long, circuitous rail journey but Emily felt that it was essential to her work, particularly as Lord Kitchener still refused to allow her into the Transvaal or even to travel as far as Kroonstad. But if she imagined she was being kept away from the worst camps, she was soon proved wrong. A few hours in Springfontein were enough to change her mind.

Springfontein was a new camp, small, isolated, and far from any town that could supply the basic necessities. The inmates were the poorest Emily had met and the camp commandant, a humane man, could do little to help them. There were appalling shortages at the camp. So scarce were clothes that most people wandered about semi-naked; a few women had made petticoats out of coarse khaki blankets but the girls wore nothing under their tattered print frocks and everyone was barefoot. Emily arrived with three cases of clothing and on her first day she fitted out about sixty persons. Sitting on the stoep of a farmhouse, she handed out clothes and listened to the all-too-familiar stories of distress. Most of the tents were unfurnished, there was no wood to make tables and beds and very little fuel for cooking: Emily was humbled to see people avidly eyeing her deal packing cases, and disgusted to be told that British soldiers had arrived at the camp offering to sell furniture from looted Boer houses. She stayed at the camp for almost a week. When she left she was comforted by the thought that at least Springfontein was cared for by a kind-hearted commandant. She was not to know that this popular officer was soon to die of pneumonia, a sickness he caught from children in the hospital.

On her way to Kimberley Emily stopped for a night at Norval's Pont, where the admirable Mr Cole Bowen was introducing further reforms. The rest of the journey was long, arduous and tiring. For three days Emily was jolted about in the guard's vans of crawling trains, enjoyed very little sleep and arrived at her destination on the point of collapse.

Like many another English visitor, she found the famous Diamond City disappointing. Its mine dumps, she thought far less picturesque than those of Cornwall, and she dismissed the town as an ugly, straggling, untidy looking place. But what really made her heart sink was her first impression of the women's camp. Surrounded by an eight-foot-high barbed-wire fence, patrolled by sentries and squeezed into a smaller area than any she had yet seen, the Kimberley camp could not be mistaken for anything other than a prison. Inside, the place was dirty and smelly, the tents were closely packed and overcrowded; a marquee that was meant to serve as a hospital was empty and unfurnished, measles and whooping cough were rife but there was no nurse; the commandant was old, lazy and negligent, and the camp's only doctor seemed to know nothing about children's ailments.

For all that, Emily found there was little for her to do at Kimberley. Not only were her supplies running low, but there was already a well-organized committee of Afrikaner women in the town, to whom she donated money for future use, and as these women were working for the same aims as the Distress Fund she was happy to leave the practical relief work to them. Her own activities were confined to badgering the authorities for extra provisions and comforting the women in the camp.

Emily's South African mission was, in fact, coming to an end. She still had a couple of places in the northern Cape to inspect but her path in other directions was blocked. On her first day in Kimberley she had written to Milner – or Alfred the Great as she mockingly called him – and made a final appeal for help. After telling him of Kitchener's refusal to allow her into the Transvaal, she placed her fate in his hands. If Milner could do nothing, she said in a letter to her brother, she intended to 'send him a sort of Ultimatum and retire from the scene'.[7]

Exactly what she meant by this is not clear, but she was obviously near to despair. A week later she paid a hurried visit to Cape Town. She gave various reasons for this, including the need to replenish her supplies, but high on her list of people to see was the new governor of the Cape, Sir Walter Hely-Hutchinson (Milner was now in the Transvaal), who gave her permission to visit Mafeking and helped solve her travel problems. But he could do nothing about the Transvaal: Milner was not apparently prepared to intervene on her behalf.

Emily's visit to Mafeking was brief and uneventful. The camp was completely isolated, six miles from the town, and reaching it was like driving into space. 'They have *no one* to visit or care for them', wrote Emily. '. . . For miles round no habitation can be seen and Mafeking folk are too bitter to do anything to help them.' Yet all was not gloom. In spite of the usual shortages – clothes, soap and candles – the people were well fed and they were encouraged by Emily's assurance that there were women in England who sympathized with their plight. Before returning to Kimberley she formed a committee of seven women to distribute the clothes she had brought, and showed them how to organize work in the camp.

This was more or less the end of the road for Emily. In the middle of April she paid a final visit to Bloemfontein, where she discovered there had been sixty-two deaths since she left and the population had doubled to four thousand, with hundreds more expected. Then, finding she was still forbidden to visit Kroonstad, she decided to return to England. For the past few months she had been writing to her aunt, begging her to write to *The Times* and other newspapers to make the conditions in the camps known. Now, having acquired contacts throughout the country and visited a wide variety of camps, Emily was ready to do battle herself. On 7 May 1901 she sailed from Cape Town on board the RMS *Saxon*.

10

A Camp in the Transvaal

ON 16 APRIL 1901, shortly before Emily returned to England, a letter was published in the *New York Herald* which drew international attention to the concentration camps in South Africa. It was written by the American wife of General Maxwell, the military governor of Pretoria, who was then visiting her husband in the Transvaal. Launching an appeal for funds, Louise Maxwell claimed she was writing 'in the name of little children who are living in open tents without fires, and possessing the scantiest of clothes.'[1] The reason she was asking for help, she explained, was that British charity had been exhausted by other claims made by the war. The letter, which appeared to carry the stamp of authority, was widely read.

There can be no doubting Louise Maxwell's sincerity. She had visited some of the Transvaal camps and seen the conditions there for herself. Well intentioned, if politically naïve, she seems to have been following the example of her husband who, a month earlier, on being made responsible for the concentration camps in the Transvaal, had opened a subscription list 'to provide necessaries' for the camp inmates. There was, however, an important difference between the two Maxwell appeals. The general's subscription list, published in South Africa, merely invited local donations; his wife's letter not only sought funds in America, but in doing so broadcast the scandal of the camps to the world. What was worse, she made it appear that she had the approval of high authority. This landed poor Louise Maxwell in serious trouble.

Propagandists quickly got to work. If to some she seemed to be a well-placed pro-Boer seeking to undermine British morale, there were others who saw her as a brave woman who, driven by 'cruel necessity', had boldly exposed the darker side of the war. 'My letter', Mrs Maxwell later admitted, 'has been frequently misrepresented both by the foreign Press and by a large number of unscrupulous people at home, who quote me as an authority when they wish to accuse the Government of neglect.'[2] But concern about the letter was not confined to partisans in the press; hackles had been raised in much higher circles. This was made clear by the intervention of Lord Roberts, who was now safely installed as Commander-in-Chief of the British army. Having no direct authority over Louise Maxwell, he wired Lord Kitchener on 19 July 1901 to say that the Tory Cabinet had taken exception to General Maxwell's appeal for subscriptions to aid destitute families. 'It has given rise to statements', he said, 'that Boer families have been neglected by the government.'[3]

That Lord Roberts's complaint applied equally to General Maxwell's wife there can be little doubt. The letter to the *New York Herald* had caused a greater stir than the general's subscription list, and was far more likely to have been remarked upon by members of the Cabinet. This is probably why, just over a week later, Louise Maxwell – who had returned to England – wrote a long defensive letter to *The Times*. She emphatically denied that by appealing for clothes for Boer women and children she was accusing the British government of neglect. She had simply intended, she said,

> to provide those necessaries for the refugees, such as baby linen, children's clothes, warm petticoats etc. which do not generally form part of any stores in the field. I have been through some of the camps and no one can affirm more strongly than I that everything has been done that could be done to provide the necessary comforts and make the camps healthy and safe . . . I proceeded to raise this fund with a view to obtaining those luxuries which women and children need, but which the British taxpayer may not see the necessity of providing.[4]

Apart from its obvious contradictions – 'necessaries' become 'luxuries' within the space of a paragraph – this letter smacks too strongly of self-justification to be convincing. The impression it leaves is not of scantily-dressed children: it reads more like a letter written to order, a letter which was meant to dispel doubts about the camps and soothe General Maxwell's political critics. No doubt it helped to ensure that when some months later General Maxwell left the Transvaal, he did so with the blessings of his superiors and the reward of a knighthood.

ady Sarah Wilson in her self-
esigned war correspondent's
niform

Lady Sarah Wilson at the
entrance of her bomb-proof
shelter

The interior of Lady Sarah Wilson's bomb-proof shelter

Baden-Powell and staff in Mafeking. Seated, left to right, Colonel
Baden-Powell, Lord Edward Cecil and Captain Gordon Wilson

An idealized portrait of Lady
Sarah Wilson

Baden-Powell, 'The Hero of
Mafeking'

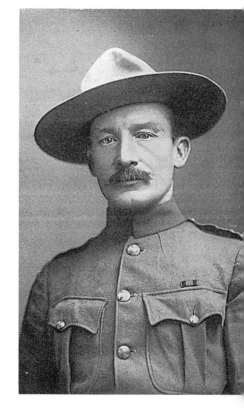

ord Roberts with his wife, elder daughter, Aileen, and his only son, rederick, who was killed at the battle of Colenso

Sir Alfred, later Lord Milner

Johanna ('Hansie') van Warmelo in her nurse's uniform

Pillars of smoke from burning Boer homes in the Transvaal

Boer families with their salvaged possessions after being evicted
from their homes

Boer families unloading from railway trucks at a concentration camp

The steely-eyed Lord
Kitchener

General John Maxwell, the
friendly military governor of
Pretoria

Emily Hobhouse, the heroine
of the concentration camps

Mrs Van Warmelo, Hansie's
redoubtable mother

The Bloemfontein concentration camp as Emily Hobhouse first
saw it

Irene concentration camp. A Boer mother holds the last surviving of her seven children

Boer women setting up home in a concentration camp

A Boer mother with her emaciated child

A brave attempt at making a garden in a concentration camp

A Camp in the Transvaal

The impact of Louise Maxwell's original letter should not, however, be underrated. It was the first public admission, from a military source, that all was not well in the concentration camps. Emily Hobhouse welcomed it with mixed feelings. Pleased with the support it gave to her own pleas for aid, she was less happy to be told, just as she was about to return to England to raise funds, that British charity was too exhausted to help Boer women and children. Since when, she wanted to know, had England 'not money enough and to spare for destitute women and children, taken willingly or unwillingly under her protection?'[5] All the same, she recognized Louise Maxwell as a potential ally and wrote to her from Bloemfontein asking for further information about the Transvaal camps. Unfortunately, by the time her letter reached Pretoria, Mrs Maxwell had already left the country. The reply Emily eventually received from General Maxwell was sympathetic but not really helpful.

Emily, it seemed, was doomed to be denied the Transvaal. Forbidden to go there herself, she had endless difficulty in making the contacts she needed to complete a comprehensive report on the camps. But she was to be put in touch with a valuable informant before she sailed from Cape Town. She mentions meeting Mrs Hendrik Cloete who, it seems, offered to act as an intermediary between Emily and her mother and sister in Pretoria. Mrs Cloete was, of course, the elder sister of Hansie van Warmelo who, through her amateur espionage activities, was already sending secret messages to Cape Town. This same secrecy was to cloak the Van Warmelos' transactions with Emily Hobhouse. The only surviving evidence of contact between the three women is a report which Emily received from Hansie and later published: it is a report which – like the one Mrs Van Warmelo sent to W. T. Stead – exposed the miseries of the unhealthy Irene concentration camp.

Situated beside the railway line to Johannesburg, about 15 miles south-west of Pretoria, the Irene camp was one of the largest in the Transvaal. It had been established in December 1900 to accommodate refugees who were then housed in the so-called 'rest camp' in Pretoria. Many of these refugees were surrendered Boers, 'hands-uppers', but, as had happened in other camps, they were soon outnumbered by families who had been brought in by the military after their homes had been destroyed.

The camp's first superintendent was an English army officer, Captain Hime-Haycock but, in February 1900 he was replaced by a forty-three-year-old Afrikaans-speaking civil servant named N. J. Scholtz. Little is known about Commandant Scholtz other than that he had served in the Cape civil service for fourteen years and had applied for a post in the Transvaal shortly after the British occupied Pretoria. What soon became obvious, however, was that his appointment as superintendent at Irene was singularly ill-advised. As an Afrikaner working for the enemy he was unable to command the respect of the people in his charge and, being inexperienced and insensitive, he ruled the camp with the bluster and petty-mindedness of a tin-pot tyrant. Scholtz, says Hansie, was 'hated and feared by all'.[6]

Hansie was one of six volunteer nurses working in the camp. They had been recruited by the *Hulpkomitee* (Relief Committee), a group of Boer women who had banded together to give practical assistance to the camp inmates. The nurses had no medical training and were there simply to perform routine duties. Their motto, according to Hansie, was: 'I cling to Thee – we cling to one another.'[7]

One of the first women to volunteer as a nurse was Mrs Henrietta Armstrong, a prominent member of the *Hulpkomitee*. Despite her English-sounding name, Mrs Armstrong was a true and proud Afrikaner. She had been born Henriette Oberholzer in the Orange Free State, and at the age of twenty-eight had married John Armstrong, a Scots bank clerk who, she later discovered, was a heavy drinker and a hopeless husband. Their far from happy, childless marriage lasted – on and off – for over nine years. They were finally forced to separate when John Armstrong, a British citizen, was refused permission to remain in the Transvaal when war was declared. How much her unfortunate marriage affected Mrs Armstrong's attitude towards the British is not certain, but there can be no doubt about her loyalty towards her own people. It was a loyalty which intensified after the departure of her husband. During the early months of the war she worked as a field nurse with the Transvaal Red Cross, accompanying the wounded on ambulance trains to Pretoria. After the British occupation she became an early visitor to the refugees in the 'rest camp' and when the camp was transferred to Irene she helped to found the *Hulpkomitee*. At the beginning of April 1901 she and a younger woman, Christina Malherbe, were the first two volunteer 'nurses' to be allowed to work in the Irene camp.

A glimpse of what the camp was like under Commandant Scholtz is given in the makeshift diary kept by Mrs Armstrong. The two volunteers were clearly not welcome. On their first day, after a perfunctory interview with Scholtz, they were handed over to an army doctor who immediately passed them on to the camp's only nurse. The nurse was less off-hand but no more encouraging. She pointed out where they could pitch their two bell-tents, took them on a tour of the camp, explained what was expected of them and then, at the first opportunity, departed for a three-day jaunt in Johannesburg, leaving them to cope as best they could.

They found themselves adrift in a sea of misery. Not only were there well over three hundred reported cases of sickness in the camp, but a stream of new arrivals was admitted almost every day. More than eighty families arrived during the first week, some of them injured on the journey, others with children missing, a few almost too weak to walk and all of them exhausted and needing attention. Children and old people died daily. The two women divided the camp between them; when they met in the evening they would report how many deaths had occurred in each section and how many cases had been sent to hospital. Mrs Armstrong quickly came to dread making a round of the tents for fear of what she might hear or see. She had her favourites among the sick children and was heartbroken when one of her 'little pets' died. Things were not helped by the repeated rainstorms, which made sleeping in the tents almost unendurable. Appeals to Scholtz for the most basic assistance had little or no effect. 'A man without a heart', wrote Mrs Armstrong bitterly; 'I would like to see his wife and children in a camp and receive such treatment as he gives.'[8]

When the flighty nurse eventually returned she was sacked and replaced by the more efficient Nurse Walsh. But this in no way lessened the demands on Mrs Armstrong and Christina Malherbe, who sometimes had to take over night duty at the hospital to give the overworked nurse a rest. It became more and more obvious that, with the rapid overcrowding and the lack of a paid staff, the burden placed on the two volunteer nurses was too great for them to shoulder alone. Mrs Armstrong, going over Scholtz's head, protested to General Maxwell. He gave her permission to enlist four more women. Two of these new recruits started work on 3 May and the other two, Hansie van Warmelo and Hester Celliers – sister of a well-known Afrikaans poet, Jan Celliers – arrived just over a week later.

Irene, unlike some of the camps seen by Emily Hobhouse, appeared in the early days to be a planned and orderly settlement. The tents were laid out with military precision in rows of thirty, each tent and each row being numbered. A brick hospital, with two large wards, was situated a little way from the camp and around it were pitched seven marquees to accommodate additional patients. There was also a small tent which served as a dispensary. Shortly after Hansie arrived, the volunteer nurses were prevented from working at the hospital, where the staff was exclusively English-speaking. Consequently, she told Emily Hobhouse, it was 'in very little favour with the Boers. We seldom succeeded in persuading the women to allow their children to be sent there, which was a great pity, because the hospital patients have every care and comfort. When there are quite 500 serious cases in camp, there are from 15 to 20 in hospital, never more, and many of these are brought in by force or after much persuasion.'[9]

The work of the 'Irene Camp Sisters', as they were known, was governed by a set of regulations drawn up after consultation with General Maxwell. Signed by the secretary of the *Hulpkomitee*, they included certain rules to be observed: no one was to stay in the camp more than a month at a time; no one could leave her post, except for serious illness, without permission; no politics were to be discussed and anyone found doing so would be dismissed immediately; no favouritism or prejudice (that is, no distinction between hands-uppers and people whose homes had been destroyed) was to be shown towards any of the inmates; no medicine was to be administered without the permission of a doctor. These rules were not always followed to the letter; there were times when they were used to discredit the volunteer nurses.

Hansie van Warmelo was assigned to a section of the camp which was later described as 'much worse' than any other in Irene. She had 150 tents to inspect every day and she had to make a note of any sickness, sending the more serious cases to the doctor. Most of the tents were woefully overcrowded – in one tent there were three families, twenty people in all, eleven of whom were ill – and living conditions were intolerable. 'Some of my tents', says Hansie, 'were the oblong ones, lined, but the majority were bell-shaped and unlined, bitterly cold at night and intensely warm during the day. Even in the winter the heat during the day is almost unbearable in those bell-tents . . . I made many complaints about the overcrowding, and earned for myself the name of "Agitator". Once I appealed directly to the Governor, General Maxwell, but he said there was nothing to be done, the empty tents would be required for new arrivals.'[10]

By the end of her first day she was utterly exhausted and found it difficult to overcome her feeling of depression, but things were to get much worse. That week there were twelve deaths in the camp but this increased steadily until, by the middle of June, the weekly toll had risen to twenty-seven. Then, says Hansie, 'the following week, to our horror, it was 47 and since then it has been 45 each week.' There was an epidemic of measles raging through the camp at the time, she explained, 'the children died in hundreds of the complications which followed – bronchitis, pleurisy and bronchial pneumonia. For the month of June we had no less than 137 deaths . . . and of these quite 100 were children under 5 years of age.'[11]

Attending victims of the measles was a nerve-shattering experience. Hansie found herself stepping through rows of wasted children, packed together 'like herrings' with hardly any standing room between them, in stifling tents with little or no bedding. She had almost nothing to offer in the way of comforts and often had difficulty persuading them to collect their medicine. 'Poor people,' she wrote in her diary. 'They must wait so long, sometimes hours, before they can be helped.'

'Conditions in camp', she noted on her second day, 'are a hundred times worse than I expected, and there is much more to do than I could possibly have imagined . . . Oh! the little ones suffer unspeakably . . . It breaks my heart and I feel so helpless. I am still not used to my work. The doctor was cross with me because I took him to the patients . . . he said that those who could walk must go to the surgery to see him, that he had no time to go round the camp: this is true – the doctors have more to do than they can manage, but why only two doctors?'[12] She was apparently unaware then that the following day one of the doctors, Dr Hamilton, was to be transferred to a camp at Volksrust and his replacement would not arrive for two days. In the meantime, regulations had to be stretched to allow Henrietta Armstrong to assist the remaining doctor with operations.

Hansie was not given a tent of her own until she had been at the camp for two days. She moved in with a deep sense of relief. 'Bed, beloved bed is the most pleasant of all,' she confessed, 'and I am thankful that I have brought my own sheets and pillow cases. Everything is so wonderfully clean after tramping from early morning till late night in the sun, over rocks.'[13] Even so, surrounded by so much suffering, she found it difficult to sleep. 'For my spirit there is no rest,' she wrote after a restless night. 'I'm not complaining about the physical discomforts – that is nothing – but the gnawing pain in my heart! Thoughts of the future depress me. What will happen to all these people, when will they be allowed to return to their devastated farms? Not one will have a roof over their heads, not a stick of furniture, no money, no clothes . . .'

Hansie estimated that when she started work at Irene, there were about 5000 people in the camp, but she was exaggerating somewhat. Two months before she arrived the population was put at 3703, and after that it is thought to have fluctuated between 4000 and 4700 (although at one time it did rise briefly to 5641). Precise figures are difficult to arrive at but, whatever those figures might be, it is certain that during 1901 Irene – like most of the concentration camps – experienced a huge increase in population. This was due to the more brutal tactics adopted by the new British Commander-in-Chief, Lord Kitchener.

Chillingly handsome and steely eyed, the fifty-year-old Lord Kitchener was a dedicated, strong-willed and ambitious soldier. Like his predecessor, Lord Roberts, he had set his sights beyond the outcome of the war in South Africa. Where Roberts had aimed at becoming Commander-in-Chief of the British army, Kitchener was every bit as intent on becoming Commander-in-Chief in India.

That post had fallen vacant on the premature death, in March 1900, of Sir William Lockhart, and although an acting Commander-in-Chief had taken over until 1903 (when Lockhart's term of office should have expired) Kitchener remained determined, despite opposition in the War Office, to claim the permanent appointment. This made him increasingly impatient to end the war in South Africa; for, unlike Lord Roberts, he had no desire to leave the country before a final settlement was reached. He was far too conscious of his reputation as a hero of past campaigns to leave this one undecided. The Boer commandos, he insisted, must be defeated at all costs. In a confidential memorandum circulated shortly after Kitchener assumed command, an indication of the methods he intended to adopt was made clear.

The General Commanding in Chief is desirous that all possible measures shall be taken to stop the present guerrilla warfare.

Of the various measures suggested for the accomplishment of this object, one which has been strongly recommended . . . is the removal of all men, women and children and natives from the districts which the enemy's bands presently occupy. This course has been pointed out by surrendered burghers, who are anxious to finish the war, as the most effective method of limiting the endurance of the guerrillas as the men and women left on farms, if disloyal, willingly supply burghers, if loyal, dare not refuse to do so. Moreover seeing the unprotected state of women now living out in the Districts, this course is desirable to ensure their not being insulted or molested by natives.

Lord Kitchener desires that General Officers will, according to the means at their disposal, follow this system in the districts which they occupy or may traverse . . . It should be clearly explained to burghers in the field that if they voluntarily surrender they will be allowed to live with their families in the camp until it is safe for them to return to their homes.[14]

Those removed from their homes in this way were to be taken to the nearest concentration camp where the families of surrendered Boers were to be given preference over those whose menfolk were with the commandos. No 'natives' were to be removed from their kraals and only 'such kaffirs and their stock as are on Boer farms' were to be removed to camps, where they would be employed at 'native rates' of pay. All of which was very different from anything officially condoned by Lord Roberts. No longer was there talk of reprisals for attacks on railway lines, or of isolated farms and suspect families being singled out for punishment: now it was entire districts that were to be cleared of families, be they loyal or disloyal, white or black, surrendered Boers or commandos' dependents. All decisions were to be left to officers who settled in or passed through a district and no questions were to be asked before removals were ordered.

The implementation of Kitchener's orders, which were circulated at the end of December 1900, accounted for the influx of 'refugees' which Emily Hobhouse saw or heard about at Bloemfontein, Aliwal North and Springfontein as well as the stream of new arrivals who daily crowded into Irene. Later it was to be claimed that the military had magnanimously provided shelter for women and children who had been left to fend for themselves while their menfolk were on commando. The indiscriminate nature of Kitchener's orders shows this to have been far from the case. Although mention is made of possible insults or molestation from the 'natives', this is incidental to the primary purpose of clearing the districts. Nor is it easy, against this background, to accept Alfred Milner's explanation of the high rate of mortality in the camps. This, he claims, was 'mainly due to the deplorable state of starvation and sickness in which great numbers of the people arrived at the camps, and which rendered them easy victims to the attack of epidemic diseases.'[15] Why should people who had lived healthily in the veld all their lives, suddenly become debilitated in great numbers on their way to the camps? Why should women whom Kitchener accused of supplying the commandos with food, be starving when his soldiers removed them from their homes? Even Milner later had second thoughts about the offering of such lame excuses.

Kitchener, at first, made no attempt to copy Lord Roberts in sending the women through the lines to the commandos. On the contrary, he regarded the women as bait for luring the men back to their farms. He said as much in a telegram to the War Office, and later employed Boer renegades – such as Adriaan Hofmeyer and Piet De Wet (brother of the guerrilla leader) – to try to talk the women in the camps into getting their husbands and brothers to surrender. It took him a long time to realize that these tactics simply strengthened the women's determination to keep the commandos in the field. The surprising thing is that Kitchener thought such a gambit would work. He had no illusions about the women who, he had earlier told Roberts, were 'keeping up the war and are far more bitter than the men'.

In January 1901, Kitchener embarked upon his great series of 'drives'. These were part of a plan by which thousands of soldiers were sent into the country to burn farmhouses, destroy livestock and confiscate supplies in a determined attempt to starve out the commandos. It was an extension of Roberts's scorched earth policy and was to lead to the building of lines of blockhouses and barbed-wire fences which criss-crossed the veld and acted as barriers, preventing the guerrillas from moving easily from one area to another. The effect of these drives on the civilian population was catastrophic. Typical of the many accounts given of the widespread devastation was that of a British woman, Mrs Bodde, who returned to England from the Transvaal where she had visited the camp at Irene.

There is no truth in the statement, which to my surprise I find repeated in London, that the women and children went to the camps by their own consent, or are willing to remain there. In almost every case, these women, with their little ones, have been taken by force from their homes at a moment's notice. They have not even been allowed to take a morsel of food, or to be removed in their own carts. They were taken by the soldiers, and put into open cattletrucks and waggons, while their own beautiful waggons, carts, and vehicles were burnt before their eyes.

The work of the destruction of the goods of these unfortunate people was not by any means confined to food-stuffs or to houses that might shelter the enemy. Thousands of bales of valuable wool . . . were destroyed by first saturating them with paraffin oil, and then setting them on fire. Bales of wool cannot be used for food.

The impression seems to prevail in this country that the work of farm-burning has ceased. Nothing could be further from the truth. When a sweeping operation takes place, and a column goes out for the purpose of denuding the country of supplies, the farmhouses are uniformly first gutted and usually set on fire . . . The work of destruction is usually done in a desperate hurry, for the soldiers are afraid that they might be surprised by the Boers in the midst of their work. They therefore usually set a house on fire, or blow up the walls with dynamite if it is strongly built. The crops are destroyed, hundreds of bags of grain are ripped open and trampled under foot, fruit trees are cut down, and all this is done in a few hours. In most of these homes are stored excellent tents . . . but no woman was allowed to bring with her a tent to protect her from the sun by day or the cold by night. The tents were burnt with all the other furniture of the household; and, thus beggared and homeless, they were carted off across the veld, and consigned to the camps, in which they remain prisoners to this day.[16]

Endless stories were told of the wanton destruction of personal goods by the soldiers. Word of this got back to Kitchener, who was also told of cases where 'sick and delicate women and children have been moved without adequate arrangements being made.'[17] To his credit, he immediately tried to check this brutal behaviour. 'Where it is impossible to make provision,' he ordered, 'the inhabitants are not to be moved until proper arrangements can be made.' But, as Professor S. B. Spies has pointed out, no steps were taken to punish officers who did not comply with this order.

That Kitchener should have concerned himself with the fashion in which the women were treated was, in a way, surprising. As Emily Hobhouse had noted, he was notorious for his dislike of the opposite sex. His attitude towards women refugees was not so much one of malevolence, as of disdain: he appeared to regard women as a completely alien species. This had been made apparent to Queen Victoria and her daughter when he visited Balmoral after his Egyptian campaign. During dinner he happened to mention that, after the capture of Omdurman, he had been greatly inconvenienced by having been left with two thousand Sudanese women on his hands. When Princess Beatrice asked what these women were like, Kitchener looked puzzled: 'They talk a great deal,' he said, after a pause, 'like *all* you women do.' A lady-in-waiting considered him 'very brusque and dumb'.[18]

There can be little doubt that Kitchener would have welcomed the end of the concentration camp system. He saw himself as a soldier, not a civil administrator, and resented having to accept responsibility for non-combatants. The Boers, in his opinion, were little more than 'savages with only a thin white veneer' and he would gladly have packed them all off to a remote island. At one stage he actually suggested sending all prisoners-of-war to Fiji or Madagascar and letting their families join them there. 'We should then only have the surrendered burghers left,' he said, 'and the country would be safe and available for white colonists.' For the most part he kept well away from the camps, but this did not prevent him voicing his opinions about the inmates. 'The Boer woman in the refugee camp', he declared, 'who slaps her protruding belly at you and shouts "When all our men are gone, these little Khakis will fight you," is a type of savage produced by generations of wild lonely life. Back on their farms and their life on the veldt, they will be just as uncivilized as ever and a constant danger. Change their country and they may become civilized people to live with.'[19]

This anti-Boer outburst was part of a letter which Kitchener wrote, in June 1901, to St John Brodrick, the Tory minister who had succeeded Lord Lansdowne as Secretary of State for War. Both in its tone and in its wild proposals, it reflects the Commander-in-Chief's frustration and impatience with the progress of the war. Not only had he failed to trounce the commandos but there was reason to think that his military reputation was under threat. This was reflected in the growing scandal surrounding the concentration camp policy. As early as 26 April, St John Brodrick had warned him that most Liberals and quite a few Conservatives were 'hot on the humanitarian tack'.[20] The more pressing the problem became, the more people were herded into camps, the louder grew the political criticism which could affect his promotion. Kitchener's mind was as much on India as on South Africa.

'At night the camp is very quiet,' wrote Hansie van Warmelo on 20 May. 'Most tents are dark and only the sound of coughing can be heard. Here and there a light burns where people are singing psalms, or a child's voice can be heard, or where bibles are being read, mostly by a young girl in the family, the one who is better "educated". It is wonderful to see how resigned some of the poor people seem. Sometimes, when I wake, I hear singing in the camp . . . On Sundays there is no end to the music and in various tents people come together to sing psalms.'[21]

Tranquil interludes in the Irene camp were rare. The inmates had too much to battle against. With the approach of the southern winter the weather had turned bitterly cold and in the tents most nights were spent nursing sick children, comforting them and trying to keep them warm. In their diaries both Hansie and Mrs Armstrong complain about the effects of the cold winds, the inadequacy of the tents, and wonder how families without blankets manage to survive. Many of them, of course, did not. Every day Mrs Armstrong totalled the number of deaths in the camp and found that there were few nights when one or more of the children did not die. 'Sometimes,' wrote the dispirited Hansie, 'I feel as if I will go mad with all the sorrow. My poor children are dying by the dozen.'[22]

There were then two doctors – an Afrikaner, Dr Neethling, had replaced Dr Hamilton – and two trained nurses in the camp but, even with the help of the volunteer nurses, the hospital was pitifully understaffed. The volunteers could only undertake the simplest medical duties and professional nursing was urgently needed for the seriously sick children. This was a need which could, and should, have been met, for there was no longer a shortage of trained nurses in South Africa.

Following the tragic typhoid epidemic in Bloemfontein, well over a hundred additional nurses had been despatched from England and many of them had followed the army to the Transvaal. Arriving in Pretoria, shortly after the occupation, Violet Brooke-Hunt, a voluntary social worker, had found the hospitals 'well staffed and amply provided for'; indeed, she says, 'many of the more enthusiastic nursing sisters complained that they had "not enough to do".'[23] At that time the typhoid scare had not ended; in November 1900, for instance, Queen Victoria's grandson Prince Christian Victor was among the soldiers in Pretoria who died from typhoid, and that same month Lord Roberts had to delay his departure from South Africa because his elder daughter, Aileen, was seriously ill with the fever. But the outbreak of measles at Irene came months later, and by then there must have been enough idle nurses in Pretoria to assist at the camp's understaffed hospital.

Dreadful as was the catalogue of disease and death, tensions were made worse by the divisions which plagued the camp. Kitchener's policy of granting privileges to surrendered Boers had created hostility and suspicion between them and the families of men on commando.

The fact that in the early days there had been differences in the rations given to the two sections – only hands-uppers were allowed meat – had sparked off feuds which lasted long after such blatant partiality ended. The wives of fighting men could never forget that their children had been denied food because their fathers were on commando. Hansie shared their resentment of the hands-uppers to the full.

'It was a terrible life in the camp,' she wrote. 'We were ringed in by enemies and traitors; spies listened to every conversation; no one was safe or relaxed; no one could trust anyone; and everywhere the bleeding hearts of mothers, who must see their children starve; of women anxious and tense about their fighting husbands and sons; and yet the longer they suffered the more worthy they were of honour and respect for their heroic qualities, their trust and their unshakeable belief in God.'[24]

Attempts were made to break the spirit of any rebellious women. The 'punishment kraal' for trouble-makers was a wire enclosure, surrounded by thorn branches and set among bare rocks, some distance from the rows of tents and close to the latrines. Here any woman judged to be subversive or simply defiant – 'unruly' was the word most often used – could be penned up for a day or even longer, depending on the offence. Hansie considered it a 'most barbaric institution'. One of the worst cases she heard of occurred after she had left the camp. A certain Miss Lotter, she says, was shut up in the wire enclosure with a 'Kaffir' and two 'coolies' (Indians) for a whole day. It had rained the day before very heavily and she was on wet ground all day without food; when she returned to her tent that night, she gave birth to a stillborn child. Hearing about this Mrs Armstrong had protested heatedly to General Maxwell, only to be told that it had been necessary to 'make an example of the woman'.

Hansie was appalled. 'This scandalous deed,' she fumed: 'imprisoning a "daughter of the Transvaal" with coloured people.'[25] The mere suggestion of racial mixing put Hansie on the defensive. Such were her prejudices that she firmly believed black people should be taught their place and kept under the thumb of the Boers. She refused to accept that there were women who sought refuge in the concentration camps because they could not look after themselves or manage their African labourers.

'The absence of their menfolk on commando made no difference to them,' she told Emily Hobhouse; 'sowing and ploughing and reaping went on as usual under the superintendence of the women, who were better off for native servants during the war than in times of peace, because the Kaffirs were afraid of the Boers, and eager to remain friends with them.' A Boer woman, she insisted, was better able to control her workforce than was any Englishman. 'Throughout the whole war,' she boasted, 'the attitude of the natives has been most favourable, and it is only in the districts occupied by British troops that they became insolent and aggressive.'[26] Hansie seems never to have forgotten the spectacle of Africans dancing on the pavements when the British marched into Pretoria.

There was little variation in the routine of the volunteer nurses. Most of the morning would be spent in visiting the tents, issuing orders for milk, medicine and food where necessary, making a note of any serious illnesses so that they could bring the doctor to them in the afternoon, and giving whatever encouragement, comfort and advice they could. According to Hansie, the people came to look on these visits as 'the one bright spot in their dreary existence'.

From time to time members of the *Hulpkomitee* would arrive with supplies of clothing collected from sympathizers in Pretoria. They were always welcome but, in the early days, the clothing had to be kept out of sight of the camp authorities. 'If it falls into the hands of the Commandant [Scholtz],' noted Henrietta Armstrong, 'no fighting man's wife will ever get a yard of it.'[27] Later, as a result of an appeal made through the *Hulpkomitee*, boxes of supplies began to arrive from abroad. A Dutch support group sent dress materials and flannelette for the women to make their clothes; an English pro-Boer charity sent warm children's garments for the winter months. ('It's nice to know', Mrs Armstrong wrote in her diary; 'there are a few English women who care for us here in the Camp.') So great was the response, from Pretoria as well as overseas, that an extra tent was needed to house all the stores; but, as Hansie ruefully observed, it would have required more than private charity to 'make life in the camp endurable for women and children.'

On 21 May, Mrs Van Warmelo visited the Irene camp for the first time. Like most new visitors she found it a harrowing experience. The sight of the gaunt, helpless women with their hollow-eyed, pathetically thin children was to haunt her for months. Returning to Harmony that night she was unable to sleep and, says Hansie, lay awake wondering what she could do 'to save her country-women from suffering and death.' Then it was that she hit upon the idea of drawing up a petititon and presenting it to the diplomatic corps in Pretoria. Getting up at three in the morning, she took her writing materials to the dining room and dashed off a passionate appeal for help in the name of the women of Pretoria. After describing the conditions at Irene, she attacked those responsible for the suffering.

> We are convinced that this pitiful state of affairs is aggravated by rough and heartless men such as Superintendent Scholtz at Irene. The women prefer to starve and suffer with their children, even when twenty are herded together in one tent, almost without bedding, rather than expose themselves to insults when they approach with their needs. Is it considered such a crime in these present days to fight for home and independence, that it is wreaked on defenceless women and helpless children, in order to compel the brave little handful of lion-hearted men to surrender? We earnestly beseech you to take steps without delay to relieve the sufferings of these unfortunate beings . . . With the approaching winter in view there is no time to be lost. Help us, in God's name and in the name of humanity.[28]

She took the petition first to the consul for the Netherlands, Mr Domela Nieuwenhuis, who advised her to consult her old friend, the Portuguese consul and doyen of the diplomatic corps, Mr Cinatti. After reading it, Cinatti agreed to support it and suggested that his hand would be strengthened if it were signed by some of the leading women in Pretoria. Nine prominent women readily gave their signatures which, by common consent, were kept secret. Cinatti then met with his fellow consuls, who endorsed his proposal to have the petition translated into French – with simply the words 'nine signatures' at the bottom – and sent to their governments. A copy was also sent to Lord Kitchener.

Mrs Van Warmelo waited anxiously for Kitchener's reply. She was disappointed. The only reaction from the British authorities came a few days later when General Maxwell sent for Mr Cinatti and demanded the names of the women who had signed the petition. These Cinatti refused to disclose. He explained that even the consuls had not been given the names of the nine signatories, although they did know who had drawn up the petition. When Maxwell asked who that was, Cinatti again pleaded diplomatic privilege and refused to name Mrs Van Warmelo. Hansie was immensely proud of the risks taken by her mother. She claims the military were relentless in their efforts to find out who was behind the petition.

Receiving no reply from Kitchener, Mrs Van Warmelo waited five weeks and then drew up a second, more sharply worded, petition. This drew attention to the rise in the death rate during the winter months and pleaded with foreign governments to intervene. 'For our men we ask nothing . . .' it argued, 'but for their imprisoned families we demand from mighty and wealthy England, sufficient and better food, warm clothing and bedding.'[29] This time the consuls in Pretoria decided to act. They formed a committee of three – Portugal, Austria and Germany – and applied for permission to inspect the Irene camp. General Maxwell knew better than to refuse. He invited 'the entire Diplomatic Corps' to spend a day with him at the camp.

Hansie was not at Irene when the consuls visited the camp in July. She had finished working there a few days earlier after assisting Dr Kendal Franks – who had been asked by Kitchener to report on all the concentration camps – on a day-long inspection. She had guided the doctor through rows of her 'prize tents' and was rewarded by seeing that he 'seemed much struck by the extreme poverty and misery there'. In one tent he examined two little boys who were dying and admitted that there was no hope for them. Later, in his report, he conceded that the condition of the inmates 'in the ward under Miss Van Warmelo . . . was much worse than in any other portion of the camp' and deplored the appalling overcrowding in tents where 'all had measles'.[30] This was the legacy which Hansie handed over to her replacement, Miss Westmaas.

The only report of the Diplomatic Corps's visit is that which the consuls produced themselves. It supported everything said by Mrs Van Warmelo and the volunteer nurses. Comparing what they had seen at Irene with official statistics for the other concentration camps, the consuls concluded that unless something was done to arrest the death rate the Boer population in the camps would be extinct within three years. The number of deaths in the camps, they claimed, was fourteen times the normal rate for Pretoria, and child mortality was increasing alarmingly. They agreed that lack of nutritious food, inadequate shelter, scarcity of clothing and blankets, overcrowding, shortage of medical facilities and poor sanitation had all contributed to this abnormal death rate.

Hansie was convinced that this report and her mother's petitions were responsible for the British government appointing a commission to investigate conditions in the camps. There may be some truth in this, but there were also other agencies at work. Not least of those advocating a full-scale investigation was the indefatigable Miss Emily Hobhouse, who was then alerting Britain in a well-publicized and highly controversial one-woman crusade.

11

Reporting Back

EMILY'S VOYAGE home on the RMS *Saxon* had not been without
interest. She made friends with Mrs Van Warmelo's younger sister
Catherina and her husband, P. J. Potgieter, the former mayor of
Pretoria, who having been ordered to leave South Africa by Lord
Roberts were on their way to Germany with their ten children. 'What
a family to travel with!' wrote Emily to Mrs Murray. 'A host, an
army!'[1] Nevertheless she warmed to Mr Potgieter and welcomed his
help in brushing up her Afrikaans. A less pleasant passenger was the
time-serving dominie Adriaan Hofmeyer, who claimed to be travelling
to England at the invitation of Joseph Chamberlain. The most important person on board, however, was Sir Alfred Milner who was returning to England on three months' leave. He was the passenger Emily
most wanted to speak to but, as he kept himself aloof and let it be
known that he did not wish to see any lady, a meeting seemed out of
the question.

But Emily did not give up easily. She took to frequenting the upper
deck, where Milner was known to sit, and she claims that he did once
speak to her there. Unfortunately it was a very gusty day and no sooner
had Emily plunged into what she called 'my subject' than they were
cut short by a 'cruel and noisy windlass'. Not until the ship was leaving
Madeira did she get another chance to corner Sir Alfred. She found
him sitting alone on the upper deck and again launched into her
'subject'. Milner, who had just heard he was to be met by the prime
minister and received by King Edward VII (Queen Victoria had died
in January) when he arrived in London, was at his most charming.

He listened to Emily patiently and even encouraged her to talk by saying he had been sent some sixty-four reports about her activities in South Africa. This both astonished and alarmed Emily, as she was aware of what some of those reports must have contained. She immediately tried to defend herself by explaining how various officials, including the admired commandant at Springfontein, had tried to inveigle her into discussing politics, and how she refused to be caught out by them. It is doubtful whether Milner believed her. The accusation of talking politics was levelled at Emily too often to be lightly dismissed. She was a political animal with strong opinions, and it is most unlikely that she would have kept those opinions to herself. That they could be regarded as legitimate and were in no way subversive did not prevent her opponents from accusing her of treachery.

For all that, she and Milner appeared to part amicably. He even said that if he allowed anyone to visit the concentration camps again, he would prefer it to be Emily. He warned her, however, that he had not made up his mind about this and would first have to consult the Colonial Office. They promised to write to each other in England.

Milner's proviso concerning Emily's future work in the camp should have alerted her. Indeed, she had every reason to doubt his sincerity. Not only had his private secretary succeeded in having her shunned by the other passengers, but he had been heard to say that it was useless her being taught Afrikaans by Mr Potgieter as she would not be allowed to return to South Africa. This was an indication of how Milner, for all his apparent friendliness, regarded Emily. He had no intention of writing to her in England and, as she later discovered, he fully supported all the official moves made against her. She was an embarrassment whom no political administrator could publicly acknowledge. Milner's return to England was to prove one of the highlights of his career. He was fêted by politicians, hailed by the press, given the freedom of the city of London and raised to the peerage as Lord Milner of St James and of Cape Town. That the disgrace of the concentration camps should be allowed to tarnish all this was unthinkable.

Years later Emily was to sum up her feelings about Milner to her friend Mrs Steyn. 'There were two Alfred Milners', she wrote, '– there was the charming, sympathetic, gracious and cultivated man, whose abilities and culture found rather a desert in South Africa, and whose really liberal leanings were in contrast to the military men surrounding him, and there was the politician who had given his word to carry out the ideas of the English statesmen and felt bound in honour to do so.

The clash must have given him many dolorous moments of extreme agony.'[2] Others have judged the man and the politician more harshly.

On reaching England at the end of May, Emily was saddened to find that the British public still had little idea of what was happening to the Boer women and children. So widespread was the ignorance, she claims, that the editor of a prominent London newspaper was under the impression that there was only one women's camp in South Africa, somewhere in the vicinity of Cape Town. That the government was doing its best to play down the scandal of the camps came as no surprise; what shocked Emily was that neither Lady Hobhouse nor the committee of the Distress Fund had acted on her requests to have extracts from her letters published in the press. The reason for this, she discovered, was that her brother Leonard had advised against publication. He and Lady Hobhouse had discussed the matter and decided that publicity was bound to have an adverse effect, that the authorities would step in and put a stop to Emily's work in the camps. It would be better, they advised the committee of the Distress Fund, to wait for her to return, when she would be free to launch a fund-raising campaign herself. Emily later came to recognize the wisdom of her brother's caution.

But it made her task all the more urgent. She got started right away. After spending a few days with Lord and Lady Hobhouse in Oxfordshire, she returned to her Chelsea flat and set to work. On advice from her family, she decided that before doing anything else she would present her findings to the Government. This seemed all the more necessary after the Secretary of State for War, St John Brodrick, made a speech in Parliament, trotting out all the old specious arguments. Boer women, he blandly announced, were flocking to the camps for food and 'protection against the Kaffirs',[3] some 20,000 to 40,000 women had sought asylum; there was 'no occasion in which these camps' food ran short', and there had been 'immense improvements' in living conditions. This, in itself, would have been sufficient to goad Emily into action. She wrote to St John Brodrick requesting an interview, and was immediately given an appointment at the War Office for 4 June. Her brother helped her draw up a list of points to be raised.

Emily was again made nervous by the thought of interviewing a minister at the War Office. She should have known herself better. Once she got in her stride there was no stopping her. For over an hour she lectured Brodrick on conditions in the camps, stressing that 'the great majority were there by compulsion and were prisoners not allowed to leave'. Brodrick appears to have been mesmerized. 'It was nearly 2 p.m. when he glanced at the clock,' Emily reported. 'I took it as a hint and rose. He had been most willing to listen, perhaps what appalled me was finding a Minister in such ignorance of what was being done under his rule.' Later she was to elaborate on this by describing Brodrick to her brother as agreeable but slippery and mediocre. She seems to have been unable to shift his view that the military had been right in setting up the camps. He was, she said, 'ready to listen, ready also to drift.'[4]

Before she left, Brodrick asked her to write down the suggestions she had made, and that same afternoon she handed in the list at the War Office. She had got through the interview by clinging to the belief that, as she had repeatedly told the Boer women, the people of England would never tolerate the suffering in the camps once it became known. But she had reckoned without the die-hard politicians who, angered by the prolongation of the war, lacked the imagination to accept a change of policy.

While waiting for Brodrick's response to her suggestions, Emily found plenty to keep her busy. Her uncle had warned her not to expect too much from the War Office, saying that the only thing that would move the Government was public opinion. This decided Emily to waste no more time and to arrange for extracts from her letters to be published. The threepenny pamphlet appeared in the form of a report to the committee of the Distress Fund and was circulated to newspapers and MPs. It created the sort of stir for which Emily had been hoping. Newspaper opinion tended to be divided along party political lines but even *The Times* – soon to be one of Emily's harshest critics – acknowledged that there were 'a great many deficiencies' in the camps and spoke of 'some pathetic instances of children dying amid the comfortless and unfamiliar surroundings'. It would 'not appear', the paper remarked tartly, 'that the narrators were subjected to any searching cross-examination by Miss Hobhouse.' Others criticized her for the tone of the report and for her use of 'emotional adjectives'.

Among her more virulent critics were the English-language newspapers in South Africa. These accused her of having a superficial knowledge of the country, of knowing nothing of the normal rough existence of the Boers and of being unacquainted with the precariousness of veld life. One incident in particular was singled out to illustrate her naïvety. This was the account of her attacking a snake with her parasol in the Bloemfontein camp. The snake, it was said, was probably a harmless house snake, easily recognized by a South African.

Emily was stoutly defended by the pro-Boer *South African News*. 'The "Argus"' it declared, attacking its Cape Town rival, 'goes to the lowest depth by insinuating doubts of the lady's personal veracity, basing the cowardly suggestion on a little anecdote about a snake . . . She simply records the mistake which the people there made in calling the reptile a puff-adder . . . But we do not expect every lady from England to know the names of our snakes by instinct. And we know of some ladies in South Africa who would not have waited even to be told the name of the snake but would have fled shrieking and given that tent a wide berth for a month.' The paper, more pertinently, dismissed charges of distorted adjectives. 'Indeed,' it observed, 'the whole report we find singularly admirable for its self-restraint in the use of adjectives . . . And if people talk of the rough conditions of veld-life, we simply ask whether ever before among these farm folk there has been a mortality of 250 per thousand, or even one tenth of that fearful rate.'

Accusations of exaggeration and gullibility were to follow Emily for months and, trivial as it was, the snake story never failed to draw a sneer. She found these attacks more amusing than offensive and rarely replied to them. As far as she was concerned they were irrelevant to the serious issues she had raised.

To coincide with the publication of the report, the Distress Fund committee booked the Queen's Hall for a meeting to be addressed by Emily. This was more than the government would allow. 'The Bishop of Hereford promised to take the Chair,' Emily later told Mrs Steyn, 'the Hall was secured and the tickets sold, when – imagine! – the authorities got behind the scenes and pulled wires so that the lessor of the Hall broke his contract. He still owes us for the expenses incurred.' The same thing happened after the Westminster Chapel had been offered as an alternative. Emily could no longer have any doubts about what she was up against.

Nevertheless, the concentration camp issue was given a public airing on the day the report was published. It was raised by Lloyd George in an adjournment debate in the House of Commons. The indefatigable Lloyd George had never faltered in his opposition to the war. He had been physically attacked on several occasions and his public meetings had often ended in chaos, but he refused to be silenced. At a more sympathetic meeting his attack on the concentration camp system was loudly cheered. 'The Herod of old', he was reported as saying, 'sought to crush a little race by killing all the young children. It was not a success, and he would commend that story to Herod's modern imitator.' This was very much the line he took in the parliamentary debate. He accused the government of pursuing a policy of 'extermination' against women and children. It might not be a direct policy but it had the same effect. Earlier Brodrick had admitted that there were now 63,127 people, white and black, in the camps and that in May 250 children, 47 women and 39 men had died in the Transvaal camps alone. That, declared Lloyd George, proved that 'so far from this being the result of temporary conditions, it is growing worse.'[5]

But Brodrick refused to accept responsibility. The fault, he argued, lay with the commandos who had abandoned their families. He pointed out that in wartime it was hard to keep 63,000 people sheltered and fed in addition to a great army. ('So obvious is this fact', snorted Emily, 'that most people would have thought that some preparation could have been made for it.') Brodrick went on to assure the House that people returning from South Africa had told him 'that things, so far from going from bad to worse, have been steadily ameliorating.' As Emily had explained to him that any improvements in the camps had been nullified by the increasing number of families brought in, it was obvious that her pleading had been ignored. Lloyd George's motion, backed by his fellow radicals, was defeated by 252 votes against to 149 in favour.

Ten days later Emily received Brodrick's reply to her suggestions. Among other things, she had asked that women who had friends in the Cape Colony or could afford to support themselves should be allowed to leave the camps; that free passes should be issued to those wishing to work in nearby towns; that a clergyman and a bilingual matron be assigned to each camp; that new camps should be sited in healthier locations; that representatives of British philanthropic societies be given access to the camps; and that a doctor's report on the children in the Bloemfontein camp be called for and acted upon.

Brodrick's replies were evasive. Like most politicians he found it impossible to give a simple 'yes' or 'no' to a straightforward question. He agreed, for instance, to approve of women leaving the camps – a vague promise that was not fulfilled – but said there were 'grave objections' to them going to the Cape Colony. He claimed that free passes to nearby towns were issued in most camps, which was not true. He said that clergymen visited and held regular services in the camps; but, as Emily pointed out, they were needed daily for burials. He objected to the interference of philanthropic societies, saying he preferred to 'work through local committees and persons sent out by the government to act with them.' What Emily found most suspicious, however, was that wherever she had asked for equality of treatment – that is, between hands-uppers and the families of commandos – the word 'equal' had been omitted in Brodrick's reply.

Emily's response to this equivocation was polite and tactful. She appeared to take Brodrick's word seriously and was at pains to straighten out any 'misunderstandings'. Most importantly, she again pleaded for representatives of philanthropic societies to be sent to South Africa. The best persons to work with the local committees, she argued, would be those nominated by the various funds raised in England. Could not their names be submitted for government approval? 'I am not in a position to speak for other funds,' she wrote, 'but with regard to the South African Distress Fund I am authorised to state that such a mode of distribution would meet with the approval of the Committee.'[6]

What in fact she was hoping for was to be sent back to South Africa with the backing of the Government. Whether she realized it or not, there was not the remotest chance of this happening. The publicity that her brother had warned against was already producing adverse effects. The Government wanted nothing to do with the meddling Miss Hobhouse.

At the same time that Emily wrote to St John Brodrick requesting an interview, arrangements were made for her to see Sir Henry Campbell-Bannerman, the leader of the Liberal Party. At that time Campbell-Bannerman had been head of his party for just over two years and, until now, his attitude towards the war had appeared equivocal. At the outbreak of war he had supported the Government, but he had done so as a patriotic duty rather than from conviction: he had no faith in war solving the South African problem. You would never, he declared in November 1899, 'make the Boers love you by soundly thrashing them.' And why else was the war being fought? But he had to tread warily for he had the thankless task of keeping his divided party together. The war had deepened the rifts among Liberals and created two antipathetic factions: at one extreme were the pro-Boers like John Morley, Sir William Harcourt and radicals such as Lloyd George, while at the other were the Liberal imperialists (Limps) led by H. H. Asquith, Richard Haldane and Sir Edward Grey. Straddling the centre required considerable political skill. Campbell-Bannerman rarely succeeded in pleasing both factions. Not until after his meeting with Emily did he openly declare himself a pro-Boer; a position, he later told Lord Rosebery, that he had always privately favoured.

Emily went to see the Liberal leader a few days after her meeting with St John Brodrick. This time she needed no prompting from her brother. 'The interview', she was to tell Campbell-Bannerman's biographer, 'remains vivid in my mind. Of all whom I saw at that time, deeply interested as they were, he alone, greatly occupied as he was, seemed to have the leisure and the determination to hear and understand everything.' So encouraged was she by Campbell-Bannerman's obvious interest that she went into great detail; describing the camps, giving her opinion of the sub-officials she had met, retelling the stories she had heard from women whose homes had been burnt and who had arrived at the camps in tatters, deprived of clothes, bedding and other basic essentials. 'For nearly two hours', she said, 'he listened with rapt attention, now and then putting a question to elucidate a point. He left the impression of a man who spared no time or pains to arrive at the truth and in whom wisdom and humanity were paramount.'

Shortly afterwards (some accounts say it was the same evening) Campbell-Bannerman attended a dinner given by the National Reform Union at the Holborn Restaurant. He was the principal guest, and during his after-dinner speech he blurted out a phrase that was soon to become notorious. After questioning the military's demand for an unconditional surrender and echoing Emily's protests about the misery already endured by the civilian population – citing the appalling death rate in the concentration camps – he denounced all those, particularly the newspaper writers, who condoned such inhumanity.

'A phrase often used', he observed, 'was that "war is war", but when one came to ask about it one was told that no war was going on, that it was not war. When was a war not a war? When it was carried on by methods of barbarism in South Africa.'

Emily later claimed that she had heard him mutter 'methods of barbarism' under his breath while she was talking to him. How true this is, one does not know. Usually Emily was totally honest about her experiences, but on this occasion she may not have been able to resist associating herself directly with the birth of a much-quoted phrase. Strangely enough it took the press a day to recognize the significance of what the Liberal leader had said. Not until two days later did the abuse of Campbell-Bannerman begin: then it was blazoned in large type and lurid language. He was accused of having insulted the British army and of defaming the British people. He was branded a traitor and deemed not fit to lead one of the great British political parties.

The imperialist wing of the Liberal party was highly incensed. They demanded that Campbell-Bannerman explain himself more fully and pay a timely compliment to the army. But this Campbell-Bannerman refused to do. He insisted that he had meant what he said and intended to repeat it when the right opportunity arose. That opportunity came a couple of days later, when Lloyd George's motion about the concentration camps was debated in the House of Commons. Campbell-Bannerman's contribution to the debate was very much to the point.

'I never said a word', he declared, 'which would imply cruelty or even indifference on the part of officers or men in the British army. It was the whole system I consider, to use a word I have already applied to it, barbarous . . . What I object to is the whole policy of concentration, the whole policy of destroying the homes of women and children, involving them in circumstances of considerable cruelty, certainly of unintentional cruelty.' Why not, he asked, act on Miss Hobhouse's advice, and free women who could fend for themselves? Why not send out teams of properly qualified doctors and nurses to deal with the epidemics?[7]

But this was not good enough for his opponents. He was attacked in *The Times* by Lord Hugh Cecil, who claimed that the accusation of 'methods of barbarism' reflected on British army generals. Why then, Cecil wanted to know, did not Sir Henry demand the resignation of Lord Kitchener? Was he afraid that this would harm the Liberal Party? As for the suffering of women and children, had not the inhabitants of besieged towns suffered in the same way? 'We hear of women and children falling sick and dying from insanitary conditions, from insufficient or unsuitable food. Has this not happened in every blockade? . . . Yet I did not blame the Boers for so sad a consequence of their operations.'[8] This sparked off a long correspondence. One contributor remarked that the difference between a siege and the concentration camps was that a siege involved active resistance while in the camps there were only passive victims. Young Winston Churchill, probably with his aunt Sarah in mind, did not agree. 'As a matter of fact,' he wrote, 'the resistance of a hardy population scattered over a vast region and continually supplying the enemy with food and information is plainly more formidable than the resistance – if it can be called resistance – of the unhappy inhabitants of an invested town. In the former case the non-combatants undoubtedly prolong the operations; in the other, by eating up the food of the garrison, they terminate them.' He had to admit, though, that suffering in the camps had 'undoubtedly been severe.'[9]

Churchill's letter to *The Times* followed a more direct attack on Emily in the same paper. The sycophantic Adriaan Hofmeyer, anxious to prove his worth to his British political sponsors, challenged the Hobhouse report by claiming personal knowledge of the camps and their inmates. This, in the opinion of many, made his letter irrefutable. Emily's critics delighted in quoting it. According to Hofmeyer, he had been prompted to write after reading Emily's report. It would, he claimed, have been cowardly for him to remain silent. He had visited more camps than Miss Hobhouse, because he had been allowed into the Transvaal. After touring the camps he could only say that he 'thanked God that England was acting so generously and kindly towards the women and children of my poor people.' He had no doubt that the 'refugees' were grateful for the way they were treated. 'I spoke their language,' he explained, 'I met them alone and got them to pour out their hearts to me. ' (This sits rather oddly with his later admission that he was fired upon twice while on his peace mission 'amongst the people'.) Emily, on the other hand, was duped by people using her for their own ends. How could she, for instance, complain about the lack of sanitary conditions when the Boers were not accustomed to 'such luxuries, living on their farms where sanitation is never attended to?' What was so alarming about the high death rate when epidemics were frequent in the *platteland*? The cause of the death rate, he insisted, was the fact that 'it is difficult to get parents to observe doctors' orders.' The Boers enjoyed living in tents, cared little for the heat or cold and welcomed thunder-storms. No conditions, it seemed, could be too rough for his poor 'misguided countrymen'.[10]

So low, in fact, was his opinion of the people he claimed to represent that it is astonishing that anyone took him seriously. Yet they did. An editorial in *The Times* recommended that his letter be read by everyone. 'Mr Hofmeyer', it enthused, 'knows much better than she does how to get the truth from people of his own blood and his own speech . . . He is a better judge of the treatment accorded to people in these camps . . . He declares himself full of thankfulness to the British government for its humane and generous treatment of Boer families.'

In fact, news items were then reporting a new and alarming rise in the death rate in the camps.

Towards the end of June 1901, Emily began to prepare for a lecture tour of Britain. She had spoken earlier that month to a group of people, mostly women, at Lady Hobhouse's London house and had found it somewhat unnerving to address well-dressed, well-fed people so soon after leaving scenes of hunger and squalor. So she was relieved when several of them, including Mrs Humphry Ward, the novelist, came to congratulate and question her afterwards; by that time she was more used to being snubbed in London drawing rooms. Even so, Emily found the thought of a lecture tour disquieting. She discussed her prospects with Lord Ripon who, as a former cabinet minister, was well versed in public speaking. He warned her it would be hard work: it was not so much the travelling or the speaking that would tire her, he said, but the private social occasions that were all part of a lecture tour. Still, he laughed, a woman could always plead a headache.

Emily found the warning of hard work all too true. Her strength was drained by constantly having to meet new people; almost every day she found herself being greeted by an unknown host, struggling to make conversation with strangers and having to answer the same inevitable questions. One of her few consolations was that she was able to travel in comfort. Lord Hobhouse thoughtfully paid her first-class fare, which provided her with a little solitude, gave her time to think and allowed her to arrive fresh for each engagement. She soon discovered she could face an audience, even though most of them were large and occasionally rough, and was able to steel herself against the many obstacles that were placed in her way.

The opposition began to show itself before the tour began. Her first meeting was to have been in Scarborough where, on 22 June, she was booked to share a platform with Joshua Rowntree, the well-known philanthropist, who had also recently returned from South Africa. But, at the last minute, the civic authorities banned the use of the town hall and the meeting had to be cancelled. About the same time she heard that she had been refused permission to speak at the Royal Institute in Hull the following week, and her supporters had had to switch to the Friends' Meeting House in the city. This sort of thing was to happen throughout the tour, and it was invariably the Quakers who came to Emily's rescue.

Nothing interfered with the arrangements for her second meeting, in Oxford on 25 June. This was a semi-private affair held, by invitation only, at the Master's Lodge of Balliol College. Emily's speech, probably as a result of earlier criticism, was unemotional and factual. Following the line taken in her report, she acknowledged the help she had received from the military authorities, praised the efforts made by some camp officials and read from letters she had received from South Africa. She was at pains to stress that a band of women should be sent to investigate conditions in the camps, and concluded by saying she 'was sure a message of sympathy to the Dutchwomen would do more for the pacification of South Africa than the British army or the Government could do'. She was thanked by the Master of Balliol who, referring to Emily's description of the camps, declared 'this sort of thing could not possibly go on'.[11]

Emily found no reason to revise this speech during the next few weeks. Occasionally she would risk a joke or a topical remark but, for the most part, she kept to her factual account. Between 25 June and 23 July she spoke at twenty-six meetings. Most of them, she claimed, were 'a joy'. 'Their general character', she boasted, 'was orderly, interested and moved – tears I often saw. It was a feature of them that at most places the majority of the audience filed past the platform to shake hands with me.' What dismayed her was the widespread ignorance of South Africa she encountered. Few in her audiences, be they friendly or ·hostile, seemed to know the difference between the Transvaal and the Orange River Colony, the Cape and Natal.

Ignorance did not deter the hecklers. On three occasions her meetings were disrupted by organized gangs of rowdies. At Southport Emily was constantly interrupted by shouts of 'traitor' and 'where's Kruger?' and in Bristol the platform was pelted with sticks and stones (while the Quakers sang hymns to quieten things down, Emily picked up the missiles to keep as souvenirs). The demonstration staged at Darlington was an even greater challenge. Here, according to newspaper reports, a section of the audience started singing the national anthem whenever anyone on the platform rose to speak. Sir David Dale, a prominent local businessman, tried desperately to obtain order but was sung down and a plea from his wife, who was listed as a speaker, was similarly silenced. Emily remained firmly in her chair. 'We on the platform', she said, 'sat and patiently faced them while twelve or fifteen organized roughs sat in a group and howled and sang for one and a half hours. The policy of non-resistance prevailed in this Quaker town, so they were not interfered with.' The speakers sat for as long as it would have taken them to make their speeches and then left. At a meeting in Sir David Dale's house the following morning, Lady Dale apologized to Emily, saying it was the first time anybody had ever been refused a hearing in Darlington. Emily took the incident in her stride.

It was at an earlier meeting in Manchester that she was persuaded to revamp her speech. The meeting, which the authorities had tried to ban, was one of the most successful of Emily's tour. The hall was packed: included among the audience were clergymen, civic dignitaries, academics and a sprinkling of journalists. Emily, who was in good authoritative form, was given an enthusiastic hearing. In the formal vote of thanks, her speech was described as being one 'of almost fastidious painfulness in its moderation of statement. It was a woman's statement addressed to women. It was a statement that was judicious, unexaggerated and transparently true.' This, in a way, reflected the faults as well as the merits of Emily's didactic approach. Worthy as were her sentiments, she tended to present her case in a dry, somewhat schoolmistressy way, dwelling more on the facts than on the humanity of her cause. It was not that she lacked passion, indeed she was highly-strung and mettlesome, but when speaking in public she preferred to hammer home her points and keep her emotions under control. This is what struck her brother Leonard, who was in the audience at Manchester. Afterwards he tackled her about it and told her she gave too much detail. It was advice she took to heart. 'After that,' she says, 'I think I improved.'

Her brother was one of the few people whose opinion Emily respected; it is doubtful whether she would have listened to anyone else. She prided herself on being honest and objective – although others found this difficult to believe – and would rather have been judged dull than dismissed as over-emotional. She always tried to measure her arguments and was careful to guard against anyone proving her wrong. In the same way, she made a point of giving her opponents their due. What she failed to appreciate was that, in displaying fair-mindedness, she was in danger of supplying her critics with ammunition. This was something which was soon to be brought home to her.

On 4 July, two days after the Manchester meeting, the *Westminster Gazette* published a trenchant review of the Hobhouse report. Lucidly written and glibly argued it was able, by taking carefully selected passages from the report, to turn Emily's words against her.

First, I would note Miss Hobhouse's frequent acknowledgments that the various authorities were doing their best to make the conditions of Camp life as little intolerable as possible. The opening sentence of her report is, 'January 22 – I had a splendid truck given me at Cape Town through the kind co-operation of Sir Alfred

Milner . . .' In other places she refers to the help given her by various officials. The commandant at Aliwal North had ordered £150 worth of clothing, and had distributed it; she undertook to forward some of it. At Springfontein 'the commandant was a kind man, and willing to help both the people and me as far as possible.' Other similar quotations might be made . . .

Other quotations were indeed made. The article is peppered with odd incidents and remarks taken out of context. Anyone reading it might think that Emily had little but praise for the concentration camps. The more gruesome aspects of the camps are scarcely touched upon. 'There can be no doubt', it is admitted, 'that the sweeping together of about 63,000 men, women and children into these Camps must have been attended by great suffering and misery, and if they are courageously borne it is greatly to the credit of the sufferers.' But, it later remarks, 'no one can take part in war without sharing its risks, and the formation of the Concentration Camps is part of the fortune of war. In this spirit "they have agreed," as Miss Hobhouse says, "to be cheerful and make the best of it."' Only towards the end of the article is it conceded that more could be done to improve conditions in the camps.

The surprising thing about this article was not that it misrepresented Emily's words, but that it was written by a most unlikely critic. It was the work of Mrs Millicent Fawcett, a well-known Liberal crusader, the widow of a radical politician, an old friend of Emily's mentor, Leonard Courtney, and, above all, a staunch advocate of women's rights. That such a fighter for justice and sex-equality should have been unmoved by the plight of the Boer women and children was, to say the least, unexpected. Few of those who knew Millicent Fawcett's early history would have thought of her as a natural opponent of Emily Hobhouse.

She had been born Millicent Garrett, one of five daughters of Newson Garrett, an East Anglian merchant. Known to her family as Millie, she grew up in her birthplace, Aldeburgh, Suffolk. She was a bright, clever girl but not the most remarkable member of her family: that honour went to her elder sister, Elizabeth, the pioneer woman doctor who later became Mrs Garrett Anderson. The obstacles which beset Elizabeth in her struggle to become a medical practitioner – then an unthought-of profession for women in Britain – are said to have infuriated young Millie and strengthened her determination to work for the advancement of women. Millie became active in that work after her marriage, aged twenty, to a Cambridge professor, Henry Fawcett, who was then the Liberal MP for Brighton. Blinded in a shooting accident when he was twenty-four, Henry Fawcett relied heavily on the assistance of his young wife. They worked closely together for a number of radical causes, particularly the emancipation of women. In Gladstone's 1880 administration Henry Fawcett was appointed Postmaster-General, while his wife was already a leader in the women's suffrage movement. They had one child, a daughter, Philippa, upon whom they both doted. After her husband's sudden death in 1884, Millicent Fawcett continued to work for the causes they had supported and, in 1897, she was elected president of the National Union of Women's Suffrage Societies, a position she held for over twenty years.

But there was another side to Mrs Fawcett's politics. Along with her radicalism went a firm belief in the virtues of the British Empire, and she saw the unity of the Empire as essential to its benevolent purpose. This had led her, three years after her husband's death, to oppose Gladstone's proposals for granting home rule to Ireland and – like her fellow-radical, Joseph Chamberlain – to join the dissident Whig grandees who broke from the Liberal Party and became known as Liberal-Unionists. It was in alliance with the Liberal-Unionists that Lord Salisbury, the Conservative prime minister, was first elected to office in 1886; he was returned again, in 1895, at the head of a Unionist government. Salisbury's government, of which Millicent Fawcett was a supporter – although she objected to being called a Conservative – had declared war on the Boer republics, and it was as a Unionist that Mrs Fawcett had attacked Emily.

There was, however, another reason for Millicent Fawcett's concern about the outcome of the war. This was her desire to see the *uitlanders* given the vote in the Transvaal. The franchise issue had dominated the months leading up to the outbreak of hostilities and had resulted in a debate which was of intense interest to Mrs Fawcett and her friends. 'No taxation without representation' had been the cry of the *uitlanders* and this had found a response among the unenfranchised women in Britain, who were struck by the sudden change of attitude towards the vote in their male opponents. It was noticed that in the press 'the strongest opponents of the enfranchisement of women in Great Britain were among the loudest in denouncing the disenfranchisement of British men in South Africa.' The *Spectator*, for instance – which had long opposed 'political liberty for women' – was emphatically in favour of votes for the *uitlanders*. 'We dwell so strongly on the franchise', it declared, 'because it includes all other rights, and is the one essential thing.' This, crowed Mrs Fawcett, 'is exactly what we have been saying for years . . . our old enemies were doing our propaganda for us and using arguments which we could transfer without the change even of a comma to our own case. The speeches of our opponents gave us examples of this, and we were continually looking them up and filing them.'[12] The eventual success of the *uitlanders* held a special significance for the women's suffrage movement.

Emily could easily have replied to Mrs Fawcett's attack in the *Westminster Gazette*. Given that the death rate in the concentration camps was then rising to new heights, she would have had new evidence with which to back up her arguments. But it is doubtful whether she saw the newspaper article in time. During her lecture tour the only press attacks she saw, she says, were in the 'Chamberlain' papers which she sometimes found discarded in railway carriages. The *Westminster Gazette* did not fall into that category. This was unfortunate, because Millicent Fawcett's criticism carried more weight than the contrived arguments of people like the Revd Adriaan Hofmeyer. What is more, had Emily seen the *Westminster Gazette* article she might not have been surprised by later events. Mrs Fawcett was soon to reappear and to pose a new threat to Emily's plans.

During Emily's absence from London her friend Lord Ripon, who was then acting chairman of the Distress Fund, continued to press the War Office on her behalf. Early in July he wrote to St John Brodrick to suggest once again that women be sent to South Africa to give practical assistance in the camps. He volunteered Emily's name as a suitable candidate.

Brodrick's reply was prompt but unhelpful. While claiming to be impressed by the readiness of philanthropic societies to assist in the camps, he firmly turned down Lord Ripon's suggestion. The trouble was, he explained, he had received too many offers of assistance; he already had three such proposals before him and it was obvious that 'it would be impossible to introduce a variety of authorities into camps organized and regulated by the Government'. In any case, the War Office was dealing with the matter and would shortly be sending out 'certain ladies to visit the camps and cooperate with the local committees'.

On hearing this, Emily was furious. It seemed to her that, despite her pleas, Brodrick had failed to appreciate the seriousness and urgency of the situation. Breaking off her tour, she returned to London and asked for a further interview at the War Office. Precisely what was said at this meeting was not reported but there can be no doubt about its outcome: Emily was told that the Government had no intention of allowing her to return to South Africa. This so incensed her that she demanded a letter setting out the Government's reasons for imposing such a restriction. She was promised that a letter would be sent to her but when it had not arrived, after two weeks she decided to send a polite reminder. By that time she appears to have heard not only that a committee of six women – three from England and three in South Africa – had been appointed, but that the three from England had already sailed for the Cape.

> I am continually asked on all sides when I am going out again [Emily told St John Brodrick, after enquiring about the promised letter]. It is generally expected that I shall start soon, which is my own desire . . . It has occurred to me that you might say that any help on my part was unnecessary, because you have yourself selected certain ladies to visit and report upon the Concentration Camps . . . may I be permitted to urge that the number you have sent is really quite insufficient . . . and, if I may speak for myself, that my experience in the camps, my acquaintance with the people, and to some extent with their language, ought to enable me, and I trust would enable me to be a useful auxiliary to them in the discharge of their duties? I would fain hope that the delay in sending your letter may mean a disposition to reconsider my appeal for leave to revisit the camps in South Africa.

It was a last desperate attempt on Emily's part, but it failed. Brodrick replied the following day to say he had explained the Government's position in a speech to Parliament and he had hoped that this would have satisfied her. 'The only considerations which have guided the Government', he added, 'in their selection of ladies to visit the Concentration Camps, beyond their special capacity for such work, was that they should be, so far as is possible, removed from the suspicion of partiality to the system or the reverse.' Emily's request had been turned down along with other women's from philanthropic agencies because they would have had to act in an unofficial capacity. It would, he pointed out, have been impossible for the Government to have accepted Emily's services while declining others, 'the more so as your reports and speeches have been made the subject of so much controversy.'[13]

Emily was angered by this final rejection but she can hardly have been surprised. What did surprise her was Brodrick's claim that the women sent to South Africa had been chosen for their impartiality.

The fact that the committee was headed by Mrs Millicent Fawcett made this impossible to believe. By this time Emily knew about the *Westminster Gazette* article and that, in her opinion, spoke for itself. 'Mrs Fawcett,' she wrote later, 'who was made principal of the Commission, had written a criticism of my Report, which was in substance a defence of the concentration system. In one phrase she had spoken of the formation of the Concentration Camps as "part of the fortune of war." One wonders in what war Mrs Fawcett had read of such a system, unless it was the Spanish action in Cuba, which was condemned by every civilized nation.'[14] There was also one other member of the commission who, as Emily knew, had publicly displayed a similar prejudice. 'It was tragic to feel', she declared, 'that instead of a great number of good nurses, and, above all, voluntary workers as camp matrons, being despatched in early June, only six ladies started in a leisurely way towards the end of July, not themselves to work, but to make more enquiry.'[15]

12

The Ladies' Commission

EMILY'S CLAIM, which she was to repeat on a number of occasions, that the six women appointed to investigate the concentration camps were chosen and despatched in a 'leisurely way' was nothing more than wild supposition. Had she been better informed she would have had greater cause for criticism. Like so much else to do with the concentration camps, the all-woman commission was hastily assembled and ill-organized. It was the politician's response to a difficult problem: that of gaining time by setting up a committee.

Little thought seems to have been given to the commission's purpose; no guide lines were issued, no objectives were set and the only recommendations given were vague and largely irrelevant. The delay arose from the War Office's difficulty in deciding which women would best suit its requirements. The members of the commission had to appear credible to the public, yet they had to be sufficiently supportive of the Government to avoid embarrassing the military authorities in South Africa.

Millicent Fawcett's article in the *Westminster Gazette* undoubtedly influenced her appointment as head of the commission. She was an ideal choice: not only was she a prominent Liberal reformer but, as her article had made clear, she could be relied upon as an imperialist. That she would accept the position could never have been in doubt. 'In 1901', explains her biographer, 'it was an unprecedented thing for an official commission on whatever subject to consist only of women, and though Mrs Fawcett was proud to be asked to serve her country in such an important capacity, this fact added yet another argument to persuade her to accept. She had no hesitation whatever.'[1] For Millicent Fawcett, the chance of scoring a first for the women's movement would always swing the balance of any decision she was asked to make.

The two other women recruited in England were less well-known. Indeed, one of them could hardly be said to qualify for enlistment. She was Alice Knox, the Scottish wife of General Sir William Knox (he had been knighted a few months earlier), who had recently returned from South Africa where her husband was serving as one of Kitchener's senior officers. She had arrived in South Africa shortly before the war and had spent four months in beleaguered Ladysmith where she helped to nurse the soldiers. Later she claimed to have visited several concentration camps but gave no indication of where these camps were: the only vivid memory she retained of them was 'the filthiness of the children'[2] who clamoured for the sweets she had brought; so extremely dirty were these youngsters, she told Millicent Fawcett, 'that she did not care greatly for them crowding around her, so she said when she came again her sweets would be for clean children.' Fastidious Lady Knox might be, but no one could accuse her of being over-zealous in her investigations. Nor, as a soldier's wife, could she truly be described as impartial. Certainly she took a jaundiced view of the Boers. 'She thought the young Boer women', noted Mrs Fawcett, 'were showing themselves open to adopt a higher standard of cleanliness and refinement. In her opinion the Boers of today are in social circumstances where the Scottish people were 200 years ago.'[3]

Lucy Deane, the third member of the English contingent, was a far more accomplished and purposeful woman. Besides being experienced in child welfare, she had become, in 1894, one of Britain's first woman factory inspectors and more recently had been placed in charge of over 4000 women's workplaces in west London. Her daily round had made her fully aware of the effects of poverty, physical hardship and malnutrition. A serious, methodical worker and planner, Lucy Deane was appointed secretary of the commission.

The three commission members then in South Africa were undoubtedly chosen for their professional qualifications: two of them were experienced doctors, the third was a trained nurse. One of the doctors was the redoubtable Jane Elizabeth Waterston, the first woman physician in South Africa and a well-known Cape Town personality. She had come out to South Africa in 1866 as a missionary but, after working in the eastern Cape for seven years, had returned to Britain to train and qualify as a doctor. Her first medical practice had been at a mission station in Nyasaland (present-day Malawi) and she had later worked among the Xhosa people of the eastern Cape until ill-health had forced her to retire to Cape Town. Here she established a 'large and successful practice' and soon became known and admired for her work among the poor. A tireless worker, she had been prominent among those organizing relief for the British refugees who poured into Cape Town at the outbreak of war and she made no secret of her staunch support for the imperialist cause. Her imperialist sympathies, combined with her experiences as a relief worker, had prompted her to write an indignant letter of protest to the *Cape Times* shortly after the publication of Emily Hobhouse's report on the concentration camps.

> We ordinary Colonial women who have been through the stress and strain of the last two years are not very favourably impressed by the present stir in England over the assumed privation of the Boer women and children . . . Judging by some of the hysterical whining going on in England at the present time it would seem as if we might neglect or half starve our faithful soldiers and keep our civilian population eating their hearts out here as long as we fed and pampered people who have not even the grace to say thank you for the care bestowed upon them . . . This war has been remarkable for two things – first, the small regard that the Boers from the highest to the lowest have had for their womenkind, and, secondly, the great care and consideration the victors have had for the same, very often ungrateful women. Let this be well ground into the minds of our English pro-Boers.[4]

Dr Waterston was a woman of strong, if often simplistic, opinions and, although she was a close friend of Mrs Fawcett's family, she at first refused to join the Fawcett commission. Only after it was pointed out to her that, as the only colonial woman selected, it was her duty to represent the Cape, did she reluctantly agree.

The other woman doctor presented the commission members with a problem. They had all heard of her but none of them had met her, and at first there were fears that she would prove a disruptive influence. She was Dr Ella Campbell Scarlett, the eldest daughter of General Lord Abinger, and she was already working as a medical officer of the concentration camps in the Orange River Colony. She had a formidable reputation. Even the usually imperturbable Millicent Fawcett was apprehensive about meeting her and dubbed her 'the scarlet woman'.

There were no such reservations about the remaining member of the group. Katherine Brereton, the nurse, was a former sister at Guy's

Hospital in London who, in South Africa, had been in charge of one of the yeomanry hospitals organized by women in England (notably Lady Georgiana Curzon, a sister of Lady Sarah Wilson) and had earned high praise for her skill and efficiency. Like Lucy Deane, Katherine Brereton was overshadowed by the more assertive members of the commission but her role as a practical, commonsense adviser was never in doubt.

It was inevitable that this hurriedly assembled, strangely mixed group should be criticized by opponents of the concentration camps. To Emily Hobhouse and her supporters they became known as the 'whitewashing commission'. This name was unfairly applied to them before they started their investigations and was to stick to them throughout – and after – their tour of South Africa.

Emily's initial hostility is understandable. Having herself been accused of undue bias by St John Brodrick, she had every reason to resent the choice of two of her more outspoken critics – Millicent Fawcett and Dr Jane Waterston – as members of the commission. Their publicly-expressed views gave Emily scant hope of a just and constructive solution emerging from the commission's findings. How could it? From the very outset, it seemed to her, a cynical attitude had undermined the workings of the commission. 'The principle laid down as a guide in the choice of the ladies for this Commission', she wrote, 'was that "they should be removed from the suspicion of partiality to the system or the reverse." This good rule was unfortunately not followed, because two of the women selected had already expressed themselves with some warmth in the public Press.'[5] All of this made her even more bitter about her own rejection by the War Office. 'My opinions were discounted and barely tolerated', she complained in a magazine article, 'because I was known to feel sorry for the sickly children, and to have shown *personal* sympathy to broken, destitute Boer women in their *personal* troubles. Sympathy shown to any of Dutch blood is the one unpardonable sin in South Africa.'[6]

Emily was not the only one to be incensed by the War Office's appointments. Mrs Fawcett found herself opposed and shunned by some of her former friends, who accused her of abandoning her Liberal principles and allowing herself to become a tool of the Government. 'It became generally believed', says Ray Strachey, her biographer, 'by people who knew nothing about her that she was a real diehard Conservative, an ardent Imperialist, and a militarist.'[7] The kind of distorted accusations that had long been levelled at Emily were now refashioned and hurled from the opposite direction at Millicent

Fawcett. She was bombarded by insulting letters from complete strangers. Nor was the abuse confined to Britain. Continental critics of the war were quick to see perfidious Albion at work. 'How can you expect the Boer women to make you their confidante', read a postcard sent to Mrs Fawcett from Switzerland, 'when they know perfectly well (as we know too) that you have been sent to South Africa for the express purpose of whitewashing the administration of the Concentration Camp? You have been well paid for your dirty work, and that ought to be a sufficient reward to you.'

Given that emotions were running high and the lives of thousands of women and children were in jeopardy, these sorts of attack were inevitable. They were also premature. Suspicions about the commission's impartiality were not unfounded, but they took no account of the basic integrity, or the experience, of the women who undertook to investigate the concentration camps. Millicent Fawcett and her colleagues were neither emotional nor sentimental in their approach – indeed some of their opponents regarded them as hard, cold and unsympathetic – but they were efficient, sharp-eyed and not easily deceived. They were well able to recognize the inadequacies of the camps and did not hesitate to condemn and, as far as was in their power, rectify the worst faults they uncovered. Their manner was often off-putting and not all their judgements were sound, but they were businesslike, conscientious, honest and responsible in their final assessments. If they did not entirely accept Emily's findings, they agreed with her more important criticisms and recommendations.

Millicent Fawcett was enlisted to head the commission by Mrs Alfred Lyttelton, wife of the Liberal-Unionist M P who later became Colonial Secretary, and it was not until Saturday, 20 July 1901 – two days before she was due to sail for the Cape – that she was summoned to the War Office. There she was introduced to Alice Knox and Lucy Deane, who had also been sent for by the Secretary of State for War. This was the first time the three women had met, but they had little chance to talk before being called to St John Brodrick's office. Making their way along the War Office's maze-like passages, they bumped into Lord Roberts – now safely installed as the new Commander-in-Chief – who dutifully shook their hands and said how pleased he was that they were going to South Africa. This, it seems, was the only indication they were given that their mission was considered important.

At the interview with St John Brodrick and Sir Edward Ward,

serious discussion was kept to a minimum. After explaining a few routine matters – they were to be known as the Concentration Camps Commission, receive all their mail through the army post office and sail in the troopship *Oratava* – Brodrick went on to emphasize issues which would require attention. He stressed the need for ministers of religion in the camps but warned that clergymen were 'often violent propagandists' (Mrs Fawcett remarked tartly that it was a great pity that the Revd Adriaan Hofmeyer had been allowed to 'put himself forward as a representative of England'). Brodrick also suggested that matrons, other than hospital matrons, should be appointed and that the 'moral conditions' of the camps should be investigated. (He may have had in mind Kitchener's remark about the pregnant woman who claimed to be expecting a 'little khaki'.) The Commission, said Brodrick, although not formally a royal commission, would have practically all the powers of a royal commission and could, if it thought necessary, recommend the removal of a camp from its present locality. Interestingly, these were all – with the exception of the morality issue – recommendations made by Emily Hobhouse, but her name was not mentioned. The only time that Emily featured in the discussion was at the end, when Brodrick claimed that 'very few women had availed themselves of his offer, made at the insistence of Miss Hobhouse, to leave the camps'.

The more urgent problem of the rising death rate was dealt with defensively. Brodrick produced the camp reports for the first half of July which, according to Mrs Fawcett, showed that the returns for the few camps in the Cape and Natal 'were very favourable' while those for the much larger number in the Orange River Colony and the Transvaal were 'still very bad'. (Using these same returns, Emily Hobhouse was to show that 576 children died in July and 1545 the following month.) Explaining the deaths, Brodrick relied on a report from Lord Kitchener which gave the familiar excuse of inmates arriving at the camps after suffering long periods of 'great privations'. To this, noted Mrs Fawcett, 'he attributed the high mortality; also to the want of training of the women in giving to Infants condensed milk out of tins without any dilution or preparation.'

This feeble reasoning did not seem to disturb the women. Indeed, Mrs Fawcett had come prepared to counter any suggestion of misrepresentation on the part of the authorities. She was quick to produce statistics which showed that the normal death rate in England for infants under one year was '150 in 1000 and may generally be taken as 8 times greater than the death rate of the whole population.' This appeared to satisfy everyone, allaying any disquiet about the death rate in the camps.

The women were told that, unlike Emily Hobhouse, they would be allowed to visit all the camps and talk to anyone they wished. Brodrick did, though, offer a parting piece of advice. 'He spoke seriously to us', says Millicent Fawcett, 'of the discretion required and the responsibility entrusted to us; also of the admirability of working *with* the authorities.'[8]

Not until the *Oratava* was about to sail did the new commissioners receive any written instructions. A messenger dashed aboard at the last minute and handed them a despatch box containing maps, a list of the camps, and information about the women they were to contact at the Cape. There was also a letter from Sir Edward Ward, to whom they were to send a weekly report, giving them their code address: *Zenobia*, Cape Town. 'I am glad', quipped Mrs Fawcett, 'they did not select Semiramis or Jezebel.' The despatch box was not opened until some days later: for almost a week the women were prostrate with seasickness.

They did not travel alone. Lady Knox was accompanied by a maid, Lucy Deane by her sister and Mrs Fawcett by her daughter Philippa. Eleven years earlier Philippa Fawcett, then a student at Cambridge aged twenty-two, had startled the academic world by being placed above the senior wrangler in the mathematical tripos list. Her mother had hailed this as a triumph for the higher education of women, and hoped her daughter would pursue an equally remarkable career. She had wanted her to become 'in turn an astronomer, a physicist, a lighthouse designer or an engineer; or at any rate something which no woman had ever been before.'[9] But Philippa had rejected all these suggestions and returned to her Cambridge college to lecture in mathematics. It was the tour of the South African concentration camps that was to have a more profound effect on her career.

Once the women had found their sea legs, they met daily on deck to discuss methods of work. Their plans were extremely vague. One of the first things they had to decide was whether they would operate in three parties, each with two members, or whether they would act on Lucy Deane's suggestion and keep together long enough to see 'one good, one bad and one average camp', so that they could agree on standards before they separated. Millicent Fawcett, conscious of her role as leader, was delighted when the collective method was favoured. Her companions, she observed, 'had heard much the same account of the "scarlet woman" as I had and for that reason too we thought keeping together at first would be desirable. If we were five to one there could be no insuperable difficulty in coping with her.'

They drew up a list of special points to enquire about. This, under the guidance of Mrs Fawcett, was far more practical than anything suggested by St John Brodrick. It dealt with such things as sanitation, water, the slaughter of animals, the availability of fuel and the death rate. Emily Hobhouse would have approved, and there can be little doubt that the list was based on her findings. 'Read through Miss Hobhouse's report again in bed before breakfast,' Millicent Fawcett noted in her diary on 28 July. 'She speaks highly of Norval's Pont . . . Probably great improvements have been carried out at Bloemfontein since she was there. She gives much more time and space in her report to Bl[oemfontein] than to any other place.'

Mrs Fawcett was never to acknowledge her debt to the Hobhouse report, let alone publicly admit that it was responsible for 'great improvements' in the camps. She rarely mentioned Emily's name, but she did later claim that she had received no help from the Distress Fund. This angered Emily. Before the *Oratava* sailed, Lady Hobhouse had written to Mrs Fawcett, whom she knew, offering to arrange a meeting with Emily. The offer was turned down, says Emily, 'on domestic grounds'. Mrs Fawcett's reply, in fact, was curt and definite; she suggested that Emily could send information to her in writing. This Emily considered to be little short of insulting. 'It is a pity', she fumed, 'that she did not choose the far simpler method of approaching me direct, instead of employing a medium. I never saw the letter [she wrote to Lady Hobhouse] . . . but the impression made by it at the time and conveyed to me, was that she evidently did not desire any help I might be able to give her.'[10]

Mrs Fawcett's hostility towards the Distress Fund was very much in evidence when the commissioners reached Cape Town. Here, two days after they landed, they met three Cape representatives of the fund: Mrs Charles De Villiers, Mrs William Purcell and Emily's close friend Mrs Charles Murray. It was not a harmonious encounter. The two groups of women took an instant dislike to each other; tempers were kept in check but the atmosphere was electric. Mrs Murray summed up the visitors as 'quite polite, but one could not touch heart or sympathy anywhere.' Mrs Fawcett she saw as 'an able woman but cold and hard I should think by nature as well as now by intention.' Lady Knox she dismissed as 'quite commonplace', and was more amused than shocked by her story of the dirty children in the concentration camps. She could form no opinion of Lucy Deane, who spent all her time taking notes and who said very little. As far as Millicent Fawcett was concerned, it was sufficient for her to know that Mrs Murray was a sister of Percy Molteno, who was prominent among the London pro-Boers, to regard her as a natural enemy. This was soon to become apparent.

'I led off', she says, 'by asking if they were non-political but I quickly found they were intensely pro-Boer. They recited various tales of horror. At Middleburg they said there had been in June 52 deaths in 4 days.' That set the tone for the meeting. When the Cape Town women were asked what was needed in the camps, their sardonic reply startled the visitors: 'Send them calico', they snapped, 'to wrap their corpses in.' The irony of this was completely lòst on Mrs Fawcett. Over the next couple of months she was to make countless enquiries about the need for shrouds, only to end up bewildered. 'Never once', she protested, 'did a single human being utter a word which justified the Cape Town ladies' insinuation . . . They naturally wanted a great many things, but not this.'

The Cape Town women arrived hoping that they, or their representatives, would be allowed to accompany the commission. They were unlucky. 'We told them', says Mrs Fawcett, 'that we had the power to co-opt but had not exercised it at present, nor come to any decision on the subject. I pointed out how impossible the task of a commandant became if the inmates of a camp were encouraged by outsiders to resist such rules as were made for the good of the whole community and said I feared such had been the effect of Miss Hobhouse's visit. They were quite incredulous as to this.'

They were more than incredulous – they were furious. The idea of Millicent Fawcett decrying Emily Hobhouse's work before she had so much as set foot in the camps could not help but be seen as evidence of prejudice. Anna Purcell was particularly incensed. She found it difficult to remain calm when Mrs Fawcett went on to claim that the commission was non-political and only interested in finding out facts about the camps. How, demanded Mrs Purcell, could they be considered non-political when Dr Jane Waterston, an arch-imperialist, was a member of the commission? Even Mrs Fawcett recognized that she had a point: there was no sense in denying the partisanship of 'an out-and-out Britisher' like Dr Waterston. 'I replied', she says, 'that of course we all knew that Miss W[aterston] had strong political views but she was capable of seeing and advising on matters relating to sanitation . . . without bringing in political considerations.' This was hardly flattering to women who had offered to serve on the same basis and had been turned down.

But at least they were spared further embarrassment. 'Dr Waterston arrived before the pro-Boer ladies left,' noted Mrs Fawcett, 'but was safely bottled up in Lady Knox's bedroom till they were clear away.' This was just as well. By the end of the meeting, the Cape Town women were in no mood to be confronted by the truculent doctor, who had recently described the concentration camps as 'comfortable winter quarters' for the families of the commandos. Rather grudgingly they agreed to supply Mrs Fawcett with introductions to local committees formed in areas near the camps, but they had little faith in the commission's willingness to co-operate. They came away feeling, as Mrs De Villiers put it, as if they had been talking at a stone wall. Later they were formally to sever all connections with Mrs Fawcett and her colleagues.[11]

The commission spent four months in South Africa. During that time they visited thirty-three camps, some of them more than once, and lived for the most part in a special second-class train supplied by the Cape government. By the time they left Cape Town, at the beginning of August, it was decided that the six of them would remain together throughout the tour. This increased the time it took them to inspect all the camps – to the disgust of Emily Hobhouse, who considered that the entire operation lacked urgency – but they were glad of the companionship which helped make their work less strenuous.

They were an oddly-assorted group but they appear to have got on reasonably well together. 'I never quarrelled with any of my colleagues,' says Millicent Fawcett. 'Of course I did not like them all equally, but I think we were all equally eager to fulfill the work we had undertaken.'[12] Even the reputedly sharp-tongued Ella Scarlett proved to be amiable; far from being the ogress of their imaginings she, as the youngest of the group, became known affectionately as 'our baby'. Living conditions on the train were cramped but they each had a compartment of their own in which they slept and could be alone. Their meals were taken in a large, airy saloon to which a travelling kitchen was attached, and they were served by a 'young Tommy named Collins' who had been sent to them by General Knox, Alice Knox's husband. They also had their own Portuguese cook. It was all a far cry from the bone-shaking journeys endured by Emily Hobhouse. Commenting on Mrs Fawcett's progress through South Africa, Emily was to observe wryly that there was 'no need for beleaguering offices and waiting for hours for permits and passes, no need to scramble for a seat or a meal – her almost royal train could go from one camp to another with ease and the minimum of fatigue to her party.'[13]

But though they travelled in comfort, the members of the commission were not lulled into complacency. They were all professional women – with the exception of Lady Knox – well aware of the work they had to do and alive to their responsibilities. Sentiment may have been in short measure but there was no lack of efficiency. Millicent Fawcett was determined that the investigation should be conducted competently. As the leader of the first official, all-woman commission, she knew she could expect criticism from anti-feminists, as well as from pro-Boers, and she had no wish to give either faction an opening. To be dismissed as members of the 'shrieking sisterhood' – a sneer frequently levelled at Emily Hobhouse – would not help them counter the taunts of 'whitewashing'. It was in all their interests to produce a report that was lucid, thorough, humane and objective.

Although they each had their special concerns, they worked in the camps as a team. They questioned officials and inmates, inspected hospitals, water supplies, abattoirs, clothing and food stores and fuel reserves; they examined and sampled rations and enquired about such things as education, medical facilities, religious services and refuse disposal. Only one of them was given a completely free hand; this was Dr Waterston. 'Throughout our camp work', says Mrs Fawcett, 'all the most difficult and fatiguing jobs were voluntarily undertaken by our dear Dr Jane. Such things as the source of water supply to be investigated, involving a tramp of a mile or more over the veldt; slaughter places, drainage and sanitation to be inspected – these were the jobs which Dr Jane claimed as hers by divine right. Her knowledge and experience of the country were an enormous advantage to us.'

They found much to praise but more to criticize: overcrowding, poor and inadequate rations, polluted water, neglect of the elementary rules of hygiene, a shortage of beds and mattresses, sick children sleeping on the ground, failure to isolate contagious diseases: all the enormities complained of in Emily Hobhouse's report were still to be found in some of the camps, unreformed and, in many cases, unheeded by the camp officials.

The sanitary arrangements were often appalling. At Potchefstroom – a camp with 4900 inmates – there were only 65 latrine pails for women and 23 for men; while at Aliwal North, which had become hopelessly overcrowded since Emily's visit, there was one latrine to 177 women and children. At Merebank in Natal one bath-house served a population of 5154 with ten baths for women, two for men and two for boys; at Mooi River there were no bath-houses at all; the men bathed in the river and arrangements were still being made to have baths installed for the women. In the furrow which brought water from the Mooi river to the camp they – probably Dr Waterston – found 'bones and skull of oxen, old tins, old boots and rubbish in the muddy bottom.' Similar, sometimes worse, evidence of pollution was discovered in several other camps.

Disease was still accounting for hundreds of deaths. At Middleburg, in the Transvaal, 403 people died in July, 197 of them being children between the ages of one and five; in the hospital at Balmoral, also in the Transvaal, there were 106 cases of measles of whom 15 had recently died. Often the deaths were the result of obvious neglect – drinking water was neither boiled nor filtered, sheets of typhoid patients were not disinfected, and sometimes typhoid patients were found in the same tent as those suffering from measles. At Howick in Natal there had been no attempt to isolate scarlet fever cases and at Brandfort, in the Orange River Colony, an epidemic killed one tenth of the camp population in three weeks.

While they were at Heilbron, again in the Orange River Colony, ten measles patients died in one night. The fact that both the camp and the town (where some of the internees were housed) had been free of disease until a batch of 'measles-infected people' were herded into the town, during one of Kitchener's 'sweeps', made these deaths all the more shocking. The makeshift accommodation in the town was execrable. 'Though some of the houses were comfortable,' says the commission's report, 'others were miserable sheds or stables, and one hovel was surely meant for a pig or perhaps some poor native [sic], and yet a young girl dangerously ill lay in it . . . There is barely language too strong to express our opinion of the sending of a mass of disease to a healthy camp; but the cemetery at Heilbron tells the price paid in human lives for the terrible mistake.'

At Bloemfontein conditions, as Millicent Fawcett had expected, were somewhat better than reported by Emily Hobhouse. There had been an extension to the camp and the newly-built section was well laid out with wide roads and additional space between the tents. Overcrowding was no longer such a problem, there being on average five people to each bell-tent and fourteen in the large marquees. There were now ten or eleven shops in the two sections of the camp and they were well stocked with luxury goods as well as necessities. But for all that, many of the old evils persisted.

It was pouring with rain when the commission arrived and they discovered that water had flooded many of the tents, soaking bedding and leaving the ground awash. The new civilian superintendent, Mr Bennett, insisted that very few tents had suffered but 'the people in the tents told a different story'. Matters were made worse by the fact that many of the reforms started by Emily Hobhouse had been abandoned. Little effort had been made to supply beds and the commission estimated that a good two-thirds of the inmates still slept on the ground. Blankets were now plentiful – some were seen strewn about the veld – but no waterproof ground sheets had been issued and 'during the next three days there was a very general airing and drying in progress'. Firewood was practically non-existent and several people were seen at work with pickaxes 'digging up roots for burning'. A loyal Englishwoman they met in the camp said that the shortage of fuel was the one thing she found hard.

Some of the other women had more serious complaints and did not hide their feelings. They were angry about the quality of the daily meat ration which, as the commission freely acknowledged, was 'extremely poor and thin'. The superintendent claimed that this was because the meat was then at its worst; it would improve, he said, once the rains made the pasture better. But the angry women thought otherwise and, to make their point, staged a demonstration. 'The camp people', says the commission's report, 'showed their discontent with the meat by throwing large portions, which had been newly served out, of good fresh, though thin meat, into the wide roadway of the camp. It would have made very good broth or stew. We supposed that this wicked waste was a sort of bravado for the purpose of showing us how discontented they were; but we took it as a proof that, at any rate, the people in the camp were not short of food.'

But what most worried members of the commission was the disregard for the elementary rules of hygiene. Although there were wells in the camp, water was still being fetched from the noxious Modder river and no instructions had been given that this water should be boiled. The washing arrangements in the camp were described as 'extremely bad'. Women were seen washing clothes in dirty puddles, using the same water repeatedly. A large trough in two divisions had been installed for washing purposes but, reported the commission, 'the people were not using it and the taps supplying the troughs were padlocked'. There were 430 latrine pails available for a population of

6660 people but, insisted the commission, the latrines 'should be labelled "For men" and "For women" respectively'. Neglect of hygiene was particularly noticeable in the hospital. Here it was found that the pails from the enteric latrines were not disinfected, and soiled linen was left lying about in the bathrooms and store cupboards. But, says the report, 'the most serious fault to be found in the hospital arrangements is the failure to boil or disinfect enteric sheets. They are just washed in cold water with other sheets and clothes.' That the death rate had soared since Emily Hobhouse left at the beginning of May is hardly surprising.

The commission published the death rate figures without comment. From 17 February to 30 April, it noted, 'the number of deaths was 100; from 1 May to 18 September, 524 – total 624.' Of these, over half were children under the age of ten years. There were, though, signs that the number of fatalities was decreasing. In the month of September, up until the 17th when the commission arrived, there had been 48 deaths; the total for May had been 141. After the commission's recommendations concerning hygiene, the distribution of rations and the need for more fuel and proper beds had been implemented, the number was further reduced.

Mrs Fawcett and her colleagues left Bloemfontein on 19 September. They travelled straight to Pretoria where, two days later, Lord Kitchener granted them an interview. This, as they realized, was an unusual concession on the part of a notorious mysogynist. Kitchener, in fact, had been opposed to their coming to South Africa and had only agreed, as he told Lord Roberts, 'in the hopes it will calm the agitators in England'.[14] He said that he doubted whether there would be much for them to do 'as the camps are very well run'. The fact that he rarely went near the concentration camps and was seemingly oblivious to the rise in the death rate helped to confirm his conviction that agitation about the camps was politically inspired, started and financed by hostile factions in Europe. In agreeing to see the ladies' commission he was not displaying interest, but merely performing a tiresome duty.

The interview was arranged through the offices of General Maxwell. Mrs Fawcett was highly amused by the preliminaries. 'We had heard a good deal of Lord Kitchener's general opinion of the female sex,' she says, 'and rather smiled when we read his letter, for he expressed a wish that of the six of us only two should come.' The two chosen were herself and Lady Knox. General Maxwell accompanied them to Melrose House, the gabled, turreted, late-Victorian confection in which Kitchener was headquartered, and asked them to wait in the hall while he announced them. 'He left the door wide open,' recalled Mrs Fawcett, 'and we could not help hearing what he said. Again we smiled when we heard Lord Kitchener's voice inquire anxiously, "How many are there of them?"' Once the discussion got under way, however, there was no more hesitation. The women were favourably impressed by Kitchener's blunt, businesslike manner. Mrs Fawcett found it a refreshing change from the equivocation of politicians.

The main purpose of the women's visit was to press for a greater variety in the rations supplied to the camps. Kitchener was not at all encouraging. What they were asking for, he said, would entail using one of the railway trucks by which the rations of the rest of the civilian population were transported. He seemed surprised when the women suggested that the problem could be solved by employing an additional truck to those already in use. This, apparently, had not occurred to him. When the idea sank in, he agreed. The two women felt their talk 'with the great man had been very satisfactory'. But it was not only the women who were impressed. Having withstood the curiosity of two females, Kitchener surprised them by inviting all six members of the commission to dinner. Mrs Fawcett was always to refer to this as one of the 'greatest compliments' of her life. 'We did not all go,' she admits; 'but I think there were four of us. Lord Kitchener took me in to dinner.'[15]

A couple of days later the commission started their investigation of the Irene camp. 'A commission of English ladies arrived today to inspect the Camp,' Henrietta Armstrong noted in her diary. 'I would like to see their account.'[16] In time she did see it, and was none too pleased.

Before Hansie van Warmelo left Irene, an important change had taken place in the camp. The unloved Commandant Scholtz, the man regarded by the volunteer staff as the 'greatest Jingo alive', was replaced by Commandant G. F. Esselen. No one was sorry to see the back of Scholtz, but Hansie was furious to discover he had been promoted by General Maxwell and was to be a travelling inspector for the camps in the Transvaal. She saw this as a personal slap in the face; Maxwell had half-promised her a similar position. Nor were things made better when the new commandant was revealed as another renegade Boer. 'Among one's own people', Hansie protested, 'there is no one more inhumane or merciless than an English-Afrikaner and the English know this well, because they appointed in the "murder camps" such people as Scholtz and Esselen who were given power over the unhappy inmates.'[17] That Afrikaans-speaking officials might have been selected because they were best suited to communicate with the inmates did not feature in Hansie's thinking. As far as she – and many others like her – was concerned, it was all a dastardly plot. Her suspicions are understandable: few concentration camp officials were more insistent that only English be taught and spoken in the camps than men such as Scholtz and Esselen.

The rest of the volunteer nurses shared Hansie's views. Esselen, whose wife was later appointed as matron, was every bit as disliked as Scholtz had been. Mrs Armstrong had some scathing things to say about him in her diary. He kept himself aloof from the day-to-day work of the camp and although his wife tried to help she was considered to be very much her husband's lackey. 'I hope', noted Mrs Armstrong, 'she is going to work with us in true Africander feeling and love, but he [Esselen] will see that she dare not!'[18] Hansie left Irene shortly after Esselen took over, but she was kept informed of his doings by the other nurses.

A few days before the ladies' commission arrived at Irene, a new military order had caused great distress in the camp. To make room for the growing number of surrendered Boers and their families, it was decided to send the dependents of men on commando to camps in Natal. The transfer was arranged at a time of incessant rain, and women with sick children were left shivering in their tents for days, waiting for the order to move, without fuel or proper protection from the cold and damp. Esselen was ruthless in his refusal to listen to complaints or make exception in cases of serious illness. He had plenty of practice in such matters. Packing people off to Natal was his method of dealing with 'unruly' elements in the camp, making the innocent suffer along with the guilty. But, like most bullies, he was essentially a weak man. This is something the ladies' commission was soon to discover.

Mrs Fawcett and her colleagues spent two and a half days at Irene. Arriving there at midday on Monday, 23 September, they set to work immediately. Their first impressions were far from favourable. Irene had deteriorated markedly since the early days and was now seriously overcrowded. 'The ground on which the camp is pitched', Mrs Fawcett wrote in her diary, 'is rocky and stony. It's on a good slope, but is extremely untidy and ill kept and tents are pitched very close together.'[19] No effort had been made, it seems, to prepare the camp for an inspection even though Esselen had known it was to take place since July.

There was evidence of squalor and neglect everywhere. Slops were emptied on to the floors of the ill-ventilated tents and the roadways were littered with debris; the ground outside four of the latrines was 'badly fouled'; there were no bath-houses (Esselen said he intended to put up canvas shelters for baths 'as soon as possible') and at the slaughter-place, 300 yards from the camp, offal remained unburied and children were allowed to watch the animals being killed. A dead animal had recently been found in the furrow bringing water to the camp, and members of the commission were shocked to learn that Esselen, although he had been at Irene for three months, had 'never been to the source of the water'. Esselen admitted that people had suffered badly from a lack of fuel; as the commission discovered, this was entirely due to his inefficiency in allowing fuel stocks to run out before ordering a fresh supply. The commandant, declared Mrs Fawcett, 'has no resource and tact, and no settled plan of distribution.'

Esselen did, however, have his favourites. This became clear when the system of rationing was investigated. The meat ration was found to be of poor quality and 'very scanty' but Esselen claimed that he did not like to increase it on his own authority. But he was perfectly willing to provide the burger 'police' with a 'special and very liberal ration for themselves and their families' and authorize chosen workers to pick out the better pieces of meat. 'This', said the commission's report, 'evidently gave offence, and some grumbling was heard even among the issuers.' There was even more grumbling among some inmates who, disgusted with the meagre ration, made a great show of refusing to accept it. Milk was served out with boiled water, but no other concessions were made to hygiene. The wooden shanty from which the milk was issued was filthy and the whole place smelt foul and sour. Empty milk tins scattered on the floor were covered with flies. When this was pointed out to the dispenser, a half-hearted attempt was made to clean up the place by sprinkling chloride of lime on the floor.

Conditions in the hospital had improved somewhat. There were now three doctors, two trained and three untrained nurses, as well as a dispenser with two assistants. There were a few shortcomings – the typhoid sheets were disinfected but not boiled – but, on the whole, the commission found little to complain about in the administration of the hospital. The real trouble lay with the patients, or rather the lack of patients. There were forty beds available but, even when sickness was rife in the camp, they were never full. The people, claimed the commission's report, refused to accept hospital treatment and nothing was done to overcome their distrust of the medical staff. This, it was thought, was largely due to doubts sown by the volunteer nurses, who not only dissuaded patients from going to hospital but encouraged them to rely on crude home remedies and folk medicines which the nurses smuggled in from Pretoria.

No love was lost between members of the commission and the nurses. The hostility between them became obvious at their first meeting. 'We called on them about 3.30 in the afternoon,' observed Mrs Fawcett; 'they were sitting in their marquee doing knitting and crochet.'[20] The nurses were furious when they read this. 'Anybody knowing anything about South African life', protested Christina Malherbe, who claims they were resting during a dinner break, 'is aware that it is impossible for women to work between these hours; also all the crocheting done by us was for the use of the women and children.'[21] They were equally incensed about other criticisms. 'We asked them', says Mrs Fawcett, 'if they thought a soup kitchen would be useful; they replied in the affirmative but they had done nothing to set one going.' This, declared Miss Malherbe, was a downright lie. Mrs Armstrong, she insisted, had repeatedly asked for facilities to start a soup kitchen but had always received evasive answers from Esselen. 'Another thing,' she went on, 'home medicines were *not encouraged* by us, but when home remedies were used they were first obtained from the store set up by the military . . . the selling of these home remedies was afterwards stopped, but this is how they were obtained.'

There were undoubtedly faults on both sides. The nurses were openly hostile to the camp authorities and, however much they denied it, could not help but influence the behaviour of the inmates. On the other hand, members of the commission adopted a haughty, unsympathetic attitude which made any co-operation between them and the nurses impossible. This is well illustrated in Henrietta Armstrong's diary. While assisting at the hospital, Mrs Armstrong twice clashed with the commission ladies. On the first occasion she was interviewed by two of them, but she could see they did not believe a word she said. 'They asked the doctor if he could trust me with the medical comforts that we had a right to order,' she noted scornfully.[22] The following day she was even more angry when Dr Ella Scarlett mistook her for an Englishwoman. 'She was disappointed', wrote the deceptively-named Mrs Armstrong, 'to hear I was Dutch . . . Of course being Dutch, we must all be rogues and thieves, instead of the reverse. But I suppose they don't call it roguery to come and take our country away. How can they expect us ever to like them?'

But, if the commission ladies disapproved of the nurses, they were every bit as critical of the camp officials. Mrs Fawcett considered Commandant Esselen – whose name she always spelt incorrectly – 'weakly amiable; he has no authority and no force of character.' His wife was seen as equally useless. Compared with other matrons they had interviewed she appeared totally irresponsible. 'At 11 a.m., September 24th,' it was reported, 'she was sitting in a bucksail shelter doing fancy-work. On September 25th, about the same hour, she was in the same tent drinking tea and doing tambour work.' The camp schools, noted Mrs Fawcett, were 'mainly in the hands of rebels' and a resident Irish clergyman was said to have become 'very Dutch' and 'extraordinarily dirty'. Nor was she happy about the way immorality was dealt with in the camp. 'When Mr Esselin [sic] first came,' she wrote in her diary, 'he had endless trouble about moral questions; but he succeeded in getting some bad women sent to Natal. "They are under direct police supervision and they are housed and are under complete discipline of police supervision." I have written down Mr Esselin's exact words. They sound very much like a Govt system of licensed prostitution.'[23]

Summing up the commission's findings, the report has some sharp things to say about the warring factions in the camp:

During the two and a half days the Commission spent at Irene, officials repeatedly complained to them of each other. Mr Esselin complained of the Ladies' Committee [the volunteer nurses]; the Ladies' Committee complained of Mr Esselin; the Assistant Superintendent complained of the Superintendent and so on. Mrs Esselin, who held the position of matron for about a fortnight, appeared to have no grasp whatever of the duties of the post. In the opinion of the Commission Mr Esselin is not a man with power enough to contend against the difficulties of his situation . . . Mr Esselin desires cases of serious illness to be taken to hospital, but he has not the strength to enforce his will. He declared that tent flaps should be lifted, but, to quote his words, 'the women flare up and get the better' of those who order the flaps up . . . Mr Esselin contents himself with calling the Commission inside the tents to demonstrate how bad they smell. A strong man is required at Irene who will sweep away the little cliques and coteries who now successfully defy the authority of the Superintendent.

The volunteer nurses were branded 'a dangerous element in camp. They represent an antagonism to the authority of the Superintendent, and act as carriers and "go-betweens" between the camp and the town.' A recommendation that the volunteer staff be removed from Irene was put into effect two weeks later.

On the day the commission was due to leave, Millicent Fawcett was standing alone on the platform of Irene station when a train arrived. Hearing that Lord Milner was on board the train, she sent in her name and asked whether she could see him. Within minutes Milner came bounding out; finding the gate of his carriage jammed, he jumped over it on to the platform. Emily Hobhouse would have been astonished to see him so eager to greet a woman involved with the concentration camps. But Milner and Mrs Fawcett were old friends. They had known each other in London and had met again in Cape Town. 'I said', wrote a delighted Mrs Fawcett, 'I was only wishing that very morning that we could show him this camp. I told him about the Orange River Colony recommendations, especially about the appointment of a travelling inspector, and how we felt a strong man was needed to gradually get control of the camps.'[24] The man she had in mind for this job was the man whom Emily Hobhouse had suggested earlier: Cole Bowen, the admired Irish administrator of the Norval's Pont camp. The advice of Millicent Fawcett, unlike that of the powerless Emily Hobhouse, was taken seriously and acted upon; Cole Bowen was later appointed as inspector of all the camps in the Orange River Colony.

There were other, more formal, meetings between Mrs Fawcett and Milner, but this chance encounter enabled her to put across all the points she considered urgent. It may well explain why the volunteer nurses were so quickly expelled, despite the fact that visiting doctors had praised their work and the inmates had petitioned for them to remain.

Irene was one of the camps that Mrs Fawcett and her colleagues considered warranted a return visit. The second inspection took place on 12 November, shortly before the commission left the Transvaal. They found there was 'little of note in the way of improvement since their last visit'. Elementary rules of hygiene were still being ignored, the promised bath-houses had not been built, the issuing of rations was unsatisfactory and nothing had been done to improve the water supply to the camp. Mrs Esselen was now assisted by a paid clerk but she was still too lackadaisical to be efficient. There had been improvements at the school and the hospital was judged to be in 'good order', but there was little else that could be commended.

On revisiting the slaughter-house the members of the commission were overcome with disgust. They had difficulty in controlling their emotions when reporting what they saw. Not only was there the usual horde of children watching the killings but, as the women approached, they passed a small child carrying a bucket of blood, followed by others clutching sheep's heads. There was worse to come. At the main slaughter area, they reported, a 'long trench had been dug; on the edge of this trench, closely packed together, squatted a line of *little girls* and boys with eager faces, holding in their hands small dishes. Across the trench were laid several sheep with their throats stretched out, each held by a man. Slowly across the first throat was the knife drawn, severing the blood vessels, but far from killing the sheep. Eagerly these little children held their vessels to catch the dripping red blood, never caring for the struggles of the sheep, so long as they got the blood. The sight was too horrible.' One member of the commission – probably Dr Waterston – was so appalled that she turned on the crowd and harangued them 'in strong and forcible language'. The rest, feeling decidedly sick, turned and hurried away.

When they tackled Esselen about it, he at first tried to deny responsibility; then he reluctantly agreed to dismiss the butcher. But the commission had had enough of the prevaricating Mr Esselen. 'After this second visit', their report concludes, 'the Commission again urged upon the Military Governor that the Superintendent at Irene was not fitted for his post, and he was superseded.' In fact, the Esselens did not leave the camp until January 1902. They were replaced by Lieutenant L. M. Bruce, a middle-aged, extremely capable quarter-master of the recently dissolved yeomanry hospitals, who succeeded in transforming the ill-famed Irene, with its tragically high death rate, into what has been described as a 'model camp'. When Hansie revisited the camp, a few months later, she found things there were 'much better'.

Having completed their inspection, Mrs Fawcett and her team went to Durban in December to work on their report. It took them a week and resulted in a competent, factual, forthright document which, although not without bias, was far from being the 'whitewash' that had been predicted. Even the highly critical Emily Hobhouse had to admit, on reading it, that they did not shrink from condemning ill-chosen sites, dismissing incompetent superintendents, reforming entire hospitals, urging improvements in food, fuel and water, recommending beds and ameliorating sanitation. If the report contained flaws, these can be attributed to the personalities and prejudices of its authors. As one critic put it: 'No one would dream of charging Mrs Fawcett or any of the ladies forming her Committee, with "hysteria" or "sentimentality" . . . In the whole of their report there is not one word of pity for the misery they witnessed.'[25] The businesslike ladies would probably have taken this as a compliment.[26]

Mrs Fawcett's association with South Africa did not end with the breakup of the commission. Her daughter Philippa was so impressed with the pioneer work in education being done in the camps that, in 1903, she returned to the Transvaal to help establish a permanent education system. She was visited there by her mother and returned to England to pursue a life-long career in educational administration. In Durban the Honourable Ella Scarlett, MD, married Lieutenant Synge, a young army officer she had met while working in the Norval's Pont concentration camp, and Mrs Fawcett, who knew the bridegroom's parents, gave away the bride.

13

Defiance and Deportation

EMILY HOBHOUSE'S approval of the Fawcett commission's findings was offset by her more deeply felt criticisms. She particularly resented the insinuations in the commission's report that ignorance, superstition and unhygienic practices on the part of Boer mothers had played a large part in the deaths of their children. It was bad enough, she argued, that government ministers 'hard up for excuses' had repeatedly disparaged Boer women, but 'one hoped that English women would have been above such accusations'. How much, in fact, did members of the commission know about the Boers? They had never spent more than two or three days in a camp, and this precluded them from getting close to the inmates. The Boers, she pointed out, 'are not a race inclined to open their hearts to strangers of a day's acquaintance.'

The implication that the women in the camps were at fault because they resorted to home cures was unwarranted, Emily maintained. Among the 40,000 to 50,000 women they had seen, the commission could only cite a few isolated cases where weird or extreme practices were followed. The rest of the women had been condemned simply for using the sort of old-fashioned remedies that could be found in any English village. 'Today', she asserted, 'one hears of mouse-pie in certain parts of England, of snails to cure consumption, those found creeping *up* a churchyard wall, those crawling *down* are of no avail, and in a northern county blacklead is used to anoint wounds in sore legs . . . and we are all familiar with a potato carried in the pocket for rheumatism, and a dead spider tied in a bag for measles. But does one ever hear of deaths arising from these remedies?'

Nor would Emily accept that the inmates of the camps were naturally dirty. To stigmatize them in this way, she protested, was both unfair and untrue. It was unfair because 'we had placed them in conditions where all the things that go to help cleanliness were scarce or altogether lacking. Water, soap, towels, brooms, utensils, were all hard to obtain or unobtainable in camp. For many months there was *no soap at all*, except what the women made from the fat of their rations. It is untrue, because, in spite of these drawbacks, the women were quite wonderfully neat and clean.' She admitted that there were in camp, as there would be in any community of a similar size, a few feckless and dirty families, but insisted that their habits could not be quoted as though they were universal. This was a point which needed to be made. Defenders of the camps spread many untrue stories by their tendency to generalize from the particular. Accounts of the so-called 'dirty habits' of the Boers lingered on for years.

What undoubtedly pleased Emily was that nearly all the Fawcett commission's recommendations followed lines she had earlier laid down. 'The Commission', she observed, 'reiterated the facts, and urged the recommendations made months before and made some useful improvements which they had the power to do. One of their best pieces of work was securing the appointment, as Inspector, of Mr Cole Bowen, an idea proposed months previously.'[1]

Emily had reason to congratulate herself. Later it was suggested that Mrs Fawcett was the real heroine of the concentration camps because it was only after her visit that substantial improvements were made. But this is manifestly unfair. While Mrs Fawcett certainly deserves credit, it is obvious that Emily Hobhouse was the true pioneering genius of the camps. Had it not been for Emily's report and the controversy surrounding it, it is doubtful whether Mrs Fawcett – who had shown no previous interest – would ever have been sent to South Africa. Mrs Fawcett studied the Hobhouse report on her way to the Cape and it enabled her to compile a list of urgent matters that needed attention; if the Fawcett commission's recommendations are similar to Emily's, it is hardly surprising. Where the missions of the two women differed was in Mrs Fawcett having the backing of the Government and being able to get things done, while Emily battled alone and was actively opposed by the Government. There was a difference also in the later attitudes of the two women. Emily did not agree with everything done by Mrs Fawcett, but she publicly gave her credit where she considered it was due. Mrs Fawcett, on the other hand, did not acknowledge Emily's work in her report and, years later, did not so much as mention her name in the chapter of her memoirs devoted to the concentration camps.

One of the criticisms Emily made of the Fawcett commission passed almost unnoticed. It involved a pressing problem which she had also neglected, and about which she felt guilty. 'Unable myself, from lack of time and strength', she wrote, 'to investigate the conditions or personally carry relief to the native camps, I confidently expected that the Ladies' Commission would have made it part of their work to do so.' She was disappointed. The plight of the thousands of black people, living in camp conditions which were often worse than those of the Boers, was ignored and, for the most part, unattended. This was something that had been nagging at Emily's conscience for a long time.

She had first raised the matter shortly after arriving in Bloemfontein. Then it was that she was invited to give a talk to the local branch of the Guild of Loyal Women. This recently-formed organization had come into being, according to one of its members, to oppose 'the stand taken by the so-called "Conciliation Women" [Emily's Cape Town friends] who had declared their undying hatred of Great Britain.' Yet, despite this unambiguous declaration, members of the Guild liked to pretend they were non-partisan or, as a Bloemfontein newspaper unblushingly put it, 'they belong to no party, only demand that those that join must recognize that they are daughters of the British Empire.' Although they did in fact work among both the British and Boer wounded, they made no secret of where their sympathies lay. Emily, with her unorthodox credentials, could have had little hope of them helping her. This is probably why she hinted that an alternative role was open to the Guild. There were then said to be some 400 black 'refugees' in the local 'Kaffir Camp' and Emily, who had heard there was a great deal of 'sickness and destitution' there, suggested the loyal ladies might investigate the problem. The response was less than enthusiastic.[2]

'I do wish someone would come out and take up the question of the Native camps,' Emily wrote to her brother. 'From the odd bits I hear it would seem to be much needed and I dare not spare a moment to look into the question. It is true I asked the Loyal Ladies here to investigate the matter but, although they said they would, I could see they were not the right kind of person to be of any use and they were quite sure beforehand that there was neither sickness, suffering or death amongst those people. I hear there is much of all three.'[3] She was still worrying about it when she wrote to her aunt the following month. By that time she had learned of the existence of several other 'native camps' and had been told that the death rate in the local camp was very high. Was it not possible, she asked Lady Hobhouse, for the Quakers or the Aborigines Protection Society to send someone out?

There can be no doubt of Emily's sincerity. It is also easy to understand how her work among the Boers made it impossible for her to take on any more commitments. At this time she was receiving very little help, her supplies were limited and she had more on her hands than she could cope with. There may, however, have been another reason why she was cautious about tackling the problem of the black camps. She was fully aware that to offer aid to both black and white would not only complicate matters, but could alienate those she was already helping. She had been in South Africa long enough to know that charity, like so much else in the race-torn country, had to be administered separately.

Emily had little opportunity of getting to know the black population. Her work was confined to the white camps where there were only a few black servants, mostly family retainers, who were kept very much in the background. In some camps these servants were not even recognized and had no official entitlement to rations. All the same, Emily knew of the colour prejudice that was rampant in all sections of the white population, more particularly among the back-veld Boers. This is something which could not have escaped her. Talk in the camps often centred on attacks and looting, real or rumoured, by bands of marauding Africans who were out to avenge past injustices. Equally lurid tales were told about women who had been 'humiliated' and threatened with rape by Africans employed by the military.

> A certain number of women had been taken prisoners in and around Potchefstroom . . . [runs a typical account] On this occasion Kaffirs were used and they equalled the English soldiers in cruelty and barbarity. The women knelt before these Kaffirs and begged for mercy, but they were roughly shaken off, and had to endure more impudent language and rude behaviour. Their clothes were even torn from their bodies . . . when the mothers were driven like cattle through the streets of Potchefstroom by the Kaffirs, the cries and lamentations of the children filled the air. The Kaffirs then jeered and cried, 'Move on: till now you were the masters; but now we will make your women our wives'.[4]

There is reason to think that some of these highly emotive stories were exaggerated. It is difficult to imagine even the most hardened military commander of the period openly allowing black guards to assault white women, and there were relatively few authenticated cases of women being physically harmed, as opposed to taunted, in this way. There was undoubtedly more truth in reports of Africans pillaging and murdering Boer families. This was something which provoked frequent protests from the Boer leaders and may even have weakened their resolve to continue the war. But such carnage was not confined to Africans. In this so-called 'white man's war' the black population was made to suffer by both sides; there is no lack of evidence to show that they were repeatedly attacked and killed by Boer guerrillas. Some of the worst 'atrocities' attributed to the Africans are now known to be the direct result of attacks made upon them. The predictions of a wholesale rising by the black population, which were used to excuse some of the Boer depredations, were proved false.

Scare stories told to Emily often owed more to fear than to fact. Fanciful notions of what could, or might, have happened tended to distort remembered experiences. But there was no mistaking the deep-rooted racial prejudices that inspired them, and this was something that Emily could not ignore. Not that she shared the Boer phobia about skin colour; in London she had happily shared her Chelsea flat with an Indian medical student and had nursed this girl through an illness while working for the South African Conciliation Committee. She had even interrupted her work to take the girl to Italy for convalescence. But so anxious was Emily to display her loyalty to the Boer women that she indulged their racial fears and even allowed them to influence her thinking. Not only did she publish the women's clearly-stated prejudices without comment, but at times she appeared to endorse them.

Reports of African guards using brutal or offensive methods, such as was said to have happened in Potchefstroom, Emily found especially disturbing. She did not hesitate to condemn the practice of black employees being given the right to supervise Boer women. When, for instance, she informed *The Times* of the recommendations she had made to the War Office for improvements in the concentration camp system, she included one that had not appeared on her original list. It read: 'That, considering the growing impertinence of the Kaffirs, seeing white women thus humiliated, every care shall be taken not to put them in places of authority.'[5]

Coming from Emily, this was exceptionally strong. When commenting on black people in private she was careful, even in letters to her Boer friends, to avoid such language. What it does reflect, though, is her passionate dedication to the Boer cause, a dedication which blinded her to all other considerations. This was a commitment which prevented her from extending her activities to the black camps. While it is true that she was unable to take on additional responsibilities, it is also true that she was wary of being sidetracked.

Nonetheless, the difficulty of finding others to take on the black camps was a worry for Emily. After failing to enlist the 'Loyal Ladies', she continued to receive reports of distress among the African refugees. 'Clergymen', she wrote, 'who worked among the coloured people in these camps, and others, told me sad tales of the sickness and mortality, which was then very high. Beyond giving a little relief for the sick, I was not able to do anything.'[6] But she was only too aware that more was needed. That need seemed even greater when, on reading the Fawcett commission's report, she discovered that the well-financed ladies 'had not touched this important branch of the concentration system.'[7] Determined not to let the matter rest there, Emily went to see H. R. Fox Bourne, the secretary of the Aborigines Protection Society, and told him all she knew about the black camps. He, in turn, wrote to Joseph Chamberlain, the Colonial Secretary, on behalf of his society.

His letter could hardly be described as a call for action. It was cautious, almost apologetic, and peppered with unreliable statistics from the Government's Blue Books. But it did show that the death rate in the black camps had risen dramatically between August and November 1901, the latest reports showing it to be 363 for every 1000 camp inmates. These figures, as Emily pointed out, were known to be incomplete and the situation was growing daily more serious. Fox Bourne's arguments might have had a greater impact had he not been so ready to make excuses. He appears to have known little about life in the South African kraals and conceded (before it was even suggested) that the crowded conditions of the camps were probably 'extremely insanitary' because of 'the conditions of native life'. He did not question the policy of sending supposedly neutral refugees, mostly women and children, to these camps. His letter ended by respectfully suggesting that a 'Ladies' Committee' be entrusted with 'a mission for the benefit of the natives, similar to that which has been so useful in the case of the Boer women and children.'

Whether this letter ever reached Joseph Chamberlain is uncertain. It appears to have landed on the desk of the Permanent Secretary at the Colonial Office, who dismissed it out of hand. It seemed unnecessary, he noted, 'to trouble Lord Milner . . . merely to satisfy this busybody.'

Fox Bourne did not receive a reply until some weeks later. Then he was sent fresh statistics to prove that the death rate in the black camps was declining, and a covering note from the superintendent of the Native Refugee Department in the Orange River Colony. This note, dated 2 January 1902, blithely claimed that 'the natives seem generally content, and . . . appreciate the efforts that are being made by His Majesty's Government on their behalf.' At the time that note was written, the death rate among African refugees had touched new heights, and was to continue rising for at least another month.[8]

No record exists of day-to-day life in the black concentration camps. There was no diarist like Sol Plaatje among the inmates, few of them could write letters and they were rarely visited by outsiders. The comments of the handful of missionaries who served the camps provide little in the way of intimate detail. Only official reports and a mass of questionable statistics remain, and even these are incomplete.

There is no knowing, for instance, precisely when the first of these camps was established. They do not appear to have existed as separate enclosures until the end of 1900. Before then the majority of dispossessed black people were servants of the Boers and had been taken to the same camps as their employers. They were mostly women and children, as the men were sent to work for the military and their wages were expected to support both themselves and their dependents in the camps. Occasionally women servants were allowed to live with their employers, but usually they were accommodated in settlements alongside the white camps. The women, some of whose husbands had accompanied their male employers on commando, attended the Boer families during the day but often they were allowed no rations and had to return to their own camps at night. A few of the available black men worked as labourers in the white camps and were sometimes employed as guards.

All this changed after Lord Kitchener became Commander-in-Chief. By intensifying the scorched-earth policy with his great country-wide 'sweeps', Kitchener created chaos among the black population. His original decree, stipulating that only the black employees on Boer farms were to be taken to the camps and the kraal-dwellers left alone, was soon forgotten. Once the military drives were stepped up, Africans were cleared not only from the farms 'but also from their own villages and even from mission stations.'[9] The military justified these clearances by claiming that Boer commandos often raided black settlements for food and livestock, or were willingly aided by the inhabitants. It had long been the practice of certain officers to burn kraals where commandos were thought to be hidden. But this was not the only reason, nor the principal reason, why black settlements were destroyed. From the very beginning, it is said, Kitchener had intended to use the men swept in by his columns as an additional labour force, and he needed to ensure there were sufficient refugees available.

The British were not the only ones guilty: similar upheavals were caused by the Boers. Long before Kitchener assumed command of the army, officers in garrison towns had had to deal with homeless blacks seeking protection from commando raids. However, it was not until the first three months of 1901, when Kitchener's devastating sweeps began to take effect, that the problems posed by black refugees became serious. Although the men could be put to work, the dispossessed women and children were seen to need some sort of organized accommodation. This led to the establishment of the first black concentration camps. When Emily Hobhouse confronted the 'Loyal Ladies' of Bloemfontein with the distress in the local 'Kaffir' camp, in February 1901, she was speaking of one of the earliest of these camps. The rot set in, it appears, as soon as the camps were started.

The African camps were at first administered by the superintendents who had overall charge of the camps for the Boers. Not until June 1901 was a separate Native Refugee Department, under the command of Major G. F. De Lotbinière, established in the Transvaal. Major De Lotbinière, a Canadian in the Royal Engineers, was highly thought of by his superiors and the following month his organization extended its administration to the Orange River Colony. Later De Lotbinière was to explain the dual purpose of his department. Not only did it have charge of the black refugees, but it recruited the men to replace mineworkers who had been commandeered to work for the army, but were now needed in the re-opened gold mines. Thus, says De Lotbinière, 'our first consideration was the supply of native labourers to the army.'[10] For this reason most of the camps were situated near the railway lines in the Transvaal and the Orange River Colony, giving the military easy access to them when labour was needed.

The men working for the army were paid a shilling a day, plus rations, and were often away from their families for three months at a time. This meant that the long-term residents of the camps were women and children (Fox Bourne estimated that they formed five-sixths of the camps' population). The speed with which these camps were established meant that all the worst faults of the white camps –

the lack of proper sanitation, ill-chosen sites and congested living conditions – were repeated. The diseases which swept through the camps appeared unstoppable, the death rate soared. In the six months between June and December 1901, well over 8000 deaths were recorded but there were many more that were not recorded.

The vast majority of victims were small children who died in epidemics of measles, dysentery, chicken-pox and pneumonia. This does not seem to have worried Major De Lotbinière unduly. He put the high mortality down to Africans being unable to 'thrive under abnormal conditions and sudden changes'.[11] They needed time, he thought, in which to become acclimatized.

What they needed more urgently was proper medical attention. In the Boer women's camps it was often said that the hospital staffs were second-rate because all the best doctors and nurses were tending wounded soldiers; the black refugees fared far worse. They were lucky to see a doctor. Camps in the Orange River Colony, says Peter Warwick, were visited by military doctors 'only twice a week, and at Rooiwal it was reported in February 1902 that the refugees had not been visited by a doctor for over a month.' Even the more healthy adults suffered from a near starvation diet. Their rations were even more meagre than those of the Boer women. Those African women whose husbands were working could sometimes buy extra cheap mealies (corn) but fresh vegetables and milk were practically unobtainable.

Living cheek by jowl in makeshift shanties and tents, shut off from the outside world, unable to fend for themselves and denied all but the most cursory medical treatment, it is hardly surprising that these undernourished women and children were decimated by disease. A visiting clergyman found the sickness and despondency in one black camp extremely disturbing. 'They are in great poverty and misery,' he wrote, 'and our visit was a comfort to them. Many are dying from day to day – what is to become of the survivors I cannot think. Between the Dutch and the English they have lost everything.'[12] He was also struck by the fact that, unlike the Boer women, they had no champion to plead for them. They were bound to 'go to the wall', he mused, because they were among the weakest.

Not until the war was drawing to a close was any real effort made to improve conditions in these sadly neglected camps. Then it was decided to separate the camps into small units and disperse them over larger areas. The Africans were encouraged to grow crops on land surrounding the camps, and both the children and the adults benefited from supplements to their diet. De Lotbinière was to report how cows were obtained to supply fresh milk and 'large quantities of tinned milk, Bovril, corn-flour were issued free.' He also tells of shops being opened in each camp so that the inmates could buy at cost price such 'luxuries' as coffee, sugar, Boer meal and clothing; but, he adds, he was sure the milk and food 'did more good than anything else'.

The pity is that these reforms were not introduced sooner. Had they been, it might have reduced the 14,154 recorded deaths among people who, as both sides claimed, had no role to play in a 'white man's war'.

Eleven weeks after the departure of the Fawcett commission from England, Emily Hobhouse set sail for the Cape on the *Avondale Castle*. Although her motives for returning to South Africa were mixed, there can be no doubt about her intentions. She was determined to defy the authorities and, somehow or other, resume her crusade there on behalf of the concentration camp victims. As she well knew, the chances of her being allowed to return to the camps were remote, but she still hoped to work from a base in the Cape. This, says her biographer Ruth Fry, was something that 'all her friends understood'. But it proved more difficult than she imagined.

Emily's determination was strengthened by the alarming reports from South Africa during August and September 1901. In those two months there had been another huge rise in the population of the camps, a corresponding increase in the death rate and, although the coldest months of the winter were over, there were fears that a hot summer would bring more sickness. 'Will nothing be done?' Emily demanded in a letter to the press. 'Will no prompt measures be taken to deal with this terrible evil?'[13] Urgent action was called for and she saw no hope of it coming from Mrs Fawcett and her colleagues. She had made her indignation on this score plain in an open letter to St John Brodrick a week before the *Avondale Castle* sailed. About the progress of the commission she was scathing.

We had to wait a month while six ladies were chosen. During that month 576 children died. The preparation and journey of these ladies occupied yet another month, and in that interval 1124 more children succumbed. In place of at once proceeding to the great centres of high mortality, the bulk of yet a third month seems to have been spent in their long journey to Mafeking, and in passing a few days at some of the healthier camps. Meanwhile, 1545 more children died. This was not immediate action; it was very deliberate inquiry . . . when the demands of death, instead of diminishing, were increasing.

By the time she wrote this, Emily must already have booked her passage to the Cape. She had planned the voyage well in advance and arranged to take a young nurse, Elizabeth Phillips, as a companion. Miss Phillips, she explained, 'would later, I felt sure, be of the utmost value in the shortage of nurses throughout the country.' All the same, she was careful not to mention in her letter to St John Brodrick that she was about to leave for South Africa. That, she realized, would not have gone down well in the War Office, where all her requests to be allowed access to the concentration camps had been refused. She had not been officially banned from South Africa, but she was not at all sure she would be permitted to leave England. For once she was anxious not to attract attention to herself.

Over the past few months she had received her full measure of publicity. Not all of it had been favourable but that no longer bothered her. She was now experienced enough to appreciate that it was more important to be heard than to be liked. At her public meetings she had discovered that the abuse of rowdy hecklers could often earn her sympathetic applause and even win over some waverers. Speaking at Portsmouth at the end of August, for instance, Emily had been bombarded with vegetables but the audience cheered her in the end and next day her speech was praised in the local Tory press.

She ignored most of the attacks against her in *The Times* and other national newspapers. A surprising number of these came from visiting South African women. These patriotic ladies – none of whom had seen the inside of a concentration camp – delighted in putting Emily straight about life in the veld. 'When', wrote one of them, 'Miss Hobhouse harrows her own feelings and endeavours to harrow the feelings of others by describing what she imagines to be the hardships to Boer women and children in the concentration camps she provokes a smile from those who know the habits of the Boers. Overcrowding is habitual among them to a shocking extent, as is indifference to what would strike Miss Hobhouse as the elements of comfort . . .'[14]

This was one of the letters Emily wrote an answer to, which she tore up without posting. It was useless, she decided, arguing with people who knew nothing of conditions in the camps. There were occasions, though, when she was not so restrained. One of these was when she was attacked by a delegate of the Guild of Loyal Women who, among other things, accused her of giving a false impression of 'conditions of things in South Africa where intense heat, crowded tents, flies, scarcity of milk, snakes etc. are everyday occurrences.'[15] This letter Emily dissected paragraph by paragraph, scornfully rejecting its contentions. What, she wanted to know, had such quibbles to do with the concentration camps? 'The great fact of the death rate she totally ignores. No one in their senses knowing these camps will deny that the suffering is very great and is likely to be greater.'[16] The majority of the attacks made on Emily warranted the same response.

Ill-founded and trivial as such attacks were, they were an irritation and a distraction. More serious were the critical leading articles which appeared from time to time in the national press. These Emily felt had to be answered, and sometimes she spent days defending herself from editorial blasts. In October a long article by Emily appeared in the *Contemporary Review*, having been rejected earlier by the *Nineteenth Century* for being 'too strong'. Keeping up with correspondence from friends and contacts in South Africa was another constant battle. It was all necessary but extremely time-consuming. Being tied to a desk was not how Emily viewed her mission. She was anxious to get back to South Africa and resume her practical work.

Emily was always to insist that she had no intention of breaking the ban on her return to the concentration camps. Not only, she protested, would she never have stooped to anything so undignified but, as martial law was in force throughout the interior, an open act of disobedience would have been impossible. She made the reasons she was returning to the Cape appear innocent. She claimed she had been told that the Boer women who had been deported to the coastal towns were in need of help; she wanted also to enquire into the circumstances of British refugees – something she was repeatedly accused of neglecting – who had fled from the Boer republics at the outbreak of the war. There might have been some truth in all this but it was far from being the whole story.

Emily admits that she had been reliably informed that the British refugees needed no further help, and she must have known that the Boer women in the coastal towns were not without friends and support groups. What little extra help she could have given hardly justified a journey to South Africa. Nor would it have warranted the secrecy surrounding her departure from England. According to her own account, she went out of her way to ensure that nobody knew she was on board the *Avondale Castle* by persuading the shipping company to omit her name from the passenger list. (In fact her name was definitely on the passenger list when the ship arrived at Cape Town.) What is more certain is that she told no one other than her family and a few close friends that she was leaving for South Africa, and made sure the War Office did not get to hear of it. This is understandable, but it is at odds with her protests of innocence. She may not have intended to break her ban, but it is fairly obvious that she was determined to continue her work for the women and children in the camps. That, in itself, would have been enough for the War Office to prevent her leaving England.

Her attempts at secrecy were wasted. She was far too well known to slip out of England that easily. A vigilant journalist heard of her boarding the *Avondale Castle* and not only reported it but, for good measure, added that she was on her way back to the camps. This, and another event – which occurred while she was at sea – effectively put an end to whatever plans Emily may have had when she sailed from Southampton.

On 9 October 1901, four days after the *Avondale Castle* left England, martial law in South Africa was extended from the interior to include Cape Town and all other ports. Kitchener had been arguing for this for a long time but had been unable to obtain the co-operation of the Cape Attorney-General. In the end he had had to ask Joseph Chamberlain to bring pressure on the civil authorities, who finally capitulated and yielded control of the ports to the military. It took a couple of weeks for the effect of this to be felt. Life in Cape Town went on undisturbed and it was not until the arrival of the *Avondale Castle*, with Miss Emily Hobhouse on board, that the law was put into effect.

That the first person to be arrested by the military was a woman would not have worried Kitchener; that the woman was Emily Hobhouse undoubtedly delighted him. Always touchy on the concentration camp question, Kitchener had been highly incensed by the agitation in England. Not only had he been informed of the parliamentary debates sparked off by Emily's report, but he was aware that the Fawcett commission had been set up as a result of that report and he considered this to be a criticism of the way he was dealing with the civilian population. He resented both the meddling and the person behind it. According to his biographer, Sir Philip Magnus, he 'conceived an especial prejudice against Miss Hobhouse, whom he always described to his staff as "that bloody woman".'[17] Now, when this ogress placed herself at his mercy, he did not hesitate to show her who wielded power in South Africa.

The *Avondale Castle* arrived in Table Bay, Cape Town on Sunday

27 October 1901. 'We dropped anchor as the clock struck 4 p.m.,' Emily wrote to her brother, 'and we were all dressed and ready to go ashore, ready with the readiness of those who had been twenty-two days at sea, grinding along with an asthmatic engine against strong currents and head winds . . . All was calm and lovely as we glided into the Bay and our spirits were at boiling point. Of course, we had to wait for pratique, but when the steam tug came out alongside us I saw with horror the khaki in it, and knew at once the worst had come.'

The khaki Emily had spotted was worn by Lieutenant Lingham, an army officer who had been sent to the ship by the military commander of Cape Town. It soon became clear why he was there. Once on board he established himself in the smoking room and, to everyone's dismay, announced that he intended to examine all the 450 passengers. Realizing that this meant there was no chance of getting ashore that night, Emily sadly went to her cabin and unpacked before joining the queue in the smoking room. When she eventually reached Lieutenant Lingham's desk her depression deepened. Taking note of her name, the officer said he would prefer to deal with her at the very end and asked her to wait. Emily had no option but to leave the queue. Even then she did not fully appreciate the situation and thought that she was simply to be given a more thorough grilling.

Not until the bell rang for dinner that evening did Lingham arrive and ask to speak to her. As the ship was in a chaotic state, with crowds of people milling about, Emily suggested that they go to the captain's cabin where they could talk undisturbed. The captain, with whom Emily had become friendly, welcomed them and was about to leave them alone when Lingham asked him to stay. Then Lingham turned to Emily and abruptly told her she was under arrest. He said she would not be allowed to land *anywhere* in South Africa and was forbidden to communicate, by word or letter, with anyone on shore. After explaining that he was acting on the instructions of Colonel Cooper, the military commander of Cape Town, he refused to name any higher authority and told the unfortunate captain – who, says Emily, was looking 'horribly miserable' – that he would be held responsible for Miss Hobhouse observing the conditions of her arrest.

'Next,' says the thoroughly shaken Emily, 'he gave me the alternative of returning home by the *Carisbrook Castle* on Wednesday, or remaining where I was. I replied that to return by the *Carisbrook* was out of the question, for I felt wholly unfit for another long voyage. I then asked if he would take letters for me to the Commandant and the

Governor, etc., and this he agreed to do, promising to call for them when he came to finish the ship in the morning.'

After Lingham left, Emily squared her shoulders and went down to dinner, trying to look as calm and unconcerned as she could. She managed to chatter merrily throughout the meal, although she was perfectly aware that word had leaked out and all eyes were on her. Then, leaving the dining saloon, she went to find the one woman with whom she had become friendly during the voyage. This was a Miss Steedman, a teacher who was on her way to take up the principalship of a well-known girls' school in Bloemfontein. Having first been wary of Emily's reputation as an agitator, she had gradually warmed to her and was now full of sympathy. With Miss Steedman's help and encouragement Emily wrote four letters: one each to Lord Milner and Lord Kitchener, one to the Governor of the Cape, Sir Walter Hely-Hutchinson, and a covering one to Colonel Cooper.

The letters all carried the same message. In them Emily expressed surprise at her arrest, protested that her mission was not political but purely philanthropic, and explained her wish to help women in the coastal towns, particularly the British refugees 'about whom so much has been heard'. If she was not allowed to do this, she wrote, would it not be possible for her to stay a while in the Cape with friends, as she did not feel well enough to stand the strain of remaining on board the *Avondale Castle* or of returning immediately to England on another ship. She made a special point of pleading for her nurse, Miss Phillips, who she said should be given permission to land as she intended to settle in South Africa.

'It cannot but seem to me', her letter to Colonel Cooper ended, 'that the summary arrest of an Englishwoman bound on works of charity, without warrant of any kind or stated offence, is a proceeding which requires explanation.'[18]

This was to be Emily's most persistent challenge to the authorities. She was continually defying them to prove that her work in South Africa had been, or was intended to be, subversive. As she never tired of pointing out, however much she might have disagreed with the aims and conduct of the war, she had never publicly criticized them, nor had she commented accusingly on the methods of the military. Her concern had been solely for the sufferings of the women and children in the concentration camps; she had kept her political opinions to herself. From time to time her opponents tried to disprove this by attributing to her remarks made by some of the more intemperate pro-Boers, but they were never able to make their accusations stick:

Emily had no difficulty in repudiating misquotations. Over twenty years later she was to claim that no valid reason had ever been given for her arrest; 'the explanation being that there was none to give'. But at the time it was not easy to remain cool. Trying to disguise her misgivings proved a terrible strain. After writing her letters she spent a sleepless night shuddering from head to foot. She pulled herself together the next morning; there was no question of her giving in meekly.

> I shall be very polite, [she told her brother] very dignified, but in every way I possibly can, a thorn in the flesh to them. I see already many ways of being a thorn. For instance *they* don't want it much talked of in Cape Town and I mean that it shall be. We are to move into dock as soon as the gale subsides, and I shall at once demand a guard; partly because it is extremely disagreeable for Captain Brown to be my gaoler, and partly that the guard is their witness that I keep the rules laid down. Most of all because I understand they don't want to do it because of making it conspicuous. I know soldiers hate guarding women. I also mean to refuse to return to England until such time as I myself feel willing and able, unless of course, they send me under force of arms. I shall not move a limb in that direction. If the *Avondale* unloads immediately she will be able to continue her voyage in ten days' time, and then they must find another prison for me. I have already petitioned all the authorities for a *land* prison.

When Lieutenant Lingham returned to the ship, Emily handed him her four letters, together with a more personal one she had written to her friend Mrs Charles Murray. These, she was later assured by Colonel Cooper, were passed on, and permission was also given for her nurse to land. But she was told that she must remain a prisoner. That same afternoon Colonel Cooper came to see her. He tried to persuade her to accept a passage on the *Carisbrook Castle* which was leaving on Wednesday but this she refused to consider. She wryly observed that she was perfectly willing to remain a prisoner if the honour or safety of England demanded it, but that she would prefer to do so in a land prison.

Colonel Cooper was followed by Lieutenant Lingham, who arrived in answer to Emily's request for a guard. She told him that it was unfair to expect her friend Captain Brown to act as her gaoler and she could not understand why, having placed her under arrest, the military did not guard her. This embarrassed Lingham. He replied evasively by asking her to give her word that she would not try to escape. Emily was astonished: that, she declared, would be tantamount to asking her to keep herself in prison. She wanted to know why they would trust her word at sea but not on land. Surely, she argued, the value of her word would be the same wherever it was given. When Lingham refused to answer her questions, Emily began to suspect the worst. She was afraid that, even though Lingham would not admit it, the only alternative to giving her word was that she would be forcibly removed to another ship. Fearing this, she agreed to obey orders until she heard from Lord Milner and Lord Kitchener.

The most depressing part of the day had come when the other passengers disembarked. Emily stood on the upper deck watching the little tug ferrying them across the harbour to the dockside. Left alone, she tried to amuse herself by sketching Table Mountain. So strong was the wind that she had to pin her paper to the deck and lie down flat to work at her drawing. She found it impossible to read. The only book that remotely interested her was Macaulay's *History of England* which she discovered in the ship's library. It contained an account of the imprisonment of Bishop Trelawney (her mother's ancestor) and six other bishops during the reign of James II. She read it through hoping to find guidance on how to behave under duress, and was delighted to discover that the bishops had refused to pay for their keep in the Tower of London. That showed her how to make a further 'bore' of herself. She decided that not only would she refuse to pay the ten shillings a day for her keep but that she would also refuse to pay her return fare to England. It was not much, but it could be counted as a family tradition.

The *Avondale Castle* finally moved into dock on Wednesday, 30 October. That was the day the *Carisbrook Castle* was due to sail. Emily had the satisfaction of seeing it leave without her.

If Colonel Cooper had been hoping to keep Emily's arrival a secret, it was unwise of him to have forwarded her letter to Mrs Charles Murray. Hardly had the *Avondale Castle* tied up before a party of women, led by Mrs Murray and carrying fruit and flowers, marched up the gangplank. Among them were Mrs Murray's older sister, Miss Betty Molteno, accompanied by her life-long friend Miss Alice Greene, and Emily's old friend Mrs Harry Currey. It was an emotional meeting. The talk was mostly about Emily's immediate needs. Alice Greene offered to send a cable to England saying simply 'Deported' and Betty Molteno promised to return the next day with a washer-woman. There was little else they could do, but their visit was a comfort to Emily.

Betty Molteno later described what happened when she revisited the *Avondale Castle* the following day. Her account is more reliable and detailed than that given by Emily, who was by then in a confused state. Betty Molteno was a highly competent professional woman who had recently retired as headmistress of a prestigious girls' school in Port Elizabeth. She and Alice Greene, who had been vice-principal of the school, were feminists, friends of Olive Schreiner, and ardent champions of the Boer women. Emily could have had no more dedicated allies.

The day started badly for Miss Molteno. When she arrived at Cape Town castle to get a boarding-pass for the *Avondale Castle*, she was kept waiting for a long time and then her request to take a laundress with her was turned down. Miss Hobhouse, explained Colonel Cooper, would not need any domestic help as she was leaving that day on the *Roslin Castle*. Somewhat taken aback, Betty Molteno asked for permission to say goodbye to Emily and this Cooper reluctantly allowed. Her further request to take Mrs Murray with her, however, was refused. The only real interest the colonel showed in Emily was in her relationship to Lord Hobhouse.

On board the *Avondale Castle*, Betty Molteno found Emily lying in a deck chair with her eyes closed. She woke with a start. On her lap was a large, official envelope which she handed to her friend to read. It had been delivered that morning. It was a notification from the dock authorities that she had been granted a free passage on the *Roslin Castle* and was expected to embark that afternoon. The *Roslin Castle*, Emily had discovered, was a troopship which was taking wounded soldiers back to England. She told Betty Molteno that she had been pressured all the previous evening and most of the morning to obey the embarkation order but had obstinately refused to leave the *Avondale Castle*. She was now almost too exhausted to talk and remained on deck while Miss Molteno went down to lunch.

Emily's nurse, Miss Phillips, had been given permission to go ashore and was in Cape Town when Betty Molteno arrived. She did not return until after lunch and was kneeling beside Emily, discussing her morning in town, when Lieutenant Lingham suddenly appeared. He had come to tell Emily to pack in preparation for boarding the *Roslin Castle*. Emily, struggling to control her voice, told him that she could not think of undertaking another voyage until she had recovered her strength. Repeating that he had orders that she must embark that afternoon, Lingham stalked off. Later he sent for the nurse. The nurse returned to report to Emily that she had been ordered to pack her boxes. Emily promptly sent her back to tell Lingham that Miss Hobhouse had forbidden her to do any such thing. When the nurse next came back, she had more ominous news. Lingham, she said, had ordered stewardesses to do the packing.

There was nothing Emily could do. Captain Brown had gone ashore and his chief officer could only apologize and ask Emily to ensure the nurse was present when the packing was done. At first Emily refused to let the nurse have anything to do with the packing; only when the chief officer pointed out that someone needed to check what was being packed did she relent.

The next person to arrive was Lieutenant-Colonel Williamson of the Royal Army Medical Corps. He announced that, as head of the Cape medical staff, he had been sent to examine Emily. When she protested that she had her own doctor in Cape Town – Mrs Murray's husband – and was too exhausted to undergo an examination by a strange medical man, Colonel Williamson appeared baffled. A shy, middle-aged bachelor, quite unused to women, he was at a loss to know what to do next. In the end, he did what everyone else seemed to do and sent for the nurse. Eventually Emily was coaxed into agreeing to be examined in the smoking room, with the nurse and Betty Molteno present. Her resistance was finally worn down by Williamson's suggestion that he might find her too unwell to sail on the *Roslin Castle*. Unfortunately, he found no such thing. He pronounced Emily's heart to be sound and said that with the help of a stimulant, brandy or champagne, she would be well enough to leave the ship.

According to a story Williamson told later, Emily then wedged herself behind a fixed table and prepared to do battle. Betty Molteno does not mention this. She says that after the medical examination the nurse came in to report that Miss Hobhouse's baggage, including her bicycle, had been taken from the hold and that a cab was waiting at the dockside. She was followed by the chief officer who was again full of apologies, explaining that he had removed the luggage on Lieutenant Lingham's order and was now waiting to have that confirmed in writing. Emily remained immovable. 'They may take my luggage,' she declared, 'but they will not take me.'

Colonel Williamson thought otherwise. After politely asking her to accompany him quietly, he warned her that he was acting under orders and would use force if necessary. When she protested that no English gentleman would carry out such an order, his patience snapped. Refusing to argue, he left saying that he would return with two army nurses. A few minutes later he burst into the smoking room followed, not by two army nurses but, according to Betty Molteno, by two hefty volunteer nurses who marched across the room and took up positions on either side of Emily. For once Emily remained calm. According to her own account she handled the situation with dignity. 'I spoke quietly to the women,' she says, 'asking them to lay no violent hands upon me. They answered they were under military orders, and this I said I understood, but I put before them that the laws of humanity and nature are, or should be, higher than military laws, and appealed to them not to mar their sacred office as nurses by molesting a sick woman. I had appealed in vain to the men, but I hoped I should not appeal in vain to my own sex.'

Betty Molteno says much the same thing and suggests that there was something almost hypnotic in the way Emily spoke. They all agree about what happened next. The faces of the two nurses gradually softened, their arms dropped to their sides and then, without a word, they left the room. 'I thanked them as they went,' says Emily. 'They behaved like true English women. I was left alone.'

But she was not alone. Betty Molteno and Nurse Phillips were still with her and shortly afterwards the nurse went to fetch tea, and returned followed by a steward with a plate of biscuits. Emily and Betty Molteno were then left to relax after the drama. The peaceful interlude did not last long. The nurse returned, wide-eyed and breathless, to announce an alarming new development. She had just heard that a stretcher had been sent for and that Colonel Williamson intended to have Emily carried away like a lunatic.

Emily immediately sent for the chief officer and asked him to stay with her as a witness. They were then joined by Captain Brown who, having just returned, was far from happy about what was happening on his ship. He sympathized with Emily but confessed he was powerless to help her, although he agreed to stay as a witness. Waiting tensely for the stretcher bearers, they were all relieved when the two volunteer nurses reappeared. These highly embarrassed women had been sent to make a last attempt to get Emily to change her mind. They did their best to coax her. In a whispered conversation one of them warned her that the stretcher bearers were waiting and would not hesitate to manhandle her if ordered to do so: they were, she said, army servicemen. But Emily refused to be frightened or persuaded. She made it clear that she had no intention of leaving voluntarily and once again the nurses quietly backed out.

When Colonel Williamson made a final attempt to bully her into submission, Emily appeared to waver. After a short argument she offered to leave on the regular mailship, *Kilfauns Castle*, the following Wednesday. Williamson was unimpressed. His instructions, he said, were that she must leave that day. As he walked out of the room Betty Molteno, after consulting Emily, ran after him and begged him to reconsider Emily's offer to travel in the mailship. Her friend, she said, was in no condition to sail before that. But the colonel remained adamant. It was impossible for him to make concessions, he said, as his orders came direct from Lord Kitchener.

At 7 o'clock that evening, as Emily was thinking of going to bed, Nurse Phillips rushed in to say the stretcher bearers were on their way to the smoking room. Almost immediately Colonel Williamson arrived with two burly soldiers who, assuming mask-like expressions, positioned themselves close to the door. Williamson then went up to Emily, touched her on the shoulder, and asked her whether she was prepared to leave quietly; otherwise, he said, 'there are the soldiers'. Emily answered him in her grandest manner. 'Sir,' she said, 'I cannot and will not give other reply than what I have said from the beginning. My refusal was based on principle, and principles do not alter in a day; nor can they be frightened out of me by force . . . I will not go one step voluntarily towards the *Roslin Castle*. I beg you to leave me.'

This show of pride was lost on the colonel. He signalled to the soldiers, who approached Emily hesitantly. Sensing their misgivings, she launched into another of her appeals. She begged them to show her the same respect as they would like shown to their wives and mothers; there was, she declared again, a law of humanity that was higher than martial law. But the men had fewer qualms than Emily imagined. Seizing her they lifted her off her feet and began to carry her out of the room. She put up a fierce fight. So determinedly did she struggle that Williamson had to bind her arms with her shawl. That, at least, is what Emily claims. Later a friend asked Williamson whether, in the tussle, Emily's 'frillies' had been revealed. 'I had thought of that,' said the puritanical colonel, 'and when she was picked up I threw a shawl over her feet.'[19]

More soldiers were waiting outside the smoking room. Here Emily was placed in a wickerwork chair and an attempt was made to carry her through the ship in it. However, she quickly freed herself and, calling the men brutes, planted her feet firmly on the deck. Once again she had to be lifted, and carried struggling to the dockside. Williamson bustled along behind her shouting to the men to take care she was not harmed. As she was hurried down the gangplank, Emily turned and shouted her thanks to Captain Brown and the ship's crew.

Betty Molteno, panting along behind, arrived just in time to see Emily being bundled into a carriage. The two volunteer nurses were sitting with her. What alarmed Miss Molteno most were the hoots and hisses of a crowd that had gathered and were calling for Emily to be thrown into the harbour. Whether, as was later reported, Emily 'shouted and screamed' back at them is uncertain. Martial law prevented the incident from being reported in the local press but there was no shortage of highly-coloured accounts afloat in Cape Town. One paper to defy the law was a satirical journal called *The Owl* which published its own weak-humoured version. 'The translation [to the troopship] was no easy matter,' it reported. 'It entailed the services of a stretcher, body straps, a file of Tommies, half-a-dozen nurses and a few other people and during its progress the fair subject of so much official devotion made day beautiful by her musical, albeit high-pitched warbling.' This was typical of the way Emily was ridiculed. The Cape Attorney-General found Colonel Williamson's straight-faced account 'simply excruciating; I laughed till I was tired . . . I thought Harry Piers who was sitting opposite would have had a fit.'

Emily was spared all this schoolboy mirth. On arriving at the *Roslin Castle* she kept her vow not to take a voluntary step towards the ship and had to be carried up the gangplank. She was joined shortly afterwards by Nurse Phillips, whom Betty Molteno had persuaded to return with her patient to England. Before the ship sailed the following morning, Emily dashed off scornful letters to Kitchener, Milner and Hely-Hutchinson. Her short confused note to Kitchener summed up her bitterness.

'Your brutality has triumphed over my weakness and sickness,' she wrote. 'You have forgotten so to be a patriot as not to forget you are a gentleman. I hope that in future you will exercise greater width of judgement in the exercise of your high office. To carry out orders such as these is a degradation both to the office and the manhood of your soldiers. I feel ashamed to own you as a fellow-countryman. Emily Hobhouse.'

Emily's friends in England were all impatiently awaiting her return. Her arrest and deportation had been reported in the press and had won her widespread sympathy. The mood of her supporters was reflected at a meeting held in Bath the day after the *Roslin Castle* left Cape Town. The speaker was Emily's old champion Sir Henry Campbell-Bannerman, and the event was reported in the *Manchester Guardian*.

Sir Henry delivered a trenchant attack on the Government with regard to the Concentration Camps. First, he paid tribute to Miss Hobhouse, the mention of whose name moved the audience to a remarkable demonstration, ladies and gentlemen rising and cheering her for several moments. 'That noble lady,' Sir Henry called her, 'who had the honour of having first called public attention to the matter, and who has now been further honoured by being expelled from South Africa.' The cheering which followed showed that on this subject at least, the Liberal Party as represented at that meeting is in entire accord.[20]

Her family had been alerted to her return by Alice Greene's telegram, and two letters from Emily, smuggled out by a ship's officer, had informed them of the events leading up to her deportation. When the *Roslin Castle* put in at St Vincent's Emily received a welcoming cable from her aunt, and when the ship docked at Southampton she was met by Leonard Courtney and his wife. She went straight to London to stay with her uncle and aunt at their Bruton Street house.

During the next few weeks messages of sympathy and requests for her to speak poured in from all over the country. Flattering as it all was, she felt far too weak to respond. Like her father and brother, Emily was subject to bouts of hypochondria, but now she was genuinely ill. A combination of prolonged nervous tension and a starvation diet – she had eaten very little on the *Avondale Castle* and could not stomach the food on the troopship – had drained her strength and caused her to lose weight. Her aunt's doctor insisted that only complete rest would restore her health.

But there were some things that could not wait. Emily, disgusted at the way her deportation had been misreported in some newspapers, was determined to state her side of the affair. Urged on by her uncle, she wrote a blow by blow account of her experiences – in the form of a letter to the Distress Fund – and published it as a pamphlet. She made it quite clear that she held the military authorities responsible for what had happened to her. Then she let it be known that she intended to sue Lord Kitchener and Lord Milner, Colonel Cooper and Lieutenant Lingham for assault and false imprisonment. Lord Hobhouse gave her his full backing and wrote a long letter to *The Times* challenging the current interpretation of martial law which, he maintained, should be tested in a court of law.

The fashionable solicitor Sir George Lewis was engaged to act for Emily and the War Office was notified of her intention. St John

Brodrick, however, refused the writ served on him and Lord Kitchener treated the whole matter as a joke. 'I see', he wrote to a friend in mock horror, 'Miss Hobhouse has taken action against me, and I shall probably be put in prison on my arrival in England.'[21] He knew he had nothing to fear. Even with the cleverest lawyers, Emily was no match for senior officials like Kitchener and Milner who, in wartime, had the full backing of a government with powers to protect them from prosecution. This is what Emily was told by her legal advisers, who warned her that any action she brought was likely to fail. In the end, it was decided not to risk defeat and the legal proceedings were abandoned.

As soon as she was well enough, Emily was fêted at a dinner presided over by C. P. Scott, the legendary editor of the *Manchester Guardian*, at the New Reform Club. This, the first time such an honour had been accorded to a woman, was one of the few tributes paid to Emily in Britain. Such occasions were rare indeed. Emily's critics far outnumbered her admirers. A new adversary to enter the lists about this time was Arthur Conan Doyle. Already well-known as the creator of Sherlock Holmes, Doyle had added to his literary reputation – and earned himself a knighthood – by defending Britain's imperial role in a soberly-argued book *The War in South Africa, Its Causes and Conduct*. He had written the book with the intention of counteracting widespread criticism of the war in Europe and America, but he had also taken a few digs at protesters closer to home. Discussing the concentration camps, he mentioned that 'Miss Hobhouse, an English lady' had criticized the camps unfavourably. But he added that her report had been discounted 'by the fact that her political prejudices were known to be against the Government', and then claimed that 'Mr Charles Hobhouse, a relation of hers, and a Radical member of Parliament, has since admitted that some of her statements will not bear examination.'[22]

This was a slur that Emily could not ignore. Conan Doyle was a popular author and his book was already known to have sold a quarter of a million copies. In order to defend herself, Emily wrote to Charles Hobhouse – a distant cousin – to find out whether he had been correctly reported. She soon discovered he had not. He readily admitted having criticized her report in a speech he had made at Derby, but he emphatically denied having questioned her honesty and said he had already taken Conan Doyle up on this point. His criticism, he said, had been provoked by Emily publishing statements from Boer women, who accused British soldiers of inhumanity, without giving the full names of the women or offering corroborative evidence. He had also pointed out to Conan Doyle that he was in no position to comment on Emily's statements because he knew nothing about them.

This was something Emily could understand. She accepted her cousin's criticism and explained that she had been obliged to withhold precise information about the statements in her report because Boer women could be penalized under martial law. 'All the same,' she said, 'on p.36 of my Report I particularly mention that the individual name of the person making the statement is in each case known to me and the [Distress Fund] Committee.'[23] She offered to send Charles Hobhouse privately any names he might require, on condition that they were not published. It was more difficult getting Conan Doyle to retract. Months were to pass before he made a public apology in what Emily calls 'scant fashion'.

The baseless criticism of men like Conan Doyle, together with the biased comments in parts of the Fawcett report, made Emily decide to publish all the information she had collected concerning the concentration camps, naming names and confuting her detractors. This, she realized, would mean writing a book. As she had not fully recovered from her illness and arrangements had been made for her to convalesce in France, she welcomed the opportunity to concentrate on writing while enjoying a quiet holiday. What she needed, she said, was sun and silence, not idleness. The retreat she chose was a converted Benedictine abbey at Talloires, on the shores of Lake Annecy in Haute-Savoie.

With its distant views of the snow-capped Alps, its orchards and meadows sloping down to the placid lake and its many walks, Talloires had a beauty and peace which Emily calls 'indescribable'. Nothing could have served as a greater contrast to the heartaches and sadness, the squalor and ugliness of the concentration camps about which she had come to write. Her book, *The Brunt of the War, and Where it Fell*, is a grim and detailed account of the farm-burnings, forced removals and life in the camps. Peppered with statistics, ration lists and tables of the death rates, it combines her own experiences with the statements of Boer women, voluntary workers, medical men and British soldiers. It does not make for easy reading and in no way rivals Conan Doyle's popular account of the war, but it provided a valuable and sober counterblast to the more strident trumpetings of imperialism.

14

Visitors to Harmony

DURING THE closing months of the war, Hansie van Warmelo and her mother were involved in some extremely risky ventures. Their house by then had become an espionage centre, a hide-out for Boer spies and fugitives. This development resulted from the contacts made by Mrs Van Warmelo while Hansie had been working at the Irene camp. Not until she returned to Harmony did Hansie discover the full extent of her mother's secret activities.

It had started when Mrs Van Warmelo was visited by a Mr Willem Botha. She had no idea who he was and his unexpected arrival at her house came as a surprise. An exceptionally short man, he had hobbled up the garden path on a stick and, at first glance, seemed singularly unimpressive. She greeted him warily. It was only when he handed her a card on which one of her close women friends had written 'You must trust the bearer as you would myself' that Mrs Van Warmelo became less suspicious. She was further reassured by the story he had to tell.

In February 1900, a few months after the outbreak of war, Willem Botha was serving with the commandos in Natal when he was struck by lightning. Severely incapacitated, he was invalided back to Pretoria. He was still there when the British occupied the capital and was prevented from escaping by ill-health. Some of his friends were more fortunate. One of these was the former beadle of Pretoria's main Dutch Reformed Church, Jacobus 'Koos' Naudé; he not only managed to bluff his way through the British lines but, on joining General Louis Botha, was given charge of a corps of scouts and eventually made responsible for the Boer espionage service. Promoted to the rank of captain, Naudé had since secretly revisited Pretoria and helped other burgers leave the town. But for all his resourcefulness Captain Naudé found it impossible to operate without inside help, and a group of townsmen were organized to act as his contacts. Willem Botha and four other trustworthy burgers were chosen to serve as a 'secret committee'. They were authorized to enlist ten or twelve men and women, who would not attend their meetings but would carry out their instructions. It was as a representative of this secret service network that Willem Botha called upon Mrs Van Warmelo.

He told her about his committee whose work, until then, consisted mainly of contacting and assisting men who wished to leave Pretoria. Now they wanted to extend their activities. They were particularly anxious to find a way of sending despatches abroad so that they would keep their allies and supporters in Europe informed of events in the Transvaal. The person they most wanted to contact was the ageing President Paul Kruger who, in September 1901, had been persuaded to leave South Africa and was now exiled in Holland. This is where Willem Botha thought Mrs Van Warmelo might help. 'Her fame as an exceedingly clever "smuggler" had evidently spread,' says Hansie, 'and if the plan of the White Envelope had been known to her visitor at the time, he would no doubt have been even more satisfied.' But no mention was made of Mrs Van Warmelo's methods; Botha had to take her promise to act as an intermediary on trust.

Mrs Van Warmelo's fame as a smuggler was known to others in Pretoria. She was to tell Hansie of how, shortly after Willem Botha's visit, a young woman (described as 'Miss F') arrived at Harmony with a man she called her brother and announced that he had just returned from Europe with a message for the Boer leaders. Could Mrs Van Warmelo help? It then emerged that the man's message concerned a consignment of dynamite from Europe which had been smuggled into the eastern Transvaal and buried near the frontier. It had been sent by Boer sympathizers who were worried about the 'dearth of explosives' needed to disrupt the railway lines. Miss F's 'brother' had come to Pretoria to explain where the dynamite was buried and needed someone to pass this information to General Louis Botha. He had brought two sample packets of the explosive with him which, he said, were harmless until mixed and ignited with a long fuse. He had smuggled the fuse through the Transvaal customs in the black lace and chiffon of a huge 'Parisian hat' which he had bought for his sister. Mrs Van Warmelo was impressed. She decided to consult Willem Botha, who told her he knew of some spies who were about to leave Pretoria for the Boer lines. The following day, Botha came to Harmony to study a map showing where the dynamite was hidden and took away the packets of explosive to deliver to the departing spies. The Parisian hat was also unpicked, says Hansie, 'and that night the dynamite fuse, wound closely round the body of a spy, went out to the commandos.'

All this happened while Hansie was at Irene, but shortly after her return she was also involved in the smuggling of dynamite. According to her diary, it was the middle of July 1901 when Willem Botha told Mrs Van Warmelo that two spies had arrived in town and wanted to see her about 'certain communications' she had sent to General Louis Botha. They were staying with Mrs Joubert, the highly respected widow of Commandant-General P. J. Joubert, and would be leaving the following evening with despatches. Mrs Joubert's house was considered a safe refuge because the widow was so well trusted by the British that Lord Roberts had once sent her on a mission to the Boer lines: that she might harbour spies would have seemed most unlikely. This was just as well because when Hansie and her mother arrived at Mrs Joubert's house the following day they discovered that her guests were no ordinary spies. One of them, a tall, fair, boyish-looking man in his mid twenties, turned out to be the dashing Captain Koos Naudé and the other, 'a mere youth' named Greyling, was his secretary. Hansie was thrilled to meet them: healthy, brown and hearty, '*your own men*,' she enthused, 'straight from the glorious freedom of their life in the veld.'

Captain Naudé had brought a report from a recent conference of the Boer generals which he wanted Mrs Van Warmelo to send to Europe. He also told them that some more dynamite samples had arrived from the cache in the eastern Transvaal and were being kept in another house in Pretoria until someone could fetch them. The problem was, he said, that neither he nor his secretary dare risk crossing the town in daylight and they had no one else to act as a messenger. Hansie took the hint. She immediately offered to collect the samples.

Arriving at the address given her by Naudé, Hansie was handed a brown paper parcel and told curtly to 'read the instructions and destroy them'. She was then left alone in the drawing room. Opening the parcel she found a small bottle of yellowish powder, labelled as a colic remedy, and a pot of paste disguised as 'an excellent salve for chapped hands'. According to the instructions, when the powders and paste were mixed they formed the equivalent of a pound of dynamite.

Confident that the two substances were safe if kept apart, Hansie rewrapped the parcel, mounted her bicycle and started back to Mrs Joubert's house. Half-way there, she changed her mind. Acting on a wild impulse, she decided to call at the military governor's office for a chat with her old friend General Maxwell. It would be 'fun', she thought, to visit the governor clutching a parcel of dynamite. But there was another reason for this show of bravado: if for some reason she was being watched, there was, she reckoned, 'nothing like a visit to the Government Buildings to disarm suspicion'.

And she had a good excuse for her visit. At that time Hansie was still hoping the governor would allow her to inspect and report on the concentration camps in the Transvaal and she wanted to discuss the tour with him. She was a little disconcerted to find him in a bad mood, but it did not take her long to win him over. When she told him why she had come, Maxwell brightened up. He told her that he had been thinking about her tour and was prepared to issue the necessary permits. But he warned her that travelling about the country in wartime might prove dangerous. What, he asked, 'would you think of a charge of dynamite under your train?' Glancing down at the parcel on her lap, Hansie said it was something she was prepared to risk.

They spent the rest of the time chatting about recent events, including reports of how President Steyn had narrowly escaped from a British ambush. Hansie thought this might have accounted for the governor's bad mood when she arrived. She left Maxwell's office in high spirits and cycled furiously back to Mrs Joubert's house where she handed over the parcel. After saying goodbye to Naudé and Greyling she returned to Harmony feeling pleased with her morning's work. She was not to know that Maxwell would soon change his mind about the camps. Smitten with Hansie as the governor undoubtedly was, he appears to have thought it wiser to send two older women in her place. When Hansie was told of this she did not blame Maxwell, who she was sure only acted under orders from the 'awful' Lord Kitchener.

Mrs Van Warmelo's meeting with Captain Naudé led to Harmony becoming a recognized espionage centre. In addition to the despatches that were smuggled out of the country, the Van Warmelos kept in touch with the Boer forces and passed on bulletins from the commandos to the consulates in Pretoria. This was done in the greatest secrecy – the typed document being slipped under the consulate door at night – to avoid any chance of betrayal. Willem Botha warned both Hansie and her mother never to take anyone on trust.

Mrs Van Warmelo took this warning very seriously. When, shortly afterwards, another visitor arrived – a man whom Hansie knew – and begged them to take in two men who were hiding in the town, Mrs Van Warmelo refused. Much to Hansie's astonishment, she said she had never harboured spies and had no intention of doing so. Hansie considered this heartless but could do nothing to change her mother's mind. Only later did she appreciate Mrs Van Warmelo's wisdom in refusing to shelter strangers.

Willem Botha kept the Van Warmelos informed of the activities of the agents who visited Pretoria. The increased vigilance of the military made every attempt to enter the town more hazardous. Several of the spies had narrow escapes and some had had to shoot their way out again. Captain Naudé was the man most sought after, and there was considerable alarm when it was learned that his wife and children had been arrested and that a close watch was being kept on his empty house. Hansie found this more amusing than frightening. Did they really think, she scoffed, that 'the Captain of the Secret Service would walk into the trap some fine evening?'

There was in fact little chance of Naudé arriving at this time, but he did send in young Greyling and two other men on a special mission. They had come, Willem Botha told Hansie, to obtain a copy of a highly secret railway timetable which was kept in the government offices. The commandos, he said, needed this timetable to learn which trains were carrying the goods they needed to replenish their dwindling stocks. Hansie and her mother were asked if they could help. Unfortunately neither of them had ever heard of the timetable; but, after making a few enquiries, they discovered that some of their friends were better informed.

What they learned was not encouraging. The timetable was said to be carefully guarded and only senior officials and army officers were allowed to consult it. Even so, Hansie refused to be discouraged. Remembering a man she knew who worked in the government offices, she decided to enlist his help through a mutual friend. At first the friend thought she was mad to suggest such a thing but, after a little wheedling, he reluctantly agreed to do what he could. It is obvious that she had chosen the right man to help her. Returning that evening from an interview with the anxious Mr Greyling, who was again being sheltered by Mrs Joubert, Hansie opened the front door of Harmony and found 'a small flat parcel on the floor, a book wrapped carelessly in a bit of white paper'. A glance through the book showed that it contained all the information needed by the commandos, and Hansie delivered it immediately to Mrs Joubert's house. Handing it to Grey-ling, she warned him to keep her name secret as it 'was well-known that there were traitors in the field' who passed on information to the British.

Just how true this was soon became apparent. Greyling and his companions had hardly left the town when Pretoria was shaken by an alarming development. One of the men whom Mrs Van Warmelo had earlier refused to harbour was caught, and turned 'King's evidence'. Not only did he inform on friends who had sheltered him but he gave the authorities details of other espionage activities in the town. 'More than eighty people were incriminated,' says Hansie. But neither she nor her mother had been named.

Her main concern was to discover the full extent of the informer's betrayal. She spent the next few days flying about Pretoria on her bicycle trying to find out how much harm had been done. On learning that none of the 'inner circle' had been arrested, she was somewhat reassured. All the same, everyone remained on edge. Willem Botha seemed particularly nervous. He told Hansie that when he was out for a walk one evening he had passed a man and a girl and heard the man say: 'This man has also been given away.' What troubled Hansie and her mother was the fact that the informant had been acquainted with both Captain Naudé and young Greyling. They wondered whether he also knew the names of members of the 'secret committee', and whether Greyling had told him how the timetable had been obtained. Mrs Van Warmelo thought it best to send word to Greyling telling him that his name was known to the military and warning him not to come back by his usual route.

But no further arrests were made as a result of the informer's confession. The next 'betrayal' came from an unlikely source and was obtained under ghastly pressure. A teenage boy who had performed various duties for the secret committee was captured on one of his missions, imprisoned and interrogated. All attempts to make him talk failed. He was as impervious to threats and bullying as he was to promises and blandishments. Frustrated, his captors tried a more menacing tactic. Late one evening an official arrived in the young man's cell and solemnly read out a death sentence, saying the execution would take place early the next morning. The prisoner was then left alone until daybreak when his father, sister and girl friend arrived to bid him goodbye. According to Hansie, they 'clung to him, sobbing, wailing and imploring him to give the names of his fellow-conspirators.' This, as was no doubt intended, proved too much for the young man who broke down and agreed to tell all he knew. And he knew a great deal. Not only did he name the five members of the secret committee, but he implicated several of their agents, including one of Mrs Joubert's sons.

Willem Botha was among the first to be seized. When Hansie and her mother heard of his arrest they were stunned. It took them some time to pull themselves together and decide what to do. Hansie's first thought was to go to Botha's house and comfort his wife who, after thirteen years of marriage, was expecting her first child. Mrs Van Warmelo sympathized but thought her daughter was courting disaster. But nothing she could say made Hansie change her mind. Whistling for her dog, she set off.

No one, she says, could have been more surprised to see her than Mrs Botha. Aware of the risks involved, the pregnant woman silently buried her head on Hansie's shoulder and began to sob. She then told her what had happened. After describing how two detectives had arrived on bicycles the previous evening with a warrant for the arrest of her husband, she went on to tell of the courageous way in which Botha had accepted his betrayal. She was thankful, she said, that the detectives had found no proof of her husband's connection with the secret committee. 'The house', she explained, 'was thoroughly searched for spies and all books and papers were taken away, but thanks to Mr Botha's prudence and foresight, not a single incriminating document was found.' From this she drew comfort. If there was no proof against her husband, she argued, his life would be safe 'although he would probably be sent as a prisoner of war to one of the distant islands.'

She was right. Altogether ten men were arrested that evening and taken to Pretoria gaol. They were kept there for almost three weeks. Not allowed to see each other, they were 'half-starved, threatened, told they were condemned to death, and then left severely alone with the sword hanging over their heads.' But none of them weakened. When it at last became obvious that they were not going to break, they were transferred to a 'rest camp' and treated as prisoners-of-war. While there, Willem Botha was told his wife had given birth to a baby and, surprisingly, he was allowed a two-hour visit home, under escort, to see her. The memory of this visit was to sustain him over the coming months: shortly afterwards he was sent, as his wife had predicted, to join other Boer prisoners in Bermuda.

Hansie and her mother lived in fear of discovery after the arrest of the secret committee. They found it difficult to believe that they had again escaped undetected. Every day they expected soldiers to arrive and take them away. Hansie's only consolation was that it would be difficult for the authorities to find proof of their activities: like Willem Botha, she had cleared the house of all incriminating documents.

The most damning evidence against Hansie was her diaries, of which she kept two versions. One was written in ink and told mostly of routine domestic matters, while the other – which she called her white diary – was written in invisible lemon juice and gave details of her own and her mother's espionage activities. So confident was Hansie that her invisible writing would not be revealed – and so strongly was she tempted to flirt with danger – that she left this diary open on her writing table. The legible diary and all her secret service correspondence, however, she had locked in an office safe in town. By keeping the white diary she must have known she was taking a risk, but her temerity went unchallenged. The book's 'clean and spotless pages' remained unread for eight years. It was Hansie herself who eventually applied the heat to reveal their contents so that she could use them for an account of her war experiences.

The rounding up of the secret committee disrupted but did not destroy Pretoria's spy ring. With most of the men having been caught, it was left to the women to protect any Boers who came into the town. They were soon put to the test. Shortly after the arrests Captain Naudé, unaware of what had happened, sent four of his men to Pretoria with despatches to be forwarded to President Kruger. They were experienced men who were used to entering the town. This time, though, they ran into trouble. As they approached the barbed-wire surrounds they were met by a storm of bullets and forced to retreat. One of the men got lost in the dark but the other three stumbled on, crossed the railway line, and succeeded in entering Pretoria from the opposite side. Now on their guard, they decided to avoid Mrs Joubert's house and instead made their way to her married daughter, Mrs Hendrina Malan. It was Mrs Malan who, the following morning, arrived at Harmony to beg the Van Warmelos for help.

Hansie immediately offered to send the despatches to President Kruger (without explaining how this would be done) and took charge of some other letters the men had brought. The real worry, however, was the men's plight. Mrs Malan told them the military authorities knew that the men had arrived in Pretoria despite being fired on, and were now searching the town for them. This was confirmed by two other women who arrived later. They reported that 'armed soldiers were patrolling the streets, men were being stopped to show their residential passes, and every cab and carriage was held up for inspection.' It was only a matter of time before the men were discovered and Mrs Malan insisted they leave that day, or at least as soon as night fell. Hansie promised to do what she could to help.

Once again she called in the friend who had helped her obtain the timetable. This time she told him she needed three residential passes so that the men could bluff their way out of town. If he could borrow the passes, she said, she would walk with the men to the barbed-wire fence and bring the passes back. The plan did not work as she anticipated. The men whom her friend approached for the loan of their passes refused to co-operate and Hansie was forced to accept three forged passes. Not at all sure these would stand close inspection she hurried with them to Mrs Malan's house, only to discover that Naudé's three agents had already left. Mrs Malan told her that a man with a residential pass had volunteered to walk out of town with them, and that if they were stopped the fugitives intended to escape while their accomplice pretended to look for his pass. Surprisingly this hare-brained scheme worked. The men, in fact, were not stopped and disappeared through the barbed-wire enclosure without a question being asked.

Hansie was far from happy with the way the escape had been arranged. As soon as things in the town had quietened down, she decided that the secret committee should be refashioned and that its five members should be women. Her mother agreed with her. There could be no question of an election so they simply chose three other women to help them: Henrietta Armstrong and her aunt, Mrs Honey, and the now tried and trusted Mrs Hendrina Malan. They held their first committee meeting at Harmony on 15 October 1901. It was an informal affair but they were all pledged to secrecy. Mrs Van Warmelo told them that she was in a position to communicate with President Kruger by every mail, but she still did not explain how. They also agreed that it was essential to have a hiding-place ready for Captain Naudé when he next entered Pretoria, and deciding upon the right place became the most important item on their agenda. After discussing it at great length, however, they ended up by making an almost inevitable choice. 'Harmony, surrounded as it was by British officers and their staffs, by British troops and Military Mounted Police,' enthused the delighted Hansie, 'was at last chosen as the most suitable, the only spot in Pretoria in which the Captain of the Secret Service could be harboured with any degree of safety.'

When and how Captain Naudé would again enter the town, they had no idea. Nothing had been heard from him for months and it was known that all sections of the fencework around Pretoria were now carefully guarded. But they had no doubt that he would at least make .ι attempt, and were prepared to wait for his decision 'knowing full well that if any one could find a way out, or in, he would.'

On 17 December 1901, Hansie and her mother had just sat down to their evening meal when they were called to speak to two strange girls who had arrived at the front entrance to Harmony. The girls said that two men, who were waiting at the garden gate, had sent them to fetch Mrs Van Warmelo. So unusual was this message and so furtive did the girls appear, that Hansie at first suspected that the military had set a trap for them. Mrs Van Warmelo's reaction was more decisive: if the men wanted to see her, she announced, they could come to the house and not expect her to go to them. She then stalked back indoors. Left alone with the girls, Hansie decided to follow them and see what happened. She walked slowly down the garden path behind them, but on reaching the gate she found that both girls had disappeared. Unable to see properly in the gathering dusk, Hansie was about to return to the house when she was joined by her mother. By this time she was quite sure it was a trap, and both women were startled when they heard someone approaching. Then, says Hansie, her heart stood still 'for a tall English officer, with helmet on and armed to the teeth' advanced and saluted them. The greatest shock came when this unsmiling soldier held out his hand and introduced himself simply as: 'Naudé'.

Captain Naudé delighted in passing himself off as a British officer. He adapted his disguise to suit any occasion and was never caught out. On this mission he had brought one of his men, named Venter, appropriately dressed as a corporal. After introducing him to the Van Warmelos, he said goodbye to the girls who were hovering in the background and then the four of them – Hansie and her mother and the two men in khaki – strolled back to the house. As they approached the fence separating them from the British encampment, they deliberately raised their voices and Hansie admits to a 'delightful thrill' on looking over the fence and glimpsing a sergeant-major in his tent, calmly smoking his pipe and reading, 'little dreaming that his arch enemies were within a stone's throw of his peaceful abode.'

Once inside, the men stretched out on sofas and relaxed. Hansie lit lamps and candles, opened the windows and played the piano loudly to let the sergeant-major know they were entertaining unashamedly.

Mrs Van Warmelo prepared a feast of ham and bacon, home-made bread and rusks, coffee and fruit. They sat up talking until midnight. Naudé told a long story of how they and another one of his men, Brenckmann, had got into Pretoria by wriggling under the barbed wire near the Aapies river. Then Brenckmann had gone to his home in the town and sent his sister and a friend to guide them to Harmony. Trying to find the house in the dark they had had several narrow escapes, the narrowest being when they stumbled into the nearby military police camp and then found themselves in front of the military governor's house, where Naudé had been respectfully saluted by the sentries. A man in a British officer's uniform was never questioned.

Before going to bed, Naudé reminded the women of the risk they were running. There was a heavy price on his head, he said, and in the event of an attack he did not mean to be taken alive. He intended to fight his way out and this could lead to Hansie and her mother being imprisoned. Were they prepared for this? Hansie, always one for a dramatic gesture, offered to join him in the fight; it would not, she said grandiloquently, 'be the first time Boer women have fought side by side with their men.' Mrs Van Warmelo had a far more practical suggestion. Taking the men into her bedroom she lifted a rug and showed them two loose floor-boards she had prepared which would provide access to sufficient space below for them both to hide in. That night, she said, they were to sleep in her bed, having put all their belongings under the floor, and at the first alarm were to creep into the hiding place and stay there until she signalled it was safe to come out.

The two women got very little sleep that night. They lay on the sofas in the dining room and sprang up every time the dog barked outside. When Naudé came in for breakfast he had a request to make. His 'corporal', he said, wanted to visit his family in town; could they fit him out with civilian clothes? He also pointed out that it was not wise for him to be seen in the house wearing khaki. Mrs Van Warmelo promised to find some clothes and advised them, in the meantime, to stay out of sight in the spare bedroom. Hansie was then sent into Pretoria to inform the women of the secret committee that Naudé had arrived and to collect clothes for the corporal. Both errands were successful. The committee women promised to call at Harmony that afternoon, and when Venter set off for home that evening he was wearing 'clothing belonging to six different people'.

Hansie was kept busy for the rest of the day. She spent most of the morning copying despatches, in invisible ink, to be sent to President

Kruger and making a list of things needed by the commandos. When the committee women called that afternoon they took away the list and Mrs Malan later returned with large parcels of food, clothing, soap, matches, salt and other essentials. That night Hansie and her mother slept soundly. They were thankful that, with Venter gone, they now had only one man under their roof – and he could hide quickly if necessary.

The following day, Mrs Van Warmelo lent Naudé one of her son's suits. It was a bad fit but at least it allowed the captain to wander about in the garden. His uniform was stowed under the floor-boards, but he kept two revolvers strapped securely to his waist. Hansie told the servants that the ruddy-faced Naudé was recuperating after a serious illness, and this unlikely explanation was accepted without question. Less convincing were the looks on the faces of Hansie and her mother when the neighbouring sergeant-major popped his head above the fence and watched them and their oddly-dressed guest picking strawberries. Naudé whispered to them to go on picking as if nothing had happened. 'He will go away soon,' he assured them. But when, after a few minutes, the inquisitive sergeant did disappear, the two women were so unnerved that they begged the captain to return to the house and stay there.

Hansie joined him indoors and spent the rest of the day listening to his stories of commando life. She asked him how he had got his British uniform and he told her it had come from a Colonel Thorold who had been killed in a recent battle. Riddled with bullet holes and covered with bloodstains as it was, Naudé had seen it as the perfect disguise for his next visit to Pretoria. He had taken not only the uniform but everything that went with it: revolvers, leggings, whistle, helmet, all was complete, even to the stars and crown on the Colonel's shoulders.

The captain had endless stories about the battles he had fought and the carnage he had witnessed. Hansie was extremely upset by his accounts of the slaughter, the tragic deaths on both sides; it all seemed so pointlessly cruel. There were times, though, when she sympathized wholeheartedly with Naudé. He told her, for instance, that British prisoners were set free because the commandos had no permanent camps in which they could be kept, but Boer renegades 'were shot without mercy'. This was something Hansie could appreciate. Unhappily it was Naudé's duty to oversee these executions, and he considered this his hardest task. Hansie says he called these men his 'fallen brothers'. On the other hand, any black man carrying a gun was also shot but Naudé did not seem to think that this warranted comment.

The captain's main concern was for his wife and children who had been sent to a concentration camp in Natal. He became even more concerned about them when Mrs Malan arrived with a snapshot of the family, taken in the camp, showing them to be haggard and feeble-looking. Hansie told him of conditions in the Irene camp. Would this, she asked, affect the duration of the war? She was pleased with his reply. '"No," was the emphatic answer, "never. We all feel that our first duty is to fight until our independence is assured. *We* are not responsible for the fate of our women and children, and they let no opportunity pass of urging us to be brave and steadfast in the fulfilment of our duty to our country. Our spies come from the Camps continually with messages of encouragement and hope; but the mortality among them is more bitter to bear than anything else."'

These appear to be Hansie's words, but they probably reflect Naudé's sentiments. Neither of them was to know that, only a few days earlier – on 15 December 1901 – Lord Kitchener had finally recognized the futility of the concentration camp policy and given orders that his officers were to bring in no more women and children. He had also decided 'to send out some of the women and children . . . to rejoin their relatives on commando.'[1] This was not a humanitarian gesture but, as Thomas Pakenham observes, 'a shrewd political move'.[2] Kitchener was well aware that after the devastation of his countryside 'sweeps' few families could return to their homes, and he knew the commandos would be unable to support them. By sending them to the enemy lines he hoped to silence his political critics in England and, at the same time, saddle the Boers with a burden which would force them to negotiate for peace. At last he had found a way of using the 'women question' to his own advantage.

Knowing nothing of this, Hansie could only sympathize with Captain Naudé and admire his resolution. But she could not help worrying about his safety. The nearer the time came for Naudé to leave, the more nervous she and her mother became. They found themselves speaking in lowered voices and finally ended up whispering to each other.

That evening Hansie went for a stroll in the garden to make sure there was no one about. She waited half an hour, then returned to the house. The captain had changed back into his British uniform and was waiting for his companions, Venter and Brenckmann, to join him. When the two men failed to appear, even Naudé began to show signs of alarm. Hansie again went into the garden to investigate. To her astonishment she found Venter and Brenckmann waiting under some willow trees, chatting merrily to a group of friends who had come to see them off. This made Hansie furious; rushing back to the house she begged Naudé to leave immediately.

But the excitement was not over. At dawn the following morning Hansie was wakened by her mother calling her to come to the dining-room. She found Mrs Van Warmelo staring out of the window at the activity opposite the house. In the road, close to the military camp, the neighbouring sergeant-major was talking to a man on horseback whom Hansie recognized as a detective in plain clothes. Nearby there were other plain-clothed horsemen surrounded by soldiers. They were all looking towards Harmony. This, to Hansie, meant only one thing. 'There is no doubt about it,' she whispered to her mother. 'We and our house have been betrayed.'

What had happened? They could only guess. Had the group under the willow trees attracted attention? Or had the servants been talking? Most alarming of all, had Captain Naudé been caught? Had someone who knew he was at Harmony given him away?

They decided that the only thing to do was to appear innocent and go about their work as usual. It was not easy. They had to brave the stares of the soldiers whenever they went into the garden and they were not at all sure how they should act. Mrs Van Warmelo took the situation particularly seriously; she became more and more certain that Captain Naudé had been captured. That afternoon Hansie went into town and met a man who had accompanied the captain to the barbed-wire fence. 'I am sure they got through unharmed,' he told Hansie. 'I always know when prisoners have been taken.'

A 'regular game of hide-and-seek' was played in the grounds of Harmony over the next few weeks. The activity was most apparent at night. During the day Hansie and her mother were kept busy picking and bottling fruit, but once the sun had set the garden came alive with other noises. Sounds were heard of prowlers pushing their way through bushes, stumbling in the dark and creeping round the house. The barking of Hansie's dog, Carlo, became so incessant that the two women found it difficult to sleep.

Mrs Van Warmelo found it all extremely alarming. Before Captain Naudé left he had told them that he hoped to return in January and an arrangement had been made to prevent him running into a trap. A password, *Appelkoos* (apricot), had been agreed upon, and the women had promised to fix a small wooden block to one of the fence-posts if it became necessary to warn Naudé against approaching the house. Now, thought Mrs Van Warmelo, was the time to display the danger sign. But Hansie would not hear of it. 'We are still in the house,' she told her mother, 'and Naudé is no chicken. He will reach us in spite of guards and fences.'

Hansie was not at Harmony when the next event occurred. Towards the middle of January, when the moon was on the wane and it seemed unlikely that the commandos would risk a visit, she decided to go and see a friend in Johannesburg. Her mother was not worried about being left alone and she did not intend to be away for more than a few days. 'I am well guarded, as you know,' laughed Mrs Van Warmelo as they said goodbye. But the joke backfired. For it was at this time that the military decided to invade Harmony. Less than a week after arriving in Johannesburg, Hansie received a message from her mother to say that on Sunday morning, 19 January, the house had been raided and searched. She returned home by the next train.

Expecting to be met with tears and anger, Hansie was amazed to be greeted by a smiling Mrs Van Warmelo. Far from being bowed down by her ordeal, her mother seemed to have enjoyed herself immensely. She could not wait to tell Hansie what had happened. The raid had taken place in the early hours of the morning. The officer who arrived told Mrs Van Warmelo that he had been ordered to search her house by the commissioner of police. Armed soldiers were stationed outside every entrance to the house. Judging by his accent, Mrs Van Warmelo was sure the officer in charge was a renegade Boer. She accompanied him as he went through the rooms, peering under beds, opening wardrobes and moving screens. After asking him what he hoped to find, she put up a great show of indignation when he said he was looking 'for men'. She was surprised, she said, that he should have been sent to search her house for *men*. Unperturbed, the man said he was equally surprised to find her name on the blacklist. He remained remarkably cool throughout the search and politely thanked her before he left. 'It was', says Hansie, 'the peacefullest, decentest raid I have ever heard of, and it would be difficult to think of anything with a termination more tame and commonplace.'

More importantly, it meant that in all probability Harmony was now removed from the blacklist, and the watch on the house would be relaxed. There was no longer any need to put out the danger signal to warn off Captain Naudé.

That he would return they had no doubt. For three weeks they waited for him, their nerves on edge, watching the phases of the moon and trying to guess which night would be most favourable. As a safety measure, Mrs Van Warmelo decided to keep Carlo locked up in case his barking, when Naudé arrived, gave the game away; but then she had second thoughts and, fearing the servants would become suspicious if she hid the dog, she let him loose again. And it was, as she expected, Carlo's barking that announced the arrival of strangers late one Sunday night. Mrs Van Warmelo was in bed, but she threw on a dressing-gown, rushed to the garden door, opened it and asked who was there. '*Appelkoos*', came the whispered reply. Then Captain Naudé and Venter emerged from the shadows. They were quickly ushered into the sitting-room, told to take off their boots and not to make a sound. 'You have never been in greater peril,' warned Mrs Van Warmelo. Captain Naudé was again wearing a British uniform.

That night the two men slept, as before, in Mrs Van Warmelo's bedroom while Hansie and her mother lay on the sofas in the dining-room. Towards dawn Hansie fell into a fitful sleep but her mother stayed awake. She was worried that the servants might have been made suspicious by Carlo's barking, half suspecting that one of them was in the pay of the British. This so troubled her that she eventually went into the garden and scattered grapes about so that it would look as if someone had raided the vines. So readily did the servants accept this planted evidence the following morning that no questions were asked about the late-night barking.

Hansie woke at six that morning to find Captain Naudé chatting cosily to her mother and drinking coffee. The rest of the day was not so relaxed. She spent most of it taking dictation from Naudé, transcribing despatches and hunting out clothing and other 'necessaries' for the commandos. Her most important mission came when Naudé asked her to contact the man who had accompanied him to the barbed-wire fence on his last visit and tell him he was wanted at Harmony. This she promptly did and later asked Naudé why the man was wanted. It was a matter of urgency, he told her. His flying column of scouts, he explained, were now scouring the country and 'doing the enemy incalculable harm', but their horses were underfed and worn out and replacements were desperately needed. Recently he had heard that there were some magnificent horses, kept for British officers, at a place called Skinner's Court. 'Those horses', he declared, 'we must have.' The man he had sent for could help get them. When the man arrived he was closeted with Naudé for almost an hour and left with a 'look of steadfast determination on his face'.

The atmosphere during this visit was far more tense than it had been when Naudé was last sheltered at Harmony. No friends were encouraged to come to the house and no strawberry picking or wander-

ing about the garden was allowed. Mrs Van Warmelo, mindful of the
recent raid, insisted that the men stay in her bedroom where she had
arranged for a bath, half-filled with soapy water, to be placed together
with sponges and towels so that if the police arrived she could rush
in, lock the door from the inside, and Hansie could say she was
bathing. This, she thought, would give the men time to creep into their
hiding-place beneath the floor-boards before the room was searched.
Hansie considered this hilarious and, to add to the fun, she chose a
moment in which to dash to the bedroom shouting: 'Danger, danger
– hide yourselves!' Later she was to double up laughing at 'the
recollection of those two men, diving for the hole in the floor.' She
was the only one to think it funny.

Captain Naudé and Venter left late that night. This time their
departure was silent, with no group under the willow trees to see them
off. The same man accompanied them out of town, this time beyond
the barbed wire, and the next day Hansie and her mother had the
satisfaction of hearing that Skinner's Court had been raided and every
horse taken.

This proved to be Naudé's last visit to Harmony. However, he did
not forget the debt he owed to the women of Pretoria. When he came
to write his memoirs, *In Doodsgevaar* (In Danger of Death), he paid
tribute to the 'faithful South African mothers and daughters' who
supported his men during the war. He returned to live in Pretoria
after the war and later retired to his farm in the northern Transvaal.

On 11 April 1902 a delegation of Boer leaders arrived in Pretoria to
bargain for peace. The following day they met Lord Kitchener at
Melrose House and laid before him the terms they hoped would
provide a basis for an honourable settlement, agreeable to both sides.
As these terms made it clear that the Boers were insisting that the
independence of their republics be recognized – a condition that
had led to the breakdown of earlier negotiations – Kitchener, after
consulting London, rejected them. A second conference was held two
days later, this time attended by Lord Milner, and lasted for another
three days. It ended inconclusively, but it was agreed, to Milner's
disgust, that provision be made for the Boers to consult their burgers
who, in turn, would elect delegates to attend further discussions in
May at the Transvaal town of Vereeniging. It was not a recognized
armistice but what Kitchener described as a 'slowing up', a rest period
for both sides.

Throughout their stay the Boer leaders were an irresistible attraction for the people of Pretoria. The Transvaal contingent was accommodated in a double-storied building, Parkzicht, close to Melrose House and, although they were not allowed to mix with the crowds who flocked to see them, they could be glimpsed at the windows or on the balcony of their guarded quarters. Opposite Parkzicht were the botanical gardens, Burgers Park, which became a popular rendezvous for news-hungry Pretorians. Not a great deal was known about the proceedings in Melrose House but this did not stop the gossips from speculating. Throughout the month, says Hansie, there were 'rumours of an early peace . . . Uncertainty, excitement, expectation filled the air.'

Hansie and her mother regularly joined the parade in and around Burgers Park. With them went Hansie's sister, Mrs Cloete, who had succeeded in obtaining permission to visit her family after an interminable battle with the Cape Town authorities. It was her first return to Pretoria since before the war; she could hardly have chosen a more stirring time to come. Walking up and down in the vicinity of Parkzicht, the women were delighted if they were rewarded by a tentative finger-wave from one of the windows of the house. Their greatest thrill came when, chancing to see Louis Botha – the man for whom they had despatched so many messages – standing alone on the balcony, they had fluttered their handkerchiefs at him and he had answered by taking off his hat, waving it, and kissing both his hands to them. After the war, says Hansie, Louis Botha had gallantly greeted Mrs Van Warmelo by clasping her hand, looking earnestly into her eyes and saying: 'You have done and risked what even I would not have dared.'

The conference of Boer representatives at Vereeniging, a small coal-mining town on the banks of the Vaal river south of Pretoria, began on 15 May 1902 and lasted until the end of that month. From the assembly of delegates, elected by the commandos, a five-man team was chosen to act as spokesmen: it was made up of Generals Botha and De la Rey and State Attorney Jan Smuts, for the Transvaal, and General De Wet and Judge J. B. M. Hertzog for the old Orange Free State. A last desperate attempt was made to negotiate a form of internal self-government for the two former republics, and when this failed the Boer spokesmen were forced to acknowledge defeat. They did so reluctantly, bitterly, and some of them defiantly, but there was no escaping the inevitable. Smuts and Hertzog drafted a resolution setting out the reasons why the commandos had no alternative but to lay down their arms. Heading this list was the plight of the Boer women and children. In the first place, it was stated, the devastation caused by the enemy – the farm-burnings, the destruction of villages, the slaughter of livestock and the confiscation of supplies – made it impossible for Boer families to survive and for the commandos to continue the war. Secondly the resolution cited the sufferings of those in the concentration camps and the appalling death rate.

Since then, there has been a great deal of debate about the validity of these assertions, some historians claiming that they were included in the resolution for their propaganda value. It has been pointed out, for instance, that the farm-burning had been started by Lord Roberts in the middle of 1900, but that this had not deterred Boer guerrillas from attacking communications or forced them to surrender in appreciable numbers. If anything, these tactics had hardened the commandos' resolve to fight on, some of them saying that with their homes destroyed and their families in concentration camps they had no place to which they could return. Nor was it accepted that the widespread devastation was depriving the commandos of the means of sustenance. When supplies were needed, it was argued, the Boers could, and did, raid African kraals and seize whatever food was available. This was something to which guerrilla leaders freely admitted. There were some, however, like Louis Botha, who recognized the danger of plundering kraals and so making enemies of the Africans. Botha also warned that if they were forced, as they eventually would be, to abandon the devastated districts altogether, their guerrilla activities would no longer divide the British forces and they would dwindle into a single target upon which the enemy could concentrate. To that extent, therefore, the claims of the resolution held good.

To what extent can the sufferings of the concentration camp inmates be said to have influenced the commandos? This was the second reason given by Smuts and Hertzog for making peace. And it was firmly believed. An official account of the Vereeniging negotiations, published five years after the war, states unequivocally that it was 'not the arms of the enemy which directly compelled us to surrender, but . . . the awful mortality amongst our women and children in the Concentration Camps.'[3] There can be no doubt about the awful mortality, but was this a pressing reason for ending the war in May 1902? By then most of the camps had been transformed almost beyond recognition. The reforms advocated by the Fawcett commission had been put into effect and this had resulted in a dramatic drop in the death rate of the white camps. Visitors to those camps at this time found it difficult to believe the stories they had been told about squalid conditions and widespread suffering. Even Louis Botha is said to have remarked that 'one is only too thankful nowadays to know that our wives are under English protection.'[4] It was later suggested that the Boers in the field knew little or nothing about these improvements and therefore accepted that the existence of the camps was a valid reason for laying down their arms. But this has been disputed. 'The general set-up in South Africa', argues A. C. Martin in his book on the camps, 'made it quite impossible to keep information from the Boers in the field. Who, in any case, would try to keep the good news from the camps from them?'[5] All the same, some of the commandos returning after the war were both surprised and relieved to find their families well cared for.

How much the commandos knew about conditions in the camps is difficult to ascertain. The evidence is conflicting, often contradictory. Louis Botha's alleged remark, for instance, was later denied by his secretary. Botha, he maintains, would never have said that the women and children were better off in the camps than in the 'healthy surroundings of their own homes'.[6] Certainly the subject was widely discussed and roundly condemned at the Vereeniging conference and this, if nothing more, would have accounted for it being cited as a reason for the Boers' capitulation.

Hansie would have resented the plight of the women being seen as a cause for surrender. She knew that conditions in the Irene camp had improved after the departure of Commandant Esselen and, in any case, she was convinced that most of the women were prepared to endure anything rather than cede their country's independence. An unyielding 'bitter ender', she had said many times that it was more honourable to fight to the finish than to accept inequitable peace terms. Her immediate reaction to the terms accepted at Vereeniging can only be guessed at. She was not in the country when the conference ended. A week or so earlier she had sailed from the Cape on the weekly mail ship, and was at sea when news that the war had ended reached her.

Amid all her other activities, Hansie had not neglected her correspondence with Louis Ernest Brandt, the recently-ordained Dutch minister whom she had met when studying in Europe. The earlier misunderstanding between them had, despite military censors, been patched up by post, and in the delightful exchange of letters that followed Hansie had accepted Brandt's proposal of marriage. Now, with the war almost over, she felt she could safely leave her mother in the care of a young girl companion and join her fiancé in Holland, where they were to be married. Getting permission to leave the country was not easy but she eventually succeeded and travelled to the Cape with her sister.

As only British mail ships sailed regularly to Europe, Hansie had no alternative but to travel first to England before crossing to Holland. This meant that most of her fellow-passengers were British citizens or English-speaking South Africans. They were not the most congenial of companions for a young Afrikaner in the dying days of the war but, by then, Hansie was well trained in keeping her feelings to herself. Her forbearance, however, was truly tested when, as they neared Tenerife, news was wired to the ship that the war in South Africa had ended. Details of the peace terms were scrappy but they were sufficient for Hansie to realize that the worst had happened. As all the ship rejoiced, she remained numb: it was impossible for her to accept that the Boers had surrendered their independence. 'There was peace in South Africa,' she wrote bitterly, '– peace "with honour" for England, peace *and defeat* for the Boers.'

On that very day, on the shores of Lake Annecy, Emily Hobhouse heard the same news. Like Hansie, she was numbed on first reading it. Only later did the full significance of these momentous events sink in. When it did, she burst into tears.

15

After the War

ON 16 DECEMBER 1913, ex-President Steyn of the Orange Free State presided over the unveiling of a monument on the outskirts of Bloemfontein. Simple in design, the monument was the work of Anton Van Wouw, the Dutch-born South African sculptor. At the foot of a sandstone obelisk soaring over a hundred feet into the sky was a sculptured bronze group comprising three figures: one of a young woman gazing clear-eyed into the future, the others of a seated mother holding a dead child on her lap. Mother and child are curiously reminiscent of the famous *Pietà* by Michelangelo, and as the sculptor was in Rome when he first visualized the statuary, the comparison is not too fanciful. The plinth supporting this symbolic group carried an emotive inscription.

To our heroines and dear children
'Thy Will Be Done'
This National Monument was erected to the memory of the
26,370 women
and children who died in the
concentration camps and to
the other women and children
who died elsewhere as a result of
the Second Anglo-Boer War of 1899–1902

Emily Hobhouse was partly responsible for the composition of the sculptured group. As she was living in Rome at that time, she was able to work with Van Wouw and to describe to him a scene similar to that which he depicted. Her advice also helped the sculptor fashion the bas-reliefs of concentration camp life which flank the obelisk. So closely involved was Emily with the conception of the monument that President Steyn invited her to perform the unveiling. Flattered as she was by the invitation, she had doubts about accepting it: an unspecified illness made her fear she would not have the strength to travel to South Africa. In the event, she did reach the Cape but then, on her way to Bloemfontein, she was so overcome by the heat and altitude that she was forced to return to Cape Town. Mrs Steyn, the ex-President's wife and Emily's friend, stood in for her at the ceremony.

The speech Emily had intended to make was read out to the crowd. In it she spoke of her experiences in the camps, the suffering she had witnessed, the deaths, the loneliness, the squalor and the hopelessness. And she railed against the 'rich and highly placed, the financiers who wanted war, the incompetent Statesmen who were their tools, the men who sat in the seats of the mighty, the blundering politicians of that dark story – all the miserable Authorities incapable of dealing with the terrible conditions they themselves had brought about.' She went on to stress the need for unity in South Africa, a need which was then seen as a matter of vital importance.

Only three years earlier a significant step had been taken towards overcoming the divisions that had long plagued South Africa. In May 1910, after months of deliberation, the Transvaal, the Orange Free State, Natal and the Cape Colony had officially become the Union of South Africa. While this act of unity did not please everyone, for most whites it seemed to herald the dawn of a new era. With Louis Botha, the former Boer commandant-general, as the Union's first prime minister, there was hope that the scars left by the war would be healed. Unfortunately it was to take many years for this hope to be realized. Even more regrettable was the unwillingness of those who devised this supposedly all-embracing political settlement to tackle the more serious obstacles to racial peace. The magnitude of what was then called the 'native question' was acknowledged but shelved: there was a reluctance to face up to the demands of the voiceless black population which, although a numerical majority, had few political rights in the Cape, fewer still in Natal and none at all in the former Boer republics. This was something which worried Emily. Reluctant as she was to offend her audience on such a solemn occasion, she took the opportunity to sound a warning.

Do not open your gates to those worst foes of freedom – tyranny and selfishness. Are these not the withholding from others in your control, the very liberties and rights which you have valued and won for yourselves . . . We in England are ourselves still dunces in the great world-school, our leaders still struggling with the unlearned lesson, that liberty is the equal right and heritage of every child of man, without distinction of race, colour or sex. A community that lacks the courage to found its citizenship on this broad base becomes 'a city divided against itself, which cannot stand'.[1]

Mild as this warning appears today, there can be no doubt that it hit home. Emily's message must have startled many of those who heard her speech being read. The liberty and equal rights that her audience was seeking were not those advocated by Miss Hobhouse. Indeed, when fifty years later the Bloemfontein newspaper *Die Volksblad* published a commemorative issue which included Emily's speech, it decided – as Rykie Van Reenen has pointed out – to omit these observations along with Emily's more direct challenge: 'Does not justice bid us remember today how many thousands of the dark race perished also in the Concentration Camps in a quarrel that was not theirs? . . . Was it not an instance of that community of interest, which binding all in one, roots out racial animosity?' These were words which could not have gone down well in 1913; they were certainly not welcome in the days of apartheid fifty years later.

The Women's Memorial, as it is known, soon became one of Afrikanerdom's most sacred shrines. It would have been more appropriate, however, had it been called the Children's Memorial, for the vast majority of deaths it honours were of infants or youngsters under the age of sixteen.

Exact figures for the concentration camp death toll are difficult to arrive at; for some camps, such as Irene, it is admitted that it is 'almost impossible' to ascertain how many inmates died. British estimates, perhaps unsurprisingly, tend to be much lower than the 26,370 white women and children recorded on the Women's Memorial, some giving a toll as low as 18,000. But the figures accepted by most responsible historians, British as well as Afrikaners, are those given by the archivist P. L. A. Goldman, who was appointed by the Transvaal government to compile a list of Boer casualties after the war. His detailed investigation established that 27,927 whites died in the camps; of these 22,074 were under the age of sixteen, while 4177 women and 1676 men were above that age. If to the total are added the conservative 14,154 recorded deaths in black camps, where documentation was far from reliable, it means that over 42,000 persons are known to have died as a direct result of the concentration camp policy.

For many years little attention was paid to the tragedy of the black camps. No official enquiry was instituted to assess the extent of the suffering and both sides preferred to forget that black people had paid a huge penalty as a result of the war between the whites in South Africa. The same cannot be said about the misery endured by the imprisoned Boer population: there was never any chance that those victims would be forgotten. For the significance of the concentration camps far outlived the end of the Anglo-Boer war; they became part of the mythology of the Afrikaner nation. Not only does the Women's Memorial stand as a permanent reminder of those who died but, until quite recently, the annual ceremonies held at the sites of the camps – occasions for fervent prayers and patriotic speeches – provided nationalist politicians with an opportunity to play on the emotions, and the fears, of their followers. Nowhere has the war been refought with more passion than at these highly emotive ceremonies, and no single factor has done more to perpetuate the divisions between the English- and Afrikaans-speaking sections of South Africa's white population than that evoked by reference to the horrors of the concentration camps.

From the very outset, the war was seen by the burgers of the Boer republics as an attempt to exterminate them as a nation. President Kruger's adamant refusal to grant the franchise to the *uitlanders* of the Transvaal was not so much a matter of obstinacy as it was a means of ensuring the survival of his people. To have allowed the foreigners the vote would soon have led to the Boers of the Transvaal being rendered politically impotent and this, he feared, would have resulted not only in a loss of power but in the destruction of the Boers' identity, language, customs, and hard-won, but still fragile, nationhood. His fears were shared by his countrymen, for whom the advent of war was evidence that force was being used where stealth had failed. This is what inspired the commandos to hold out so long; not only were they defending their country but, as they saw it, they were fighting for the very existence of their race.

Nowhere did that existence appear more directly threatened than in the concentration camps. Lloyd George summed up what most Boers felt when he likened the internment policy to Herod's attempt 'to crush a little race by killing all the young children.'[2] The higher the camp death toll mounted, the more certain some of the inmates became that a plot to exterminate the Afrikaner nation was being put into effect.

So firmly was this believed that for years descendants of the Boers were convinced that many of those who died in the camps had been deliberately killed. Stories were told of poison being administered as medicine – said to be one of the reasons why the sick often refused medical attention – and particles of ground glass, supposedly found in camp food, were produced as proof of lethal intent on the part of the British authorities. These accusations, based on rumour and hearsay, were rarely subjected to impartial investigation and came mostly from the more fanatical fringes of Afrikanerdom. Nevertheless they had a wide circulation. During the Second World War, Nazi propagandists seized upon the more lurid of these unsubstantiated scare stories to justify their own, overtly racist and intentionally evil, concentration camps.

Neither in their origin nor in their ultimate purpose can the Anglo-Boer war camps be compared with those of Nazi Germany. The camps in South Africa were makeshift settlements, hastily established to help solve a wartime problem of the military; those in Germany were designed and equipped in peacetime as punishment centres for Jews, gypsies, homosexuals and the political opponents of the Nazi regime. Inmates in both sets of camps suffered and died but, whereas the Nazi camps were built with the acknowledged intention of penalization, the Anglo-Boer war camps were simply examples of appalling mismanagement, hasty erection, ill-chosen sites, polluted water, poor sanitation, overcrowding, food shortages, lack of medical staff and facilities and exposure to epidemics; all of which contributed to the ghastly conditions in which the inmates of the Anglo-Boer war camps were obliged to live.

Lord Roberts and Lord Kitchener, as Commanders-in-Chief, must share most of the blame for this tragic state of affairs. They were both more concerned with early victories, which would consolidate their reputations and earn them promotion, than they were with the fate of the women and children they arbitrarily confined. The extent of their neglect can be judged by the speed with which conditions in the camps improved after the Fawcett commission's brisk and effective inspection. With so many lives at risk, this could and should have been organized much sooner. Kitchener, in particular, could not plead ignorance after the publication of Emily Hobhouse's report, yet he left it to the politicians in London to rectify the situation which he had helped to create. His indifference to the suffering in the camps was both characteristic and chilling.

But to suggest that the military commanders were guilty of culpable negligence is a far cry from accusing them of genocide. No serious, unbiased study of the concentration camps has found evidence of a plot to exterminate Afrikaners; nor did those who were closely involved in the life of the camps – women like Emily Hobhouse, Hansie van Warmelo, Henrietta Armstrong and various Quaker missionaries – acknowledge the existence of such a plot. That the maladministration which led to the loss of so many lives was in no way influenced by racial hostility can be seen by a study of the British army casualty lists. Out of an estimated 22,000 soldiers killed in the war, no fewer than 13,350 died of disease. Most of these deaths were caused by enteric fever, which was also responsible for a further 31,000 men being invalided home. The most significant outbreak of this fever was, of course, in Bloemfontein, and it was Lord Roberts's failure to ensure an adequate medical auxiliary force that allowed the epidemic to spread and follow the troops on their march to the Transvaal. If this could happen to the British army, is it surprising that disease devastated the camps? The deaths of innocent children cannot properly be compared with those of soldiers who, for whatever reason, die in a war. But the way the disease spread in the army camps is an illustration of how easily it could contaminate the closely-packed concentration camps; if soldiers could succumb to it, children were even more vulnerable, and in both cases neglect was all too obvious. There was no need of a plot to depopulate the camps.

It is also worth remarking that among those responsible for the well-being of the concentration camp inmates, it was not British superintendents who were the most hated but renegade Boers like N. J. Scholtz and G. F. Esselen of Irene. Indeed, when new superintendents were being recruited in the Cape, General Maxwell stressed that 'men with pronounced anti-Boer feelings should be avoided'.[3]

'A barrier of dead children's bodies', warned Lloyd George, 'will rise up between the British and Boer races in South Africa.'[4] He was proved right. Whether one accepts that the internment of Boer civilians was part of a conspiracy or believes that the concentration camp disaster was the result of mismanagement, there can be no doubt about the outcome. The Women's Memorial stands as a sombre reminder of those who died, and all over South Africa the graves of the concentration camp victims are still religiously tended. In her commemoration speech, Emily Hobhouse called for unity and warned of the pitfalls that had to be avoided. 'Alongside the honour we pay the Sainted Dead,' she counselled, 'forgiveness must find a place . . . To harbour hate is fatal to your own self-development, it makes a flaw; for hatred, like rust, eats into the soul of a nation as of an individual.' She also made it clear that her view of unity included the Africans. 'May it not come about,' she went on, 'that the associations linked with this day will change, merging into nobler thoughts? . . . The plea of Abraham Lincoln for the black comes echoing back to me: "They will probably help you in some trying time to come to keep the jewel of liberty in the family of freedom."'

Respected as was Emily, her speech struck few responsive chords in those to whom it was addressed. The wounds of war were too deep to heal quickly; many years were to pass before those who fought on opposing sides were ready to forgive and forget. It was to take even longer before the possibility of an interdependent bond with the black people of South Africa could be considered. This is a crucial lesson which, almost eighty years later, has still to be learned.

One person who would have found Emily's vision of a united South Africa bewildering was that popular heroine of the early war years, Lady Sarah Wilson. She was to view the country and its inhabitants with very different eyes.

On her return to England, in July 1900, Sarah had been fêted as the intrepid 'Sally Wilson of Mafeking'. No one seemed to doubt she had won lasting fame. 'When the history of the South African campaign comes to be written,' declared a journalist, 'there is one Englishwoman whose wonderful pluck and valour in face of terrible and depressing difficulties will need no fine language to enhance the glory of that simple record of fact. That Englishwoman is, we need hardly say, Lady Sarah Wilson, "the heroine of heroic Mafeking."'[5] For the next few months she was in great demand at smart dinner parties, where her merry accounts of her African adventures were guaranteed to silence all other conversations. She spent the rest of the war energetically supporting fashionable charities, often appearing in her self-designed war-correspondent's outfit – a tailored serge tunic and skirt, white silk cravat and wide-brimmed military-style hat – photographs of which were later to feature in books evoking the Anglo-Boer war period. Sarah was extremely proud of these photographs. She set great store by her ability to carry off any style of dress, and never failed to enchant the gossip columnists. 'What a delightful dresser is this clever descendant of the great Duke,' enthused a reporter of a charity bazaar; 'she was a perfect lesson in silhouette as well as in blending of colour.'[6]

Two months after the war ended, Sarah returned to South Africa.

She and her sister Georgiana toured the country, travelling from Cape Town to Bloemfontein and Kimberley and then on to Mafeking. Here Sarah was surprised to find herself almost a stranger. 'Beyond the Mayor of the town', she wrote, 'and a nigger coachman who used to take me out for Sunday drives, I failed to perceive one face I knew in the town during the siege.'[7] But the nuns at the convent gave her a warm welcome and she was pleased to find that their shell-shattered buildings had been completely restored. Curiously, she makes no mention of some less pleasant news she had received concerning the Keeley family, with whom she had sheltered at Mosita. She had learned of their misfortune in Cape Town but, in Mafeking, she made no attempt to contact them.

The Boers were not the only ones to have had their homes destroyed in the war. Reprisal attacks were made on a few English-speaking farmers and, although these attacks were rare, they were every bit as devastating. At the beginning of September 1901, Mrs Keeley – who had for so long lived in terror of a Boer attack – had her worst fears realized. Her husband was away from home when it happened. 'Boer Fire Fiends', reported the local newspaper, 'swooped down unawares, turned Mrs Keeley and the children out into the bush, forbidding them to take anything with them, and set fire to the whole place.'[8] The family spent the night huddled together in a barn and staggered to safety the next morning.

Sarah had been shocked to hear this and dashed off a note of sympathy, but she had no desire to visit Mosita. Nor did she linger long in the northern Cape. Six hours in Mafeking, she says, 'were more than sufficient and it was astounding to think of the many months it had been our home.' Turning their backs on the dusty, deserted little town, she and Georgiana caught the train to Rhodesia, where they met Dr Jameson and a few other friends, and then returned by way of Johannesburg in order to investigate the post-war prospects of the mining industry. In all their visit lasted a little over three months.

Sarah left South Africa in a suspicious mood. She had been told, and obviously believed, that the defeated Boer generals 'were not in the least cast down by the result of the war; that they simply meant to bide their time and win in the Council Chamber what they had lost on the battle-field; that oft-reiterated sentence "South Africa for the Dutch", was by no means an extinct volcano or a parrot-cry of the past.'[9] Sarah was to retain a long-lasting distrust of the Afrikaners. Years later she was still warning that if they were 'to be assimilated with British colonists' they needed first to be thoroughly understood.

On two further occasions Sarah visited South Africa. In 1903 she and her husband spent six weeks in Rhodesia, on a big-game-hunting expedition, passing through the Cape and the Transvaal on the way; and in 1924 Sarah stayed as Sir Abe Bailey's guest at Muizenberg in the Cape. Each time she arrived in the country she was welcomed as a celebrity, while in Britain she was regarded, by her circle, as an expert on all things African. Unfortunately her views were such that they tended to perpetuate rather than dispel misunderstandings about the continent. All too often she simply reflected the worst prejudices of her bigoted friends and acquaintances.

After her hunting expedition in 1903, for example, she wrote an article for the *Pall Mall Magazine* in which she held forth on the 'native question'. She claimed to be qualified to write on this subject after listening to conversations 'between native commissioners and others – kind, genial, just Englishmen'. Her expressed aim was to correct those 'people who remain in England, and who give vent to strange doctrines on the rights and privileges of the black man'. Needless to say, her inside information came from men whose opinions were as biased as they were forthright.

They maintained, observed Sarah, 'that the chief characteristic of the native is laziness, that the young men of the tribe, who do not work, sleep and smoke all day . . . They will tell you that the more you pamper the native the less he will respect you; that civilization in the shape of European clothes and boots and shoes, at present, only deteriorates him; that you are educating him, are teaching him to run without first making him walk.' She agreed with the contention that allowing Africans to carry rifles would lead, in the not too distant future, to a 'desperate struggle before which any previous wars will fade into insignificance.' This touch of fear, mixed with racial superiority, brought her to an uncompromising conclusion. All in all, she argued, black men were 'not to be mentioned in the same breath as white men. They are, and will ever be an inferior race, full of good points, capable of enormous improvement, and deserving of the kindest and most considerate treatment. But to call these races our "black fraternity" strikes those who have any acquaintance with them, their pleasures, and their modes of life, as absurd; and the white man who talks to them in this strain, or who associates with them as his equals, is certainly not their best friend.'[10]

Lady Sarah Wilson's conception of the future of southern Africa was a far cry from that of Emily Hobhouse.

For all that, there is no mistaking the effect that Africa had on

Sarah's life. It had provided her with a brief moment of glory, lifting her out of the ranks of conventional society women and establishing her, among her contemporaries, as an adventurous and exciting personality. But she did nothing to cultivate this reputation and, by neglecting it, allowed herself to be forgotten. Those who knew her well were amazed at her subsequent modesty. Sonia Keppel – daughter of Sarah's great friend Mrs Alice Keppel – was, for instance, to remember Sarah playing with her as a child, and classed her among the legendary figures of her youth. 'I put Lady Sarah Wilson in the same category as Miss Florence Nightingale . . . ' she wrote. 'Both ladies had been heroines and as such were awe-inspiring . . . [but] Lady Sarah seemed cheerfully forgetful of her former heroism and content to let it lie in lavender.'[11]

This did not mean that Sarah was indifferent to the lure of fame. She certainly appreciated notoriety in others, and in no one more than in Sonia's mother, Alice Keppel, the last mistress of King Edward VII. During the Edwardian era the Wilsons lived in Leicestershire (for the hunting) but Sarah kept up her contacts with London society and it was during these years that she became known as Mrs Keppel's 'lady-in-waiting'. The two women remained close friends after the King's death, and at the outbreak of the First World War memories of Mafeking were revived when they jointly organized a field hospital in Boulogne. Sarah took charge of the hospital in November 1914, shortly after learning that her husband – then a lieutenant-colonel – had been killed while leading his men into action at Ypres. She worked unsparingly throughout the war but once it was over she again drifted back into comfortable anonymity.

The last years of Sarah's life were spent in London, playing bridge, assisting at charity functions, attending the races and being seen at the smartest of social occasions. To her attendance on Alice Keppel she added another quasi-royal role by acting as chaperon to Nancy Leeds, the rich American widow who, in 1920, married Prince Christopher of Greece. But in society she was more often a guest than a hostess, invariably asked to balance a dinner table rather than to shine as the celebrity she had once been. 'Lady Sarah Wilson', commented a journalist when she died, on 22 October 1929, 'affords a striking example of a woman whose name was on everyone's lips rather more than a generation ago, but who lapsed into almost complete obscurity. Cynical people may add that, considering she was an aunt of Mr Winston Churchill, this was even more curious.'

Hansie van Warmelo had her own ideas about the future of South Africa. Like the majority of Afrikaners, she bitterly resented the Boer republics' loss of independence and the fact that they were now regarded as part of the British empire. But she was not entirely pessimistic. She had hopes of a new dawn once the old enmities dividing the white population had been overcome. Writing in 1913, the year the Women's Memorial was unveiled, she remarked: 'South Africa is united in *name*, if not yet in reality, but the time will surely come . . . when under the softening influence of time, a great united race will be born.' If in this she was close in spirit to Emily Hobhouse, she also shared Lady Sarah Wilson's prejudice towards the Africans. Hansie could not accept Emily's vision of an undivided, non-racial South Africa. The great united nation envisaged by Hansie was to be white in colour, Christian in faith and paternal in its responsibilities towards the black population. Like so many of her countrymen, she saw the separation of the black and white races as God-ordained.

Unlike Sarah Wilson, Hansie had to wait for the war to end before she could enjoy her moment of glory. Not until she arrived in Holland for her marriage was she publicly hailed as a heroine. Close friends of her future husband already knew of her activities in Pretoria and she was soon being fêted. Not only was the part she had played in the war acknowledged but, as one of the first South Africans to arrive in peacetime, she was sought out as a source of information. Functions, attended by Afrikaner exiles, were arranged and receptions held to allow her to meet as many admirers as possible. She was bombarded with questions about the war and some of her replies may well have surprised the uninitiated. When asked, for instance, what part the concentration camps had played in ending the war, her answer was dismissive. 'No,' she said, 'no it was not the Concentration Camps. The high mortality was past, the weakest had been taken, and there was no cause for anxiety for those remaining in the Camps. Their rations had been increased and improved – there was no more of that awful suffering.'

Never would Hansie have admitted that the women in the camps were responsible for the Boers' capitulation. She was equally adamant in denying that Boer leaders had feared a mass African uprising. An 'army of natives', she scoffed, 'would have been the last thing to induce the Boers to surrender.' Her own explanation for the ending of the war was the betrayal of the 'Judas Boers' – the renegades who had collaborated with the British. '*They* broke our strength by breaking our ideals,' she fumed, 'by crushing our enthusiasm, by robbing us of our inspiration, our faith, our hope . . .' By insisting that it was inside traitors, not outside foes, who had weakened Boer resistance, Hansie was able to hold to her republican pride.

As the day of her wedding drew near, Hansie became the centre of widespread attention. The Boer generals sent her telegrams and she received personal congratulations from Queen Wilhelmina, whom she now, in a swift change of loyalty, acknowledged as *'her* Queen'. But most treasured of all was the photograph forwarded to her from President Kruger – who was then living at Menton, on the French Riviera – on which he had inscribed 'in his illegible hand, "For services rendered during the late war".'[12]

Hansie remained in Holland for over a year after her marriage. During that time she transcribed entries from her carefully-guarded diary to form the basis of a book detailing her experiences in the Irene concentration camp. This book, which was probably written with the help of her husband, was published in Dutch as *Het Concentratie-Kamp van Irene* in 1905, the year after Hansie returned to Pretoria. Louis Brandt had decided to settle in South Africa and his career was to follow a pattern similar to that of Hansie's father. After being accepted for the ministry of the Hervormde Kerk, the thirty-one-year-old Brandt was appointed to a district in the northern Transvaal which included the Zoutpansberg, where Nicolaas van Warmelo had been a minister when he met Hansie's mother. Brandt remained there for four years and was then transferred south to the Witwatersrand region where he was to serve for the best part of the rest of his life.

Hansie's early married years were taken up with raising her large family – the Brandts had seven children – and caring for her mother. She was able, however, to find time to write another book about her wartime adventures, *The Petticoat Commando or Boer Women in Secret Service*, which was published in 1913. The following year saw the outbreak of the First World War, and this led to Hansie becoming involved in politics. Her sympathies were entirely with those Afrikaners who, in October, rose in armed rebellion against the decision of Louis Botha's government to side with Britain and invade German South West Africa (present-day Namibia). How far she actively assisted the rebels is not clear but in July 1915, after the uprising had been quashed, she launched and became honorary president of the Women's National Party, which campaigned for the release of the rebels. In the general election of that year Louis Brandt stood, unsuccessfully, for the parliamentary National Party, which had also opposed the invasion of South West Africa. Hansie's organization was later to extend its activities to welfare work and the championing of political rights for white women; it also assisted in furthering the political aims of the National Party – the party which, when it was reformed and gained office, was to introduce legal apartheid to South Africa.

The year 1916 was notable for more than politics in Hansie's life. In December of that year her mother, then in her late sixties, died. Her death was to have a profound, if bizarre, effect on her daughter. According to Hansie, she was sitting at her mother's bedside, praying, on the night before Mrs Van Warmelo died. Then it was, she says, that 'a bright angel with wings of transparent gold and a crown on his head, more blazing than the sun, entered the room and called me by my name.' This apparition, she claims, informed her that she had been chosen to prepare her country 'for great things and to save the South African races from complete destruction.' Apparently this did not surprise Hansie because she had already decided, by reading her Bible, that the war then raging in Europe heralded the second coming of Christ and the end of the world. As a token that he had been sent by God, the 'glorious Visitor' predicted the time of Mrs Van Warmelo's death and told Hansie precisely when her comatose mother would regain consciousness and be able to say goodbye to her family. All of which, says Hansie, proved true: the household was assembled at five the next morning, Mrs Van Warmelo remained conscious for an hour, said her farewells, and died at ten o'clock that night.

Hansie, whose religious faith was of a fundamentalist, unquestioning nature, had always been close to her mother and, praying alone in the middle of the night, was probably in a confused emotional state. But her hallucinations did not end with her mother's death. Five days later, again in the middle of the night, the 'Messenger' returned. He had come to show her what was about to happen throughout the world. During the following day he remained with her, inspiring visions that were both glorious and frightening. There can be little doubt that Hansie was delirious. She was under the impression that, in the coming upheavals, South Africa had been selected to give a lead to the rest of the world. 'They would find us brave and fully trusting in the face of the greatest dangers,' she claimed, 'keeping calm under the howling fury of the storm . . . they would accept the testimony of our example and be forced to follow it in order to be saved in the great Day which is to come.' It was to be Hansie's duty to prepare her countrymen, particularly the Africans, for the role they had to play: the warning had to be given *'not later than March* 1918'.

Extraordinary as this all was, Hansie's reaction was every bit as outlandish. For she appears to have believed that even with the end of the world approaching, South Africa's racial divisions would remain and that, whatever else happened, the black population must wait for the word of the white men. This was stressed in a pamphlet, *The Millennium. A Prophetic Message to the Native Tribes of South Africa* which she published the following year.

> When the first blast strikes this country, the Native and the coloured peoples must know it is no ordinary storm . . . The Natives of this land must sit still when the dreadful afflictions come over the white peoples. They must have no hand in any of the tribulations, they must not seek to pay off old scores . . . It was revealed to me by the Messenger of the Lord that the perils in store for South Africa, would be a thousand times more severe if the Native tribes mixed themselves up in them . . . When human beings are scattered homeless over the land, and when the elements rage, when the mighty roar of destruction shakès the very earth, they must remain as quiet as possible and only protect themselves.[13]

This venture into oracular writing was an extreme example of Hansie's incurable flights of fancy. It illustrates not only her romantic nature but her lack of emotional security. There was a vein of eccentricity running through most of her later career. Nowhere was this more apparent than in her involvement with the empirical aspects of naturopathy. She had her own ideas about natural medicines; she published *The Fasting Book* and, shortly before her mother died, founded and became honorary president of a body called the World Harmony Movement. In time she was to establish the Harmony School of Naturopathy, a sanatorium for whites near Johannesburg, where her unproven theories were practised. The most controversial of her treatments was the subject of a book, *The Grape Cure* (1928), in which she advocated the use of grapes as a remedy for cancer. For her work as a naturopath she received an honorary degree from the now obscure American School of Natural Physic.

Besides producing a number of pamphlets and tracts, she also wrote two novels in English. *Patricia*, published in two volumes, with five years between each volume, appeared under the pseudonym Marcus Romondt; *Elinda*, published in 1938, led to her being made an honorary member of the Eugene Field Literary Society in America that same year.

In June 1939 Louis Brandt died, aged sixty-five, in what was described as a 'domestic accident'. Hansie survived him by twenty-five years, living for the last part of her life in Cape Town. She was eighty-seven when, on 21 January 1964, she died peacefully in her sleep. As a young woman, sixty-two years earlier, Hansie had stood alone on a ship bound for England, mourning the passing of the old Boer republics; as an old woman, on 31 May 1961, three years before she died, she had rejoiced when a republic was again proclaimed in South Africa, a republic which embraced not merely the Transvaal and the Orange Free State but the entire country. The fact that it was a republic in name only, retaining the constitutional framework established under the British crown, would not have bothered her. As a girl she had vowed to fight for the restoration of her 'beloved country's' independence and, to all outward appearances, it seemed her cause had at last triumphed.

'Miss Hobhouse is anathema out here – a person who believed Boer lies and talked "politics",' wrote Lawrence Richardson, a Quaker who was visiting Bloemfontein in November 1903. 'We don't mention that we know her, though it goes against the grain to have to sit by and hear her abused.'[14] Richardson was recording the British reaction to Emily's return to South Africa almost a year after the war ended. It was a journey she had been planning for some months.

Emily had left Lake Annecy for London soon after hearing that the peace treaty had been signed. She had wanted to be in England to greet her friends from South Africa whom she knew would be arriving as soon as they were free to travel. Among the first to dock at Southampton were the three Boer generals – Louis Botha, Christiaan de Wet and 'Koos' de la Rey – who had come to Europe to seek help for their devastated country. In South Africa they were known as 'The Glorious Trio', and elaborate preparations had been made to welcome them to England. Great crowds had gathered at the docks, Lord Roberts and Lord Kitchener were there to meet them, and King Edward VII had invited them to attend his coronation naval review at Spithead. But Emily managed to get in ahead of everyone else. Betty Molteno was on the same ship as the generals and Emily went to Southampton to meet her. Betty's sister, Mrs Charles Murray – who had arrived in England earlier – went with her and the two women were allowed, with the help of a Molteno brother, to go out to the ship in a tug before it docked. 'I was thus', Emily wrote to her aunt, 'the first English person to welcome them [the generals] to English soil as they stood at the top of the gangway with their staff to receive us. They are a striking trio . . . I felt they were not merely great soldiers but great men.'[15]

The generals refused the royal invitation to the naval review – Emily, although a great royalist, is said to have advised against it as they would have been seen on show at a British triumph – and left for London by train. 'We all went up to London together,' reported an ecstatic Emily; 'I sat between Botha and De Wet with De la Rey opposite.' She was to entertain the generals at her Chelsea flat during their stay in England. In her talks with them she was made fully aware of the poverty and distress in South Africa where Boer families, returning to the ruins of their burnt-out homes, were often left to fend for themselves. Most of them were penniless, the much-vaunted repatriation schemes were bogged down by bureaucracy and the £3 million compensation promised by the British was not only proving inadequate but, all too often, did not reach those most in need. All this was confirmed by other friends arriving from South Africa as well as in the letters Emily continued to receive from the Cape.

Once again the urge to be of service – the urge that first sent her to the concentration camps – began to quicken in Emily. But she was unable to go to South Africa immediately. She had speaking engagements, her book had still to be published and she had not yet fully recovered her strength. Not until the end of April 1903, after a short break in Paris with her brother, was she able to sail for the Cape. She arrived there on 12 May.

Emily was to describe the next seven months as the most physically, mentally and emotionally exhausting period of her life. She toured the ruined districts of the former Boer republics and was aghast at what she discovered. The despair, the hopelessness, the suffering and the near starvation conditions seemed to exist on a much wider scale than before and pose equally intractable problems. There were areas, mostly close to the railways, where repatriation work was going ahead but these were show places, acclaimed in the newspapers; it was in the more remote, neglected regions that real hardship was encountered. These were the regions through which Emily travelled, and she became angry at the bland optimism of those who did not follow her example. Some of this anger spilled over in the letters she wrote to the press, describing the wretchedness and squalor in which families were living, appealing for relief funds and accusing the government of mismanagement.

All her old critics were quick to respond. Once again she was derided as hysterical, unpatriotic, intemperate, an Anglophobe and a trouble-maker. Her letters, sneered the *Birmingham Daily Mail*, 'are too transparently those of a credulous lady who went forth to discover evidence of Boer suffering and hardship, and who was too ready to believe anything that a Boer with a grievance cared to tell her.'

These were not opinions shared by the Quaker Lawrence Richardson, who with his South African companion James Butler was on a similar mission. His letters, while not uncritical, were full of praise for the work Emily was doing.

> I do not approve altogether of Miss Hobhouse's attitude, it is too one-sided, but she is not hysterical but remarkably calm and business-like . . . She has managed to cover a good deal of ground and has accomplished many times more good than Jas. Butler and I between us are going to manage . . . [she] has rather an attitude of opposition to the authorities which is most unfortunate, though perhaps not to be wondered at after her experiences. The officials are sore at her criticism. But she has won the hearts of the people and is worshipped by them . . . one sees her photo in a place of honour in their houses.[16]

Certainly nobody could fault Emily's endeavours. She was tireless in distributing food and clothes among the needy, supplying destitute farmers with grain and seed and even buying oxen to help with the ploughing. But it was not all toil and tears. On this visit she made two new friends who were to feature prominently in her later life. While still in the Cape she had stopped at Beaufort West, where she was met by Betty Molteno and Alice Greene who introduced her to Olive Schreiner. Emily was already an admirer of the famous novelist, having read her classic book *The Story of an African Farm*, and had been thrilled to receive a congratulatory letter from Olive on the publication of *The Brunt of the War*. But this was the first time the two women had met. They became friends immediately; they had a great deal in common. Olive Schreiner had made no secret of her pro-Boer sympathies and in 1900 had twice spoken at protest meetings condemning the war. This had resulted in her coming under suspicion from the British authorities and she had spent most of the war years confined to the little Cape village of Hanover, virtually under house arrest. That she and Emily should have warmed to each other was inevitable. Their friendship, conducted mostly by correspondence, was to last until Olive's death in 1920. The other friend Emily made was General Jan Smuts, at whose house she stayed in Pretoria. Smuts, always at his best with women, charmed her with his easy manner and relaxed attitude – which contrasted with his wife's lingering bitterness – and, perceptively, Emily predicted a great future for him. It was a future in which she was to play a part, for she remained in close contact with him – again chiefly by letter – for most of her life.

Perhaps the most important event of this visit, however, was the *Volks Vergadering* (national rally) which Emily attended at Heidelberg in the Transvaal. This first great Afrikaner meeting since the war was arranged by Louis Botha for a public airing of the Boers' political grievances. People flocked to it from all over the country. Botha arrived, accompanied by eight Boer generals, and spoke from the church steps in the market square; Emily, who was made dizzy by the altitude, sat listening in a carriage, almost unnoticed by the crowd. But at a garden party afterwards she was given a place of honour with the generals and was deeply touched when presented with a basket of flowers. Botha then revealed who she was by introducing her to the crowd. 'How well I remember the scene,' recalled Emily, 'and how those two thousand men cheered as I stood beside Botha and clung to the little tree for support.'[17] Leaving Heidelberg she travelled on to Pretoria where she was again publicly fêted. She also spent an afternoon at Harmony with Mrs Van Warmelo – the newly-married Hansie was still in Holland – but unfortunately she left no record of this visit.

These were the highlights in what was otherwise a sad and energy-sapping tour. Emily arrived back in England in December 1903 still feeling weak and in need of rest. But before settling in with her uncle and aunt in their Bruton Street house, she managed to address a public meeting in Manchester and interview officials at the Colonial Office about conditions in South Africa. During the months that followed she was influential in keeping Liberal opposition leaders informed about Boer political opinion. Over a year was to pass before she returned to South Africa, in February 1905.

Her visit this time had a more definite purpose. Having become concerned, not only about the poverty of the ruined districts but about the idleness, bitterness and waste of talent among the younger Boers, she was determined to find employment for some of them. Her intention was to organize home industries for Boer girls. 'I had seen so many sitting in their ruined homes where every means of occupation had been destroyed,' she wrote. 'I knew they had the skill with the needle and had detected here and there a latent sense of art. They appeared to cling to home and family life and time was theirs in abundance. This tranquil existence, combined with brilliant skies, all helped to suggest lace-making as a most suitable occupation.'[18]

She was advised against it. Lace was a luxury article which only the rich could afford; it would be far more suitable to train the farm girls in spinning and weaving. Recognizing the sense of this, Emily changed her plans. Helped by a Quaker friend, Margaret Clark, and encouraged by Mrs Steyn's father, the Revd Colin Fraser, she opened her first spinning and weaving school at Philippolis in the Orange River Colony in March 1903. Five months later she started a similar school at Langlaagte on the Witwatersrand.

Shortly after arriving in the Transvaal, Emily received news of her aunt's death – Lord Hobhouse had died a year earlier – and this blow caused her again to change her plans. Instead of returning to England that summer, she decided to remain in South Africa. The following year she had a cottage built in the Johannesburg suburb of Bellevue. So began the longest period she was to spend in her adopted country. She lived in the Transvaal, with one short break, for the next two years. They were years in which she was kept fully occupied supervising her schools and arranging for the marketing of the cloth they produced. In time there were to be no fewer than twenty-six of these schools in the former Boer republics. Emily finally left South Africa in October 1908 after her schools had been taken over by the governments of the Transvaal and Orange River Colony.

Plagued by ill-health, Emily found it impossible to settle in England now that Lord and Lady Hobhouse were dead. She felt the need of a warmer climate. So she moved to Rome, where she rented a flat overlooking the Forum. This was to be her home for the next few years. She was still living in Rome when she was invited to unveil the Women's Memorial in Bloemfontein.

Among the people who contacted her during this visit to South Africa was M. K. Gandhi, the Indian leader, who was then waging a determined non-violent campaign against the South African government. Earlier he had been sentenced to three months' imprisonment but, having been released after ten days, was now seeking a new way to tackle the authorities. Jan Smuts was then Minister of Defence, and Gandhi appealed to Emily to use her influence with him. It was an appeal she could not ignore.

'I should not presume', she wrote to Smuts on 29 December 1913, 'to write to you, had it not been that Gandhi has *asked* me to do so . . . You see Jan. 15 is the date now proposed for another march. *Before then* some way should be found of giving private assurance to the leaders that satisfaction is coming to them. Their grievance is really *moral* not material . . . and *never never never* will governmental physical force prevail against a great moral and spiritual upheaval. Wasted time and wasted energy dear Oom Jannie . . .'[19]

Whether Emily's letter helped bring the two men together is not certain, but there can be no doubt about the effect Gandhi had upon her. His advocacy of non-violent methods of protest – *satyagraha* as he called it – awakened a passionate and positive response in Emily. There is no evidence that pacifism played any important part in her life before she went to South Africa, but her experiences in the concentration camps had left her convinced that war should be avoided at all costs. 'Mixed wrong and right there always is on *both* sides,' she was to say, 'and only misery comes of fighting about it.' Gandhi's *satyagraha* provided her with a philosophical vehicle to which she could harness her deepest convictions. Although she joined no peace societies or similar organizations, pacifism was a cause she championed for the rest of her life.

> Pacificists [she later wrote] are never, as such, the enemies of their countries . . . they are the truest patriots; Governments they may oppose if those Governments lead them into war; for well they know war brings disaster in its train as well for the victor as for the vanquished. Neither must they be accused in future of maintaining or arousing hatred when they lay open the old wounds of war. There is no valid ground for such accusations; since all nations have resorted to war and every single one has contributed its share to this age-long pain and disaster of the human race, not one can afford to cast stones . . . The pure pacifist position (as I at least apprehend it) is to own but one enemy and that one WAR itself. We have sworn vengeance upon a system – an outworn and barbarous system. So far from detracting from our country's honour, our point of view is that those who lead her into war, with its trail of horrors, are the more guilty of that . . . I doubt if a pacifist exists who would not fain see our country fearlessly place herself in the world's moral front and, taking the lead in total disarmament, win paramount honour among nations.[20]

Her aversion to violence prevented her from playing an active part in another cause close to her heart. She was always to describe herself as an 'ardent supporter' of the suffragist movement, an earnest champion of women's rights, but she refused to have anything to do with the 'destructive demonstrations' of the militant suffragettes. Ironically, her rightful place would have been with Millicent Fawcett's constitutional, non-militant, branch of the women's movement, but – or so it would seem – old enmities were too deeply ingrained to allow of such an alliance. But while disapproving of the methods adopted by the suffragettes, Emily never hesitated to speak in their defence when they were arrested. It was impossible, she protested, 'to lock up a *Spirit*'.

Emily's pacifism was not entirely negative. When action was called for she was willing, if not always able, to play her part. Her fervent opposition to the First World War provided ample evidence of her response to a challenge: it was a campaign she waged on many fronts, starting with her outspoken denunciations of the South African government.

Emily deplored South Africa's involvement in the war and, as she was quick to tell Jan Smuts, was appalled that a Boer-led government had taken sides in the European conflict. Equally distressing to her was the division the war caused among Afrikaners when, in 1914, the more irreconcilable element rose in rebellion against the alliance with Britain. As soon as the uprising had been suppressed she again wrote to Smuts, pleading with him to be lenient to the rebel leaders, many of whom were her friends. She was evidently afraid that the men she had once idolized were in danger of behaving like the imperialists they had once heroically defied. That Louis Botha's government could assume the role of aggressor, by invading South West Africa, was beyond her comprehension. So profound was her disapproval of the part Smuts was playing in the war that it led to a rupture in their friendship which, as far as Emily was concerned, was never fully healed.

But her wartime activities were by no means confined to a long-distance correspondence. In 1915 she worked for three months at the Women's International Bureau in Amsterdam, headquarters of a women's peace movement. This brought her into contact with like-minded women in Italy and Switzerland and also to the notice of the British Foreign Office where, as early as June 1915, her movements were being noted. The Home Office was informed that if she returned to England she was to be prevented from leaving the country. An even greater stir was caused when, in June 1916, it was discovered that Miss Hobhouse had ignored the threatening noises of various government officials and had actually crossed the enemy lines, to visit first German-occupied Belgium and then Berlin. In Belgium she had visited Brussels, Louvain, Antwerp and other towns but had been carefully supervised and not allowed to talk to any Belgians. She had then been given permission to travel on to Berlin where an old acquaintance of hers, Gottlieb von Jagow, was Foreign Minister. There is some dispute about her interview with Herr von Jagow. One account claims that he hinted to her that Germany was willing to negotiate a peace and that she later 'endeavoured to convey this to important people in England'.[21] Unfortunately this claim is not supported by her letters to the British Foreign Office. She did, however, contact people concerned with the welfare of British prisoners-of-war and visited the internment camp at Ruhleben where, as they later testified, she spoke to some of the prisoners. All of which was sufficient to make her, once again, a target for accusations of unpatriotic behaviour.

Later that year angry questions were asked in Parliament about Emily's visit to Germany. MPs wanted to know how her journey had been organized. Had she been issued with a passport for such a visit? Was she given the Government's permission? If not, what action would be taken against her? The Attorney-General, highly embarrassed, was forced to admit that, as the law stood, Miss Hobhouse had not committed a criminal act; but, he added, it was proposed to alter the Defence of the Realm Act to make such a visit an offence in the future. He also made it clear that Emily would not again be allowed to leave the country. Forbidden once more to enter enemy territory, Emily spent the rest of the war in England, dividing her time between Cornwall and London. Her proposed scheme for having civilian prisoners-of-war, on both sides, interned in a neutral country came to nothing.

After the war, Emily devoted herself to work for the Save the Children Fund. As a representative of the fund she travelled to Austria and Germany, helped to prepare reports on centres where aid was badly needed, and proved herself extremely effective as a fund raiser. Her appeals for financial help were not only successful throughout Europe but were extended to South Africa, where her old friend Mrs Steyn organized the private collection of £12,000 to which the South African government added £5000. What surprised those who worked with her was that, although frail and nearing sixty, Emily seemed as alert, purposeful, efficient and exacting as she had ever been. She was still very much 'the missus'. 'The thing which I admired most about Miss Hobhouse', wrote one of her helpers, 'was her tireless energy, the domination of her mind over physical weakness . . . The self-discipline, which seemed part of her nature, must have appeared often to others as harshness. She had no tolerance in doing things "rather more or less" and would accept no excuse for any inaccuracy.'[22] Later

Emily was to work independently among the children of Leipzig, and was decorated for her services by the German Red Cross.

But, efficient as she was in organizing charities, she failed dismally to provide for her own old age. In the slump which followed the First World War, her finances – always limited, often precarious – dwindled alarmingly and she was forced to sell her treasured possessions in order to exist. She was rescued from penury by her South African admirers, who by means of half-crown subscriptions raised £2300 which, in 1921, enabled Emily to buy a small Victorian house in the artists' resort of St Ives on the Cornish coast. In addition to this, the various districts of the Orange Free State took it in turns to send her, every year on her birthday, a lovingly prepared gift-box of South African produce.

Emily never went back to South Africa after her exhausting visit in 1913, but she kept in regular contact with the country. She continued to write to her friends there, and at great length to her confidante Mrs Steyn. South African visitors to England sought her out and looked to her for advice. Yet, dearly as she loved her friends and unshaken as her respect for the Afrikaners remained, it is doubtful whether Emily would have been happy had she lived permanently in South Africa. There were already many things about the country that she found disturbing. Louis Botha had died in 1919 and she no longer had any faith in Jan Smuts, his successor as prime minister. To her Smuts's behaviour during the world war, his imperialist posturing and his delight in the British social and political hierarchy, seemed a betrayal of Boer virtues, a disavowal of the simple, natural life she so admired.

She was soon also to have doubts about the Nationalist opposition led by General Hertzog. When, in June 1924, Smuts's government fell and was replaced by a coalition of Hertzog's party and the mainly English-speaking Labour party, Emily was delighted. But her delight did not last long. A month or so later Hertzog's supporters began to advocate the 'territorial segregation of the natives' as the only sound policy for South Africa. Emily feared the worst. She made her feelings known in a letter to Mrs Steyn: she warned it would be wrong to imagine that South Africa could ignore world opinion when dealing with the problems posed by its black population. 'Personally,' she wrote, 'I believe segregation of any of either race or colour and class the wrong policy and one which can only lead to discontent and ultimate disaster.'[23]

One of the saddest aspects of Emily Hobhouse's life is the failure of those she defended and worked for to live up to her ideals. There can be little doubt that she would have found the policies pursued by successive Afrikaner governments, since the Second World War, abhorrent. All that she stood for and believed in was callously swept aside. Liberalism, the political philosophy that inspired her and so many other pro-Boers, became a dirty word in South Africa. It was replaced by a nationalism which Emily–who was proud to believe 'not in narrow Nationalism, but Internationalism, the Brotherhood of Man' – would have found repugnant.[24] Apartheid, the policy of racial separation, the policy which lost the Afrikaners the sympathy they had once attracted throughout the world, would undoubtedly have aroused Emily's crusading instincts; had she lived in a later age, she would have been a prominent anti-apartheid activist. It would have been impossible for her to witness the results of this policy – the oppression, the overt racism, the sufferings, the deprivations and humiliations, the poverty and slum conditions, the uprooting of entire communities and the denial of basic human rights – without raising her voice in protest.

Almost as sad is the extent to which a later generation of Afrikaners, who claim to honour Emily's memory, have misunderstood her motives. They regard her simply as an Englishwoman who championed their cause, rather than as a woman who would have come to the rescue of the oppressed anywhere. Emily's principles are, in many ways, irrelevant to the respect in which she is held in South Africa. Since her death there have been attempts to honour Emily as a national heroine, including the naming of a Free State town after her, but not all these so-called honours have been so happily chosen. One conspicuous example of this misplaced veneration illustrates just how little Emily is understood by those who pay her homage. In 1969 the South African navy acquired three new, French-built submarines, each of them 'heavily armed with twelve torpedo tubes' and manned by a crew of fifty. The second of these formidable vessels was launched in October of that year and named the *Emily Hobhouse*. A more inappropriate memorial to a convinced and unswerving pacifist is difficult to imagine. The fact that the submarines were ostensibly meant only for defence (the excuse always used for a build-up of arms) would not have impressed Emily. Her condemnation of war was total. In her opinion the amassing of arms, for whatever reason, was evil and only made war more certain. She would have been sickened by the thought of a submarine bearing her name.

But in South Africa she is at least remembered. In her own country she is forgotten. Her rejection by the British people is said to have overshadowed the last years of Emily's life. She made the mistake of putting Britain's honour, its reputation for justice and fair play, before Britain's might, and for that she was never forgiven. Her claim that she was more pro-British than pro-Boer failed to be understood. Misguided and naïve in certain respects Emily might have been, but her honest humanitarian instincts, her compassion, and her courage in upholding, against all odds, what she judged to be right, deserves greater recognition than it has received in her native land.

Emily died in a London nursing home on 8 June 1926. She was sixty-six. *The Times* published a carping obituary but her death was not even acknowledged in the Cornish newspapers. It was the loyal Mrs Steyn who ensured that a fitting tribute was paid to her in South Africa. Emily was cremated, and at Mrs Steyn's suggestion her ashes were buried at the foot of the Women's Memorial in Bloemfontein. At a moving interment ceremony, on 27 October 1926, Jan Smuts was the main speaker. Forgetting their past differences, he did full justice to Emily's efforts on behalf of his countrymen.

'We stood alone in the world,' he said, addressing a huge gathering of mourners, 'friendless among the peoples, the smallest nation ranged against the mightiest Empire on earth. At the darkest hour, when our race almost appeared doomed to extinction, she appeared as an angel, as a heaven-sent messenger. Strangest of all, she was an Englishwoman.'[25]

Bibliography

Manuscript Sources
Millicent Fawcett's South African Diary, Fawcett Library, City of London Polytechnic.
Baden-Powell's Staff Diary, National Army Museum, London.
C. G. H. Bell's Diary, Cory Library, Rhodes University, Grahamstown, South Africa.
W. Hayes's Diary, Cape Archives, Cape Town, South Africa.
Miss Crauford's Diary, Mrs C. Cassidy, Maseru, Lesotho.
Thomasina Cowan's Diary, Mrs S. Minchin, Mafikeng, Bophuthatswana.
Trooper Fuller's Diary, Mr J. Fuller, Johannesburg, South Africa.
The Keeley Family Papers, Mrs E. M. Johnstone, Durban, South Africa.
Mafeking Convent Papers, Convent of Mercy, Rosebank, Johannesburg, South Africa.

REPORTS, PAMPHLETS AND ARTICLES

Official Reports
Cd.819 *Reports, etc., on the working of the Refugee Camps in the Transvaal, Orange River Colony, Cape Colony and Natal*, London 1901
Cd.853 (1901), Cd.902 (1902), Cd.934 (1902), Cd.936 (1902) *Further papers relating to the working of the Refugee Camps in South Africa*
Cd.893 *Report on the Concentration Camps in South Africa by the Committee of Ladies appointed by the Secretary of State for War containing Reports on the Camps in Natal, the Orange River Colony and the Transvaal*, London 1902

Pamphlets
Emily Hobhouse, *To the Committee of the Distress Fund for South African Women and Children. Report of a visit to the camps of women and children in the Cape and Orange River Colonies*, Friars Printing Association Ltd, London 1901
——, *A letter to the Committee of the South African Women and Children's*

Distress Fund [On her deportation from the Cape], Argus Printing Co. Ltd, London 1901 (?)

Johanna Brandt (*née* Van Warmelo), *The Millennium. A Prophetic Message to the Native Tribes of South Africa*, Privately printed, Pretoria 1917

Articles

Lady Sarah Wilson, 'The Transvaal War: A Woman's Reminiscences of 1899', *Book of Beauty*, London 1902

——, Six Weeks in North-Western Rhodesia', *Pall Mall Magazine*, London 1903

——, 'In Tight Corners': copy of an unidentified newspaper article, supplied by the Mafeking Convent

Lady Randolph Churchill, 'Letters From a Hospital Ship', *Anglo-Saxon Review*, June 1900

BOOKS

Aitken, W. Francis, *Baden-Powell: The Hero of Mafeking*, London 1900

Allen, Vivien, *Kruger's Pretoria*, Cape Town 1971

Amery, L. S. (ed.), *The Times History of the War in South Africa*, London 1905

——, *My Political Life*, London 1953

Armstrong, Henrietta, *see* Van Rensburg, Thariza

Arthur, Sir George, *Life of Lord Kitchener* (2 vols), London 1920

——, *Life of General Sir John Maxwell*, London 1932

Baden-Powell, Lord, *Lessons from the Varsity of Life*, London 1933

Baillie, F. D., *Mafeking: A Diary of the Siege*, London 1900

Balsan, Consuelo, *The Glitter and the Gold*, London 1953

Batts, H. J., *Pretoria From Within during the War 1899–1900*, London 1901

Beak, G. B., *The Aftermath of the War: Repatriation of Boers and Natives in the Orange River Colony*, London 1906

Bean, Lucy and Heyningen, Elizabeth, *The Letters of Jane Elizabeth Waterston 1866–1905*, Cape Town 1983

Bishop, George, *A Parish Album of St Ive*, Plymouth 1988

Brandt, Johanna (Van Warmelo), *Het Concentratie-Kamp van Irene*, Amsterdam 1905; *The Petticoat Commando*, London 1913; see also pamphlet listed above

Bron, Alice, *Diary of a Nurse in South Africa*, London 1901

Brooke-Hunt, Violet, *A Woman's Memories of the War*, London 1901

Cecil, Lady Gwendoline, *The Life of Robert, Marquis of Salisbury* (2 vols), London 1921

Childs, Sir Wyndham, *Episodes and Reflections*, London 1930

Churchill, Randolph S., *Winston S. Churchill: Youth 1875–1900*, London 1966

——, (ed.), *Companion Volume I to W. S. Churchill, parts 1 & 2*, London 1966

Churchill, Viscount, *All My Sins Remembered*, London 1947

Churchill, Winston, *London to Ladysmith via Pretoria*, London 1900

——, *Ian Hamilton's March*, London 1900
——, *My Early Life*, London 1930
Comaroff, J. L. (ed.), *The Boer War Diary of Sol T. Plaatje: An African at Mafeking*, Johannesburg 1973
Creswicke, Louis, *South Africa and the Transvaal War*, Edinburgh 1902
Davenport, T. R. H., *South Africa: A Modern History*, London 1987
Davey, Arthur (ed.), *Lawrence Richardson: Selected Correspondence 1902–1903*, Cape Town 1977
——, *The British Pro-Boers 1877–1902*, Cape Town 1978
De la Rey, Mrs, *A Woman's Wanderings and Trials during the Anglo-Boer War*, London 1903
De Souza, C. W. L., *No Charge For Delivery*, Cape Town 1969
Dennison, Major C., *A Fight to the Finish*, London 1904
Devitt, Napier, *The Concentration Camps in South Africa*, Pietermaritzburg 1941
De Wet, C. R., *Three Years' War*, London 1902
Doyle, A. Conan, *The War in South Africa, Its Causes and Conduct*, London 1902
——, *The Great Boer War*, London 1903
Engelenburg, F. V., *General Louis Botha*, Pretoria 1929
Farwell, Byron, *The Great Boer War*, London 1977
Fawcett, Millicent, *What I Remember*, London 1924
Fisher, John, *The Afrikaners*, London 1969
——, *That Miss Hobhouse: The Life of a Great Feminist*, London 1971
——, *Paul Kruger: His Life and Times*, London 1974
Flint, John, *Cecil Rhodes*, London 1976
Forrest, Sir George, *Life of Lord Roberts*, London 1915
Fry, Ruth A., *Emily Hobhouse: A Memoir*, London 1929
Fulford, Roger, *Votes For Women: The Story of a Struggle*, London 1957
Gardner, Brian, *Mafeking: A Victorian Legend*, London 1966
Gibbs, Peter, *Death of the Last Republic*, London 1957
Ginsberg, Morris, *L. T. Hobhouse: His Life and Work*, London 1931
Godley, Sir Alexander, *Life of an Irish Soldier*, London 1939
Gooch, G. P., *Life of Lord Courtney*, London 1920
Grigg, John, *The Young Lloyd George*, London 1973
Hamilton, J. Angus, *The Siege of Mafeking*, London 1900
Hancock, W. K., *Smuts: The Sanguine Years 1870–1919*, Cambridge 1962
Headlam, Cecil (ed.), *The Milner Papers*, London 1933
Hibbert, Christopher, *Edward VII: A Portrait*, London 1976
Hobhouse, Emily, *The Brunt of the War, and Where it Fell*, London 1902
——, (ed.), *Tant Alie of the Transvaal: Her Diary 1880–1902*, London 1900
——, (ed.), *War Without Glamour: Women's Experiences written by Themselves*, Bloemfontein 1927
Hobson, J. A., *The War in South Africa: its Causes and Effects*, London 1900
Holt, Edgar, *The Boer War*, London 1958

Bibliography

James, D., *Lord Roberts*, London 1954

Jeal, Tim, *Baden-Powell*, London 1989

Keppel, Sonia, *Edwardian Daughter*, London 1958

Knight, E. F., *South Africa After the War*, London 1903

Koss, S. (ed.), *The Pro-Boers*, London 1973

Kruger, Rayne, *Goodbye Dolly Gray*, London 1959

Laidler, P. W. and Gelfand, M., *South Africa: Its Medical History*, Cape Town 1971

Le May, G. H. L., *British Supremacy in South Africa 1899–1907*, Oxford 1965

Leslie, Anita, *Jennie: The Life of Lady Randolph Churchill*, London 1969

Magnus, Sir Phillip, *Kitchener: Portrait of an Imperialist*, London 1958

Mallet, Victor, *Life With Queen Victoria*, London 1968

Marquard, Leo, *Letters From a Boer Parsonage*, Cape Town 1971

Martin, A. C., *The Concentration Camps: Facts, Figures and Fables*, Cape Town 1957

Meintjes, Johannes, *De La Rey: Lion of the West*, Johannesburg 1966

——, *President Steyn*, Cape Town 1970

——, *General Louis Botha*, London 1970

——, *The Commandant General*, Cape Town 1971

——, *President Kruger*, London 1974

Menpes, Mortimer, *War Impressions*, London 1901

Milne, Duncan-Grinnell, *Baden-Powell at Mafeking*, London 1957

Milner, Viscountess, *My Picture Gallery*, London 1951

Neilly, J. Emerson, *Besieged with B.P.*, London 1900

Pakenham, Thomas, *The Boer War*, London 1979

Pohl, Victor, *Adventures of a Boer Family*, Johannesburg 1943

Phillipps, L. M., *With Rimington*, London 1902

Radziwill, Princess, *Cecil Rhodes: Man and Empire Maker*, London 1918

Raymond, E. T., *Portraits of the Nineties*, London 1921

Reitz, Deneys, *Commando*, London 1929

Rubinstein, David, *Before the Suffragettes: Women's Emancipation in the 1890s*, Brighton 1986

Shaw, Gerald, *The Garrett Papers*, Cape Town 1984

Solomon, Vivian, *Selections from the Correspondence of Percy Alport Molteno 1892–1914*, Cape Town 1981

Spender, J. A., *Life of Sir Henry Campbell-Bannerman* (2 vols), London 1923

Spies, S. B., *Methods of Barbarism: Roberts and Kitchener and Civilians in the Boer Republics January 1900–May 1902*, Cape Town 1977

Strachey, Ray, *Millicent Garrett Fawcett*, London 1931

Sykes, Lady Jessica, *Sidelights on the War in South Africa*, London 1900

Trombley, Stephen, *Sir Frederick Treves: The Extra-Ordinary Edwardian*, London 1989

Troup, Freda, *South Africa: An Historical Introduction*, London 1972

Van Jaarsveld, F. A., *The Afrikaner's Interpretation of South African History*, Cape Town 1964

Van Reenen, Rykie (ed.), *Emily Hobhouse: Boer War Letters*, Cape Town 1984

Van Rensburg, Thariza (ed.), *Camp Diary of Henrietta E. C. Armstrong: Experiences of a Boer Nurse in the Irene Concentration Camp*, Pretoria 1980
Van Warmelo, Johanna ('Hansie') *see* Brandt, Johanna
Walker, Eric A., *A History of South Africa*, London 1947
Warwick, Peter, *Black People and the South African War 1899–1902*, Cambridge 1983
Weintraub, Stanley, *Victoria: Biography of a Queen*, London 1987
Weir, Charles, *The Boer War: A Diary of the Siege of Mafeking*, Edinburgh 1900
West, Mrs Cornwallis, *The Reminiscences of Lady Randolph Churchill*, London 1908
Willan, Brian (ed.), *Edward Ross: Diary of the Siege of Mafeking*, Cape Town 1980
Williams, Basil, *Cecil Rhodes*, London 1921
Wilson, Lady Sarah, *South African Memories*, London 1909; see also articles listed above
Wright, H. M. (ed.), *Sir James Rose Innes: Selected Correspondence 1884–1902*, Cape Town 1972
Young, Filson, *The Relief of Mafeking*, London 1900

General Reference Books
Dictionary of South African Biography (five volumes), Pretoria 1968–1987
Standard Encyclopaedia of Southern Africa (twelve volumes), Cape Town 1970–1976

Notes

When the source of a quote is indicated in the text, no reference is given.

1 Society Butterflies

1 Cecil, *Life of Salisbury*
2 Mallet, *Life With Queen Victoria*
3 Milner, *My Picture Gallery*
4 Menpes, *War Impressions*
5 Ibid.
6 Arthur, *Life of General Maxwell*
7 Menpes, op. cit.
8 Lady Randolph Churchill, *Letters from a Hospital Ship*
9 Milner, op. cit.
10 Sykes, *Sidelights on the War*
11 Williams, *Cecil Rhodes*
12 Flint, *Cecil Rhodes*
13 Le May, *British Supremacy*
14 Pakenham, *Boer War*
15 Ibid.
16 Davey, *British Pro-Boers*
17 Menpes, op. cit.
18 Fulford, *Votes for Women*

2 An Enterprising Churchill

Quotes from Wilson, *South African Memories* except as listed below.

1 Randolph Churchill, *Companion, Vol. 1*
2 Balsan, *The Glitter and the Gold*
3 West, *Reminiscences of Lady Randolph Churchill*
4 *The Times*, 15 October 1929
5 Randolph Churchill, op. cit.
6 Raymond, *Portraits of the Nineties*
7 *Daily Mail*, 3 November 1899
8 Milner, *My Picture Gallery*
9 *Daily Mail*, 3 November 1899
10 *Bulawayo Chronicle*, 20 October 1899
11 Hamilton, *Siege of Mafeking*
12 Godley, *Life of an Irish Soldier*

3 Alarms and Excursions

Quotes from Wilson, *South African Memories*, except as listed below.

1 Hobhouse, *Tant Alie of Transvaal*
2 Wilson, *The Transvaal War*
3 Ibid.
4 Hamilton, *Siege of Mafeking*
5 Dennison, *Fight to the Finish*
6 Keeley family information
7 Willan, *E. Ross Diary*
8 Dennison, op. cit.
9 *Black and White*, 3 March 1900

4 In and Out of Captivity
Quotes from Wilson, *South African Memories*, except as listed below.

1 *Illustrated London News*, 16 December 1899
2 *Daily Mail*, 8 December 1899
3 West, *Reminiscences of Lady Randolph Churchill*
4 De Souza, *No Charge for Delivery*
5 Thomasina Cowan's Diary
6 Willan, *E. Ross Diary*
7 De Souza, op. cit.
8 Ibid.
9 W. Hayes' Diary
10 Neilly, *Besieged with B.P.*
11 Willan, op. cit.

5 Under Siege
Quotes from Wilson, *South African Memories*, except as listed below.

1 Comaroff, *Diary of Sol Plaatje*
2 C. Bell's Diary
3 W. Hayes' Diary
4 *Daily Telegraph*, 23 October 1929
5 *Daily Mail*, 20 March 1900
6 Ibid.
7 Ibid.
8 Neilly, *Besieged with B.P.*
9 Comaroff op. cit.
10 Willan, *E. Ross Diary*
11 Comaroff, op. cit.
12 Ibid.
13 *Illustrated London News*, 4 August 1900
14 *Daily Mail*, 23 October 1929
15 Wilson, *In Tight Corners*
16 *Daily Mail*, 20 March 1900
17 *Illustrated London News*, December 1900
18 *Daily Telegraph*, 23 October 1929

6 Holding Out
Quotes from Wilson, *South African Memories*, except as listed below.

1 Comaroff, *Diary of Sol Plaatje*
2 *Daily Mail*, 20 April 1900
3 *Cape Argus*, 23 October 1929
4 *Daily Telegraph*, 25 October 1929
5 *Thomasina Cowan's Diary*
6 Ibid.
7 *Daily Mail*, 21 February 1900 (despatch dated 9 February)
8 *Daily Mail*, 16 March 1900 (despatch dated 20 February)
9 Comaroff, *Diary of Sol Plaatje*
10 Diary of Trooper W. Fuller
11 Aitken, *Baden-Powell*
12 Hamilton, *Siege of Mafeking*
13 Neilly, *Besieged with B.P.*
14 *Daily Mail*, 10 April 1900
15 Thomasina Cowan's Diary
16 *Daily Mail*, 25 April 1900
17 *Daily Mail*, 22 May 1900
18 *Daily Mail*, 19 June 1900
19 *Cape Argus*, 23 October 1929
20 *Daily Mail*, 21 May 1900

7 'Tommy Atkins, The War Has Just Begun'
1 Doyle, *The Great Boer War*
2 Hobhouse, *Brunt of War*; Spies, *Methods of Barbarism*
3 Forrest, *Life of Lord Roberts*
4 Brooke-Hunt, *A Woman's Memories*
5 Doyle, *The Great Boer War*
6 Ibid.
7 *The Times*, 11 April, 27 June, 30 June 1900
8 Doyle, op. cit.
9 Brandt, *Petticoat Commando*
10 Ibid.
11 Headlam: *Milner Papers*
12 Wilson: *South African Memories*
13 Godley: *Life of an Irish Soldier*

14 Ibid.
15 W. Churchill, *Ian Hamilton's March*

16 Wilson, *South African Memories*
17 Brandt, op. cit.
18 Ibid.

8 The Ladies of Harmony
Quotes from Brandt, *Petticoat Commando*, except as listed below.
1 Batts, *Pretoria From Within*
2 *Morning Herald*, 20 March 1900
3 Hobhouse, *Brunt of War*
4 Young, *The Relief of Mafeking*
5 Arthur, *Life of General Maxwell*
6 Phillipps, *With Rimington*
7 Ibid.
8 Spies, *Methods of Barbarism*
9 Hobhouse, op. cit.

9 The Archdeacon's Daughter
Quotes from Fry, *Emily Hobhouse*, except as listed below.
1 *Cornish Times*, 7 July 1900
2 Childs, *Episodes and Reflections*
3 For John Jackson episode, *see* Fisher, *That Miss Hobhouse*
4 Hobhouse, *Brunt of War*
5 Van Reenen, *Emily Hobhouse: Boer War Letters*
6 Hobhouse, op. cit.
7 Van Reenen, op. cit.

10 A Camp in the Transvaal
Quotes from Brandt, *Petticoat Commando*, except as listed below.
1 *New York Herald*, 16 April 1901
2 *The Times*, 31 July 1901
3 Spies, *Methods of Barbarism*
4 *The Times*, 31 July 1901
5 Hobhouse, *Brunt of War*
6 Brandt, *Het Concentratie-Kamp van Irene* (*Irene* hereafter)
7 Ibid.
8 Van Rensburg, *H. Armstrong's Camp Diary*
9 Hobhouse, op cit.
10 Ibid.
11 Ibid.
12 Brandt, *Irene*
13 Ibid.
14 Spies, op. cit.
15 Headlam, *Milner Papers*
16 Hobhouse, op. cit.
17 Spies, op. cit.
18 Weintraub, *Victoria* and Mallet, *Life with Queen Victoria*
19 Spies, op. cit.
20 Magnus, *Kitchener*
21 Brandt, *Irene*
22 Ibid.
23 Brooke-Hunt, *A Woman's Memories*
24 Brandt, *Irene*
25 Ibid.
26 Hobhouse, op. cit.
27 Van Rensburg, op. cit.
28 Hobhouse, op. cit.
29 Ibid.
30 Ibid.

11 Reporting Back
Quotes from Fry, *Emily Hobhouse*, except as listed below.
1 Van Reenen, *Emily Hobhouse: Boer War Letters*
2 Ibid.
3 *The Times*, 25 May 1901
4 Fry, Van Reenen and Hobhouse, *Brunt of War*
5 *The Times*, 19 June 1901
6 Hobhouse, op. cit.

7 Spender, *Life of Campbell-Bannerman*
8 *The Times*, 19 June 1901
9 Ibid. 28 June 1901
10 Ibid. 26 June 1901

11 Ibid.
12 Fawcett, *What I Remember*
13 Hobhouse, op. cit.
14 Ibid.
15 Ibid.

12 The Ladies' Commission

Quotes from *Report on Concentration Camps . . . Cd 893* except as listed below.

1 Strachey, *Millicent Garrett Fawcett*
2 Fawcett, South African Diary
3 Ibid.
4 *Cape Times*, 24 July 1901
5 Hobhouse, *Brunt of War*
6 *Nineteenth Century*, October 1901
7 Strachey, op. cit.
8 Fawcett, South African Diary
9 Strachey, op. cit.
10 Hobhouse, op. cit.
11 For Fawcett meeting with Cape Town women, *see* Fawcett, South African Diary; *What I Remember*; and Van Reenen, *Emily Hobhouse: Boer War Letters*
12 Fawcett, *What I Remember*

13 Van Reenen, op. cit.
14 Magnus, *Kitchener*
15 Fawcett, *What I Remember*
16 Van Rensburg, *H. Armstrong's Camp Diary*
17 Brandt, *Irene*
18 Van Rensburg, op. cit.
19 Fawcett, South African Diary
20 Ibid.
21 Hobhouse, *Brunt of War*
22 Van Rensburg, op. cit.
23 Fawcett, South African Diary
24 Ibid.
25 *Investor's Review*, 28 June 1902
26 For a detailed account of the tour of the Ladies' Commission, *see* their official report, CD 893

13 Defiance and Deportation

Quotes from Fry, *Emily Hobhouse*, except as listed below.

1 For her comments on the Fawcett report, *see* Hobhouse, *Brunt of War*
2 For the Guild of Loyal Women, *see The Times*, 2 July 1901; Fisher, *That Miss Hobhouse*, Van Reenen, *Boer War Letters*
3 Van Reenen, op. cit.
4 Hobhouse, op. cit.
5 Fisher, op. cit.
6 Hobhouse, op. cit.
7 Ibid.
8 Ibid.
9 Spies, *Methods of Barbarism*
10 Ibid.

11 Warwick, *Black People and the South African War*
12 Ibid.
13 Hobhouse, op. cit.
14 Sarah Heckford, in *The Times*, 5 August 1901
15 Mrs K. H. R. Stuart, in *The Times*, 2 July 1901
16 *The Times*, 5 July 1901
17 Magnus, *Kitchener*
18 Fisher, *That Miss Hobhouse*; and Van Reenen, *Boer War Letters*
19 For Emily Hobhouse's deportation, *see* Van Reenen, *Boer War Letters* (which includes

Betty Molteno's account); Fisher: *That Miss Hobhouse*; Wright: *Rose Innes Correspondence*; *The Owl*, 8 November 1901

20 *Manchester Guardian*, 2 November 1901
21 Arthur, *Life of Lord Kitchener*
22 Doyle, *The War in South Africa*
23 Hobhouse, op. cit.

14 Visitors to Harmony
Quotes from Brandt, *Petticoat Commando*, except as listed below.
1 Spies, *Methods of Barbarism*
2 Pakenham, *Boer War*
3 Spies, op. cit.
4 De Wet, *Three Years' War*
5 Martin, *The Concentration Camps*
6 Spies, op. cit.

15 After the War
1 Van Reenen, *Boer War Letters*
2 Fisher, *The Afrikaners*
3 Spies, *Methods of Barbarism*
4 Fisher, op. cit.
5 *Illustrated London News*, July 1900
6 *Black and White*, 19 July 1901
7 Wilson, *South African Memories*
8 *Mafeking Mail*, 5 September 1901
9 Wilson, op. cit.
10 *Pall Mall Magazine*, December 1903
11 Keppel, *Edwardian Daughter*
12 Brandt, *Petticoat Commando*
13 Brandt, *The Millennium*
14 Davey, *L. Richardson's Correspondence*
15 Fry, *Emily Hobhouse*
16 Davey, op. cit.
17 Fry, op. cit.
18 Ibid.
19 Hancock, *Smuts: The Sanguine Years*
20 Hobhouse, Introduction to *Tant Alie of the Transvaal*
21 Fry, op. cit.
22 Ibid.
23 Fisher, *That Miss Hobhouse*
24 Hancock, op. cit.
25 Fry, *Emily Hobhouse*

Index